Advance Praise for Conquest

"Andrea Smith offers a powerful analysis of sexual violence that reaches far beyond the dominant theoretical understandings, brilliantly weaving together feminist explanations of violence against Native women, the historical data regarding colonialism and genocide, and a strong critique of the current responses to the gender violence against women of color. As a passionate activist and a respected scholar, Smith brings her experience working on the ground to this important project, rendering *Conquest* one of the most significant contributions to the literature in Native Studies, Feminist and Social Movement Theory in recent years."
— *Beth E. Richie*, **author of** *Compelled to Crime: The Gender Entrapment of Black Battered Women*

"Whether it is our reliance on the criminal justice system to protect women from violence or the legitimacy of the U.S. as a colonial nation-state, Andrea Smith's incisive and courageous analysis cuts through many of our accepted truths and reveals a new way of knowing rooted in Native women's histories of struggle. More than a call for action, this book provides sophisticated strategies and practical examples of organizing that simultaneously take on state and interpersonal violence. *Conquest* is a must-read not only for those concerned with violence against women and Native sovereignty, but also for antiracist, reproductive rights, environmental justice, antiprison, immigrant rights and antiwar activists."
— *Julia Sudbury*, **editor of** *Global Lockdown: Race, Gender and the Prison-Industrial Complex*

Give thanks for the very great honor of listening to Andrea Smith. This book will burn a hole right through your mind with its accurate analysis and the concise compilation of information that makes it the first of its kind. *Conquest* is not only instructive, it is healing. I want every Indian I know to read it.
— *Chrystos*, **artist, poet, and activist**

"*Conquest* is the book Aboriginal women have been waiting for. It is the non-fiction work we all wish we had the time and inclination to research and write, the book we all wish had been within easy reach during the long years of our education. Andrea Smith has not only meticulously researched the place of rape and violence against Indigenous women in the colonial process, but she is the first to fully articulate the connections between violence against the earth, violence against women, and North America's terrible inclination toward war. Every single adult human being on this continent needs to read this book. If we did, we would all find the strength to face our history and alter its course."
—*Lee Maracle*, **author of** *I Am Woman: A Native Perspective on Sociology and Feminism*

"Andrea Smith has no fear. She challenges conventional activist thinking about the global and the local, sexism and racism, genocide and imperialism. But what's more, in every chapter she tries to answer the key question: What is to be done? *Conquest* is unsettling, ambitious, brilliant, disturbing: read it, debate it, use it."
—*Ruth Gilmore*, **Associate Professor of Geography, American Studies and Ethnicity, University of Southern California**

"*Conquest* radically rethinks the historical scope and dimensionality of "sexual violence," a historical vector of bodily domination that is too often reduced to universalizing—hence racist—narratives of gendered oppression and resistance. Offering a breathtaking genealogy of white supremacist genocide and colonization in North America, this book provides a theoretical model that speaks urgently to a broad continuum of political and intellectual traditions. In this incisive and stunningly comprehensive work, we learn how the proliferation of sexual violence as a normalized feature of modern Euro-American patriarchies is inseparable from violence against Indigenous women, and women of color. In *Conquest*, Andrea Smith has presented us with an epochal challenge, one that should productively disrupt and perhaps transform our visions of liberation and radical freedom."
—*Dylan Rodríguez*, **Assistant Professor of Ethnic Studies, University of California, Riverside**

This book is dedicated to Sunjay Smith,
who has shown me what it really means
to struggle against the odds,
and to Tsali Smith, future revolutionary leader.

Conquest
Sexual Violence and American Indian Genocide

Andrea Smith

South End Press
Cambridge, MA

Smith, Andrea, 1966-
Conquest : sexual violence and American Indian genocide / by
Andrea Smith.   p. cm.
Includes bibliographical references and index.
ISBN 0-89608-744-1 (cloth : alk. paper) — ISBN 0-89608-743-3 (pbk. :
alk. paper)
1.   Indian women—Crimes against—North America. 2.   Indian
women—Colonization—North America. 3.   Indian women—North
America—Social conditions. 4.   Indians, Treatment of—North
America—History. 5.   Violence—North America. 6.   North
America—Race relations. 7.   North America—Politics and
government. I. Title.

E98.W8S62   2005   305.48'897073—dc22
2004030398

ISBN: 0-89608-744-1 (hardcover: alk. paper)
ISBN: 0-89608-743-3 (pbk.: alk. paper)

Printed in Canada by union labor on acid-free, recycled paper.
05 04 03 02 01   1 2 3 4 5

South End Press
7 Brookline Street, Suite 1
Cambridge, MA 02139
www.southendpress.org
southend@southendpress.org

Table of Contents

Acknowledgments

Many thanks to the South End Press, the greatest publishers on planet Earth, for supporting this work. The professional, personal and political support South End gave me to finish this project was astounding. Not many publishers will not only help you with editing, but help you with babysitting (thanks Asha Tall and Jill Petty!) In particular, I must profusely thank Jill Petty for devoting countless hours to the manuscript. Her political commitment as well as her kindness, generosity and patience was very inspiring to me. Theresa Noll and Nina Sarnelle also assisted with the research and fact checking for this book. Donna Kiefer and Erich Strom were helpful in proofreading the manuscript. And Alyssa Hassan did a great job with the production and layout of the book. South End Press plays such an invaluable role in supporting progressive social movements in the U.S., and I am so grateful for the work they do.

I cannot claim the analysis of this book as my own. Rather, it comes from what I have learned from countless Native women and women of color in various organizing projects. I would like to thank all the women from Women of All Red Nations (WARN) in

Chicago, particularly Sherry Wilson who introduced me to
WARN. All the women from INCITE! Women of Color Against
Violence have provided the foundation for my thinking on these
issues, particularly Andrea Ritchie, Nadine Naber, Mimi Kim,
Isabel Kang, Sherry Wilson, Clarissa Rojas, Michelle Erai, Julia
Sudbury, Loretta Rivera, Beth Richie, Paula Rojas, Simmi Gandhi,
Ann Caton, Prosh Sherkarloo, Elham Bayour, Barbara
Smith,Tammy Ko Robinson, Janelle White, Kata Issari, Nan
Stoops, Jamie Lee Evans, and Shana Griffin, Val Kanuha and Inhe
Choi.The Boarding School Healing Project has also been a critical
resource. Other organizations I would like to acknowledge
include Sista II Sista, Critical Resistance, Communities Against
Rape and Abuse, and the Committee on Women, Population and
the Environment.

Numerous individuals have provided me countless insights
that have informed this book. I apologize to anyone I might inad-
vertently omit. Luana Ross and Justine Smith provided
significant input into Chapter 6. Chapter 5 is informed by the
work and analysis of Mary Ann Mills and Bernadine Atcheson.
Willetta Dolphus, Charlene LaPointe, and Sammy Toineeta informed Chapter 2. Other individuals I would like to thank
include: Pamela Kingfisher, Mililani Trask, Angela Davis, Ruthie
Gilmore, Tonya Gonnella Frichner, Sarah Deer, Peggy Bird,
Madonna Thunder Hawk, Loretta Ross, Eulynda Benally, Neferti
Tadiar, Suzanne Pharr, and Herman Gray.

I have also been informed by the analyses developing out of
Native American and Pacific studies, particularly Luana Ross,
Audra Simpson, Kimberly TallBear, Jennifer Denetdale, Angela
Gonzales, Kehaulani Kaunui, Vera Palmer, Justine Smith, Jace
Weaver, Michelene Pesantubbee, and Mary Churchill. I would
particularly like to thank the faculty of the Native Studies depart-
ment at the University of Michigan: Tiya Miles, Joe Gone, Michael
Witgen, Philip Deloria, and Greg Dowd.

The folks I worked with in the people of color caucus of Union
Theological Seminary taught me much about organizing from an
integrated mind-body-spirit framework. I would especially like
to thank Kimberleigh Jordan who has been a great friend and who
always helps me think about how to remain centered while doing

the work. In addition, I would also like to thank Sylvester Johnson, Angelica Guel, Lorena Parrish, Kanyere Eaton, Adam Clark, Harold Rhee, Yoon Jae Chang, Anthony Lee, and everyone else who was part of the people of color caucus.

To Alisa Bierria, my evil twin Andrea Ritchie, and my partner in crime Nadine Naber, I owe all countless spa treatments.

Most importantly, I have to thank my sister Justine Smith who has always been there for me, as well my nephews Tsali and Sunjay Smith, for their love and support..

Sections from the following articles were revised and included in this book: "Beyond Pro-choice Versus Pro-life: Women of Color and Reproductive Justice," *NWSA Journal,* (Spring, 2005); "Spiritual Appropriation as Sexual Violence," *Wicazo Sa Review,* (Spring 2005); "Boarding Schools, Human Rights, and Reparations," *Social Justice,* (2004); "Not an Indian Tradition: The Sexual Colonization of Native Women," *Hypatia,* (Spring 2003); "Domestic Violence, the State, and Social Change," *in* Natalie Sokoloff (editor), *Multicultural Perspectives on Domestic Violence,* Rutgers University Press, 2005; "Better Dead than Pregnant: The Colonization of Native Women's Health," in Anannya Bhattacharjee and Jael Silliman (eds.), *Policing the National Body,* South End Press, 2001; and "Christian Conquest and the Sexual Colonization of Native Women," in Carol Adams and Marie Fortune (eds.), *Violence Against Women and Children: A Christian Theological Sourcebook,* Continuum, 1995.

Foreword
Winona LaDuke

*D*ignity, love, and life. These basic principles ground social movements for justice, movements for change. We are people who are about creating, strengthening, and growing these movements. And the questions of how we build and nurture these movements are key to Andrea Smith's writing of *Conquest: Sexual Violence and American Indian Genocide.*

Movements for change, movements to make us well, to create healthy societies—whether tribal or American—are grounded in healing, are grounded in honesty. Voices of our stories as Indigenous women and the complexity of our situation are found in this amazing book, which opens parts of the mind and spirit to a healing.

Pam Colorado's poem, " What Every Indian Knows…" haunts me as I write, as I reflect on the subliminal yet constant nature of the predator culture, and its influence on my psyche.

What Every Indian Knows
Auschwitz ovens
burn bright

in America
twenty-four million
perished in the flame
    Nazi
      not a people
      but
      a way of life
Trail of Tears Humans
ends in Oklahoma
            an Indian name for
            Red Earth

Redder still
soaked in blood
of two hundred
removed tribes
the ovens burn bright
in America
Ancestral ashes
sweep the nation
carried in
      Prevailing winds
Survivors know
          the oven door stands wide
    and some like mouse
     cat crazed and frenzied
     turn
     and run into the jaws

at night
the cat calls softly
to the resting
us

As a woman who has organized across movements in this country, some truths remain constant. These truths are related to conquest, to the process of deconstructing peoples, and deconstructing Native women to be of less stature and value than others.

So it is that as a Native woman, you always know that you will be viewed as a woman of color, hence your politics will be race based, your analysis marginalized, and your experience seen as limited.

As a Native woman, you can always count on someone " little ladying" you, or treating you as a novelty. When I ran for the office of the Vice President of the United States as Ralph Nader's running mate in 2000, *The New York Times* referred to me as something like "an Indian Activist from a reservation in Minnesota, who butchers deer and beaver on her kitchen table... and has stated that the US is in violation of international law." *The New York Times* would not refer to me in the same context as my opponents, as, for instance a "Harvard educated economist and author."

As a Native woman from northern Minnesota, you can be sure that if you are killed in a violent death (which is ten times more likely to occur for Native women than white women in the state), that the National Guard will not spend hours of manpower scouring for your missing body. Compare this reality with the events which followed the terrible death of Dru Sjojin, who was abducted and murdered last year near the North Dakota/Minnesota border. More than 150 National Guard members, as well as nearly 1000 volunteers, searched for Dru, a beautiful blonde woman of the north. The search cost almost $150,000, which included expenses for payroll, fuel, and food. No Native woman would have generated this effort.

As a Native woman, you can be sure that you suffer from, what my colleague Agnes Williams calls " ethno-stress." In other words, you will wake up in the morning, and someone will be trying to steal your land, your legal rights, your sister will be in jail, your public Anglo-dominated school district will be calling about your children's conflicts with teachers or their spotty attendance, and your non-profit organization's funding is getting cut by a foundation because *you are no longer a priority*.

"Ethno-stress" is the reality of our situation as Native women, which is directly related to the process of colonization, sexual violence, dehumanization and marginalizing of who we are. The reality is that what is personal and intimate — whether your family history, the perceptions of you as an individual, or perceptions of your daughters — becomes the centerpiece of power relations between peoples and societies.

The reality is that there is no way to build a real movement for justice and peace, whether between peoples or between peoples and the land, without challenging the violence of historical and contemporary colonialism.

Andrea Smith has taken the mythology of dominance head on, putting voice to experiences we all feel, acknowledge and struggle with. Smith's writing puts these shared realities into the context of history and colonization, moving it beyond personal interactions. She links resistance to the marginalizing of Native women to broad feminist struggles for social and environmental justice. Her analysis of the relationship between these elements is clear and fierce.

Introduction

Women of color live in the dangerous intersections of gender and race. Within the mainstream antiviolence movement in the U.S., women of color who survive sexual or domestic abuse are often told that they must pit themselves against their communities, often portrayed stereotypically as violent, in order to begin the healing process. Communities of color, meanwhile, often advocate that women keep silent about sexual and domestic violence in order to maintain a united front against racism. In addition, the remedies for addressing sexual and domestic violence utilized by the antiviolence movement have proven to be generally inadequate for addressing the problems of gender violence in general, but particularly for addressing violence against women of color. The problem is not simply an issue of providing multicultural services to survivors of violence. Rather, the analysis of and strategies for addressing gender violence have failed to address the manner in which gender violence is not simply a tool of patriarchal control, but also serves as a tool of racism and colonialism. That is, colonial relationships are themselves gendered and sexualized.

This book comes out of my work in Native sovereignty, antiviolence, environmental justice, reproductive rights, and women of color organizing. During the late 1980s and early 1990s, I worked with the Chicago chapter of Women of All Red Nations (WARN). At the same time, I worked with mainstream antiviolence and reproductive rights organizations such as the National Coalition Against Sexual Assault (which no longer exists) and the National Abortion Rights Action League. I later became involved with the Committee on Women, Population, and the Environment, which focuses on policies of population control in their various forms.

Frustrated with how mainstream groups were defining issues of violence and reproductive rights in ways that were inherently oppressive to indigenous women and women of color, I became involved in co-organizing INCITE! Women of Color Against Violence. INCITE! is a national organization of feminists of color which builds coalitions around the intersections of state violence and interpersonal sexual and domestic violence from a grass-roots-organizing, rather than a social service delivery, perspective. Much of my work in INCITE! was informed by my involvement in the first Critical Resistance: Beyond the Prison Industrial Complex conference held in Berkeley in 1999. Critical Resistance organizes against prisons from an abolitionist rather than a reformist perspective. Through INCITE! I then became involved in the American Indian Boarding School Healing Project, which seeks to document the abuses perpetrated in boarding schools, provide a space for healing from these abuses, and build a movement to demand reparations in conjunction with other reparations struggles. From these organizing efforts as well as numerous others, I have had the opportunity to learn from countless indigenous women and women of color who have helped shape my analysis about violence. Consequently, while I take responsibility for all the errors in the book, I cannot claim that the analysis is original — analysis is always a group effort that arises from the context of struggle.

This book will focus particularly on sexual violence as a tool of patriarchy *and* colonialism in Native communities, both historically and today. However, this analysis has broader implications for all women. An examination of how sexual violence serves the goals of colonialism forces us to reconsider how we define sexual violence, as well as the strategies we employ to eradicate gender violence.

Putting Native women at the center of analysis compels us to look at the role of the state in perpetrating both race-based and gender-based violence. We cannot limit our conception of sexual violence to individual acts of rape — rather it encompasses a wide range of strategies designed not only to destroy peoples, but to destroy their sense of being a people.

The first chapter outlines how colonizers have historically used sexual violence as a primary tool of genocide. It also provides my theoretical framework for the rest of the book. I argue that sexual violence is a tool by which certain peoples become marked as inherently "rapable." These peoples then are violated, not only through direct or sexual assault, but through a wide variety of state policies, ranging from environmental racism to sterilization abuse.

Chapter 2 focuses on U.S. and Canadian American Indian boarding school policies, which are largely responsible for the epidemic rates of sexual violence in Native communities today. Boarding school policies demonstrate that violence in Native communities, and by extension, other communities of color, is not simply a symptom of dysfunctionality in these communities. Rather, violence is the continuing effect of human rights violations perpetrated by state policies. Consequently, these policies serve as a focal point for thinking about how we can center an antiviolence analysis in the movement for reparations, because gender violence is a harm for which the state needs to be held accountable.

Sexual violence against Native peoples takes many forms. In Chapter 3, I analyze how environmental racism can be seen as a form of sexual violence against indigenous peoples. Native lands are disproportionately impacted by environmental degradation and contamination in this country, since the majority of energy resources in the United States are on Indian lands. The effects of environmental contamination often severely impact women's reproductive systems. In addition, I will explore how the environmental movement fails to organize from an intersectional race/gender analysis and how this failure contributes to its support of policies that are both racist and sexist.

One reason why Native women have been historically targeted for sexual violence arises from the colonial desire to stop them from reproducing. In Chapter 4, I look at contemporary manifestations of what I would call state-sponsored forms of sexual violence in racist reproductive policies. In particular, I look at sterilization abuse and the promotion of long-acting hormonal contraceptives in Native communities, and in other communities of color. I also argue that the current "pro-choice" framework that undergirds the mainstream reproductive rights movement is inadequate for addressing the attacks on the reproductive rights of indigenous women, women of color, poor women, and women with disabilities.

Chapter 5 is an exploratory essay on yet another form of sexual violence: medical experimentation in Native communities. Through my work with Chicago Women of All Red Nations and the Boarding School Healing Project, I have informally heard of numerous medical experimentation programs conducted on Native peoples, generally without their informed consent. When we have tried to investigate these cases, we find that those people who have medical and scientific backgrounds are often so committed to the essential goodness of the Western medical establishment that they are unwilling to explore the nature of these programs. Meanwhile, Native peoples on the grassroots level are organizing against these programs, but because they do not have the proper "credentials," they are dismissed as alarmists.

Progressives often have no trouble seeing the inherent corruptness of institutions such as prisons or border control, and hence have no difficulty believing that those in power in these institutions may abuse power and not serve the interests of communities. However, they often have difficulty viewing the medical establishment with the same lens of suspicion, despite the fact that it is a multibillion-dollar industry. This chapter is a call for more investigation and organizing into the area of medical experimentation to bring more visibility to this form of violence and to provide clearer information as to what is going on in these programs.

Despite the more than 500 years of genocide that Native peoples have faced, they continue to survive and organize, not only on their behalf but on behalf of all peoples. Native spiritualities have always been a cornerstone of resistance struggles. These spiritualities affirm the goodness of Native communities when the larger society dehumanizes them. They affirm the interconnectedness of all things that provides the framework of re-creating communities that are based on mutual responsibility and respect rather than violence and domination. Hence, it should not be a surprise that colonialists also appropriate Native spirituality in another form of sexual violence. Chapter 6 suggests that we can see spiritual appropriation as a form of sexual violence and explores how colonial ideology attempts to transform Native spiritualities from a site of healing to a site of sexual exploitation.

Chapter 7 discusses what strategies for eradicating gender violence follow from the analysis set forth in this book. It is clear that the state has a prominent role in perpetrating violence against Native women in particular and women of color in general. However, most of the strategies developed by the mainstream antiviolence movement depend on the state as the *solution* for ending violence. In particular, the antiviolence movement has relied on a racist and colonial criminal legal system to stop domestic and sexual violence with insufficient attention to how this system oppresses communities of color. In this chapter I will focus on strategies for addressing interpersonal acts of gender violence that simultaneously address state violence. By putting Native women at the center of analysis, I will argue, we can develop more comprehensive strategies for ending gender violence that benefit not only indigenous women and women of color, but all people affected by gender violence.

Finally, in Chapter 8 I examine how an antiviolence strategy that addresses state violence requires antiviolence advocates to organize against U.S. empire. If we acknowledge the state as a perpetrator of violence against women (particularly indigenous women and women of color) and as a perpetrator of genocide against indigenous peoples, we are challenged to imagine alternative forms of governance that do not presume the continuing existence of the U.S. in particular and the nation-state in general.

We must recognize, for example, that the consolidation of U.S. empire abroad through the never-ending "war on terror" is inextricably linked to U.S. attacks on Native sovereignty within U.S. borders. This chapter looks to alternative visions of governance articulated by Native women activists that do not depend on domination and force but rely on systems of kinship, respect, and reciprocity.

Chapter 1

Sexual Violence as a Tool of Genocide

[Rape] is nothing more or less than a conscious process of intimidation by which all men keep all women in a state of fear.[1]

*R*ape as "nothing more or less" than a tool of patriarchal control undergirds the philosophy of the white-dominated women's antiviolence movement. This philosophy has been critiqued by many women of color, including critical race theorist Kimberle Crenshaw, for its lack of attention to racism and other forms of oppression. Crenshaw analyzes how male-dominated conceptions of race and white-dominated conceptions of gender stand in the way of a clear understanding of violence against women of color. It is inadequate, she argues, to investigate the oppression of women of color by examining race and gender oppressions separately and then putting the two analyses together, because the overlap between racism and sexism transforms the dynamics. Instead, Crenshaw advocates replacing the "additive" approach with an "intersectional" approach.

The problem is not simply that both discourses fail women of color by not acknowledging the 'additional' issue of race or of patriarchy but, rather, that the discourses are often inadequate even to the discrete tasks of articulating the full dimensions of racism and sexism.[2]

Despite her intersectional approach, Crenshaw falls short of describing how a politics of intersectionality might fundamentally shift how we analyze sexual/domestic violence. If sexual violence is not simply a tool of patriarchy but also a tool of colonialism and racism, then entire communities of color are the victims of sexual violence. As Neferti Tadiar argues, *colonial relationships are themselves gendered and sexualized.*

> The economies and political relations of nations are libidinally configured, that is, they are grasped and effected in terms of sexuality. This global and regional fantasy is not, however, only metaphorical, but real insofar as it grasps a system of political and economic practices already at work among these nations.[3]

Within this context, according to Tadiar, "the question to be asked…is, Who is getting off on this? Who is getting screwed and by whom?"[4] Thus, while both Native men and women have been subjected to a reign of sexualized terror, sexual violence does not affect Indian men and women in the same way. When a Native woman suffers abuse, this abuse is an attack on her identity as a woman and an attack on her identity as Native. The issues of colonial, race, and gender oppression cannot be separated. This fact explains why in my experience as a rape crisis counselor, every Native survivor I ever counseled said to me at one point, "I wish I was no longer Indian." As I will discuss in this chapter, women of color do not just face quantitatively more issues when they suffer violence (e.g., less media attention, language barriers, lack of support in the judicial system) but their experience is qualitatively different from that of white women.

Ann Stoler's analysis of racism sheds light on this relationship between sexual violence and colonialism. She argues that racism, far from being a reaction to crisis in which racial others are scapegoated for social ills, is a permanent part of the social fabric. "Racism is not an effect but a tactic in the internal fission of society into binary opposition, a means of creating 'biologized' internal enemies, against whom society must defend itself."[5] She notes that in the modern state, it is the constant purification and elimination of racialized enemies within the state that ensures the growth of the national body. "Racism does not merely arise in moments of crisis, in sporadic cleansings. It is internal to the biopolitical state, woven into the web of the social body, threaded through its fabric."[6]

Similarly, Kate Shanley notes that Native peoples are a permanent "present absence" in the U.S. colonial imagination, an "absence" that reinforces at every turn the conviction that Native peoples are indeed vanishing and that the conquest of Native lands is justified. Ella Shohat and Robert Stam describe this absence as,

> an ambivalently repressive mechanism [which] dispels the anxiety in the face of the Indian, whose very presence is a reminder of the initially precarious grounding of the American nation-state itself...In a temporal paradox, living Indians were induced to 'play dead,' as it were, in order to perform a narrative of manifest destiny in which their role, ultimately, was to disappear.[7]

This "absence" is effected through the metaphorical transformation of Native bodies into a pollution of which the colonial body must constantly purify itself. For instance, as white Californians described them in the 1860s, Native people were "the dirtiest lot of human beings on earth."[8] They wear "filthy rags, with their persons unwashed, hair uncombed and swarming with vermin."[9] The following 1885 Procter & Gamble ad for Ivory Soap also illustrates this equation between Indian bodies and dirt.

> *We were once factious, fierce and wild,*
> *In peaceful arts unreconciled*
> *Our blankets smeared with grease and stains*
> *From buffalo meat and settlers' veins.*
> *Through summer's dust and heat content*
> *From moon to moon unwashed we went,*
> *But IVORY SOAP came like a ray*
> *Of light across our darkened way*
> *And now we're civil, kind and good*
> *And keep the laws as people should,*
> *We wear our linen, lawn and lace*
> *As well as folks with paler face*
> *And now I take, where'er we go*

This cake of IVORY SOAP to show
What civilized my squaw and me
And made us clean and fair to see.[10]

In the colonial imagination, Native bodies are also immanently polluted with sexual sin. Theorists Albert Cave, Robert Warrior, H. C. Porter, and others have demonstrated that Christian colonizers often likened Native peoples to the biblical Canaanites, both worthy of mass destruction.[11] What makes Canaanites supposedly worthy of destruction in the biblical narrative and Indian peoples supposedly worthy of destruction in the eyes of their colonizers is that they both personify sexual sin. In the Bible, Canaanites commit acts of sexual perversion in Sodom (Gen. 19:1–29), are the descendants of the unsavory relations between Lot and his daughters (Gen. 19:30–38), are the descendants of the sexually perverse Ham (Gen. 9:22–27), and prostitute themselves in service of their gods (Gen. 28:21–22, Deut. 28:18, 1 Kings 14:24, 2 Kings 23:7, Hosea 4:13, Amos 2:7).

Similarly, Native peoples, in the eyes of the colonizers, are marked by their sexual perversity. Alexander Whitaker, a minister in Virginia, wrote in 1613: "They live naked in bodie, as if their shame of their sinne deserved no covering: Their names are as naked as their bodie: They esteem it a virtue to lie, deceive and steale as their master the divell teacheth them."[12] Furthermore, according to Bernardino de Minaya, a Dominican cleric, "Their marriages are not a sacrament but a sacrilege. They are idolatrous, libidinous, and commit sodomy. Their chief desire is to eat, drink, worship heathen idols, and commit bestial obscenities."[13]

Because Indian bodies are "dirty," they are considered sexually violable and "rapable," and the rape of bodies that are considered inherently impure or dirty simply does not count. For instance, prostitutes are almost never believed when they say they have been raped because the dominant society considers the bodies of sex workers undeserving of integrity and violable at all times. Similarly, the history of mutilation of Indian bodies, both living and dead, makes it clear that Indian people are not entitled to bodily integrity.

I saw the body of White Antelope with the privates cut off, and I heard a soldier say he was going to make a tobacco-pouch out of them.[14]

At night Dr. Rufus Choate [and] Lieutenant Wentz C. Miller...went up the ravine, decapitated the dead Qua-ha-das, and placing the heads in some gunny sacks, brought them back to be boiled out for future scientific knowledge.[15]

Each of the braves was shot down and scalped by the wild volunteers, who out with their knives and cutting two parallel gashes down their backs, would strip the skin from the quivering flesh to make razor straps of.[16]

Dr. Tuner, of Lexington, Iowa, visited this solitary grave [of Black Hawk] and robbed it of its tenant...and sent the body to Alton, Ill., where the skeleton was wired together. [It was later returned] but here it remained but a short time ere vandal hands again carried it away and placed it in the Burlington, Iowa Geographical and Historical Society, where it was consumed by fire in 1855.[17]

One more dexterous than the rest, proceeded to flay the chief's [Tecumseh's] body; then, cutting the skin in narrow strips...at once, a supply of razor-straps for the more "ferocious" of his brethren.[18]

Andrew Jackson...supervised the mutilation of 800 or so Creek Indian corpses—the bodies of men, women and children that he and his men massacred—cutting off their noses to count and preserve a record of the dead, slicing long strips of flesh from their bodies to tan and turn into bridle reins.[19]

A few nights after this, some soldiers dug Mangus' body out again and took his head and boiled it during the night, and prepared the skull to send to the museum in New York.[20]

In 1990, Illinois governor Jim Thompson echoed these sentiments when he refused to close down an open Indian burial mound in the town of Dixon. The State of Illinois had built a museum around this mound to publicly display Indian remains. Thompson argued that he was as much Indian as current Indians, and consequently, he had as much right as they to determine the fate of Indian remains.[21] The remains were "his." The Chicago press similarly attempted to challenge the identity of Indian people protesting his decision by asserting that they were either only "part" Indian, or merely claiming to be Indian.[22] In effect, the

Illinois state government conveyed the message to Indians that being on constant display for white consumers, in life and in death, is acceptable. Furthermore, Indian identity itself is under the control of the colonizer, and subject to challenge or eradication at any time.

In 1992, Ontario finance minister Jim Flaherty argued that the Canadian government could boost health-care funding for "real people in real towns" by cutting the bureaucracy that serves *only* Native peoples.[23] The extent to which Native peoples are not seen as "real" people in the larger colonial discourse indicates the success of sexual violence, among other racist and colonialist forces, in destroying the perceived humanity of Native peoples. As Aime Cesaire puts it, colonization = thingification.[24] As Stoler explains this process of racialized colonization:

> The more "degenerates" and "abnormals" [in this case Native peoples] are eliminated, the lives of those who speak will be stronger, more vigorous, and improved. The enemies are not political adversaries, but those identified as external and internal threats to the population. Racism is the condition that makes it acceptable to put [certain people] to death in a society of normalization.[25]

The project of colonial sexual violence establishes the ideology that Native bodies are inherently violable—and by extension, that Native lands are also inherently violable.

As a consequence of this colonization and abuse of their bodies, Indian people learn to internalize self-hatred, because body image is integrally related to self-esteem. When one's body is not respected, one begins to hate oneself.[26] Anne, a Native boarding school student, reflects on this process:

> You better not touch yourself...If I looked at somebody...lust, sex, and I got scared of those sexual feelings. And I did not know how to handle them...What really confused me was if intercourse was sin, why are people born?...It took me a really long time to get over the fact that...I've sinned: I had a child.[27]

As her words indicate, when the bodies of Indian people are designated as inherently sinful and dirty, it becomes a sin just to be Indian. Native peoples internalize the genocidal project through self-destruction. As a rape crisis counselor, it was not a surprise to me that Indians who have survived sexual abuse would often say that they no longer wish to be Indian. Native peoples' individual experiences of sexual violation echo 500 years of sexual colonization in which Native peoples' bodies have been deemed inherently impure. The Menominee poet Chrystos writes in such a voice in her poem "Old Indian Granny."

> You told me about all the Indian women you counsel
> who say they don't want to be Indian anymore
> because a white man or an Indian one raped them
> or killed their brother
> or somebody tried to run them over in the street
> or insulted them or all of it
> our daily bread of hate
> Sometimes I don't want to be an Indian either
> but I've never said so out loud before…
> Far more than being hungry
> having no place to live or dance
> no decent job no home to offer a Granny
> It's knowing with each invisible breath
> that if you don't make something pretty
> they can hang on their walls or wear around their necks
> you might as well be dead.[28]

Mending the Sacred Hoop Technical Assistance Project in Duluth, Minnesota, reports that a primary barrier antiviolence advocates face in addressing violence in Indian country is that community members will argue that sexual violence is "traditional." This phenomenon indicates the extent to which our communities have internalized self-hatred. Frantz Fanon argues, "In the colonial context, as we have already pointed out, the natives fight among themselves. They tend to use each other as a screen, and each hides from his neighbor the national enemy."[29] Then, as Michael Taussig notes, Native peoples are portrayed by the dominant culture as inherently violent, self-destructive, and dysfunctional.[30] For example, townsperson Mike Whelan made the following statement at a 1990 zoning hearing, calling for the denial of a permit for an Indian battered women's shelter in Lake Andes, South Dakota.

Indian Culture as I view it, is presently so mongrelized as to be a mix of dependency on the Federal Government and a primitive society wholly on the outside of the mainstream of western civilization and thought. The Native American Culture as we know it now, not as it formerly existed, is a culture of hopelessness, godlessness, of joblessness, and lawlessness...Alcoholism, social disease, child abuse, and poverty are the hallmarks of this so called culture that you seek to promote, and I would suggest to you that the brave men of the ghost dance would hang their heads in shame at what you now pass off as that culture....I think that the Indian way of life as you call it, to me means cigarette burns in arms of children, double checking the locks on my cars, keeping a loaded shotgun by my door, and car bodies and beer cans on the front lawn....This is not a matter of race, it is a matter of keeping our community and neighborhood away from that evil that you and your ideas promote.[31]

Similarly, in a recent case among the Aboriginal peoples of Australia, a judge ruled that a 50-year-old Aboriginal man's rape of a 15-year-old girl was not a serious crime, but an example of traditional culture. He ruled that the girl "knew what was expected of her" and "didn't need protection" when raped by a man who had been previously convicted of murdering his former wife. An "expert" anthropologist in the case testified that the rape was "traditional" and "morally correct."[32] According to Judy Atkinson, an Aboriginal professor, survivors have reported numerous incidents of law enforcement officials dismissing reports of violence because they consider such violence to be "cultural behavior." "We are living in a war zone in Aboriginal communities," states Atkinson. "Different behaviors come out of that," she says. "Yet the courts of law validate that behavior."[33]

Taussig comments on the irony of this logic: "Men are conquered not by invasion, but by themselves. It is a strange sentiment, is it not, when faced with so much brutal evidence of invasion."[34] But as Fanon notes, this destructive behavior is not "the consequence of the organization of his nervous system or of characterial originality, but the direct product of the colonial system."[35]

Tadiar's description of colonial relationships as an enactment of the "prevailing mode of heterosexual relations" is useful because it underscores the extent to which U.S. colonizers view the subjugation of women of the Native nations as critical to the success of the economic, cultural, and political colonization.[36] Stoler notes that the imperial discourses on sexuality "cast white women as the bearers of more racist imperial order."[37] By extension, Native women are bearers of a counter-imperial order and pose a supreme threat to the dominant culture. Symbolic and literal control over their bodies is important in the war against Native people, as these testimonies illustrate:

> When I was in the boat I captured a beautiful Carib woman....I conceived desire to take pleasure.... I took a rope and thrashed her well, for which she raised such unheard screams that you would not have believed your ears. Finally we came to an agreement in such a manner that I can tell you that she seemed to have been brought up in a school of harlots.[38]

> Two of the best looking of the squaws were lying in such a position, and from the appearance of the genital organs and of their wounds, there can be no doubt that they were first ravished and then shot dead. Nearly all of the dead were mutilated.[39]

> One woman, big with child, rushed into the church, clasping the altar and crying for mercy for herself and unborn babe. She was followed, and fell pierced with a dozen lances...The child was torn alive from the yet palpitating body of its mother, first plunged into the holy water to be baptized, and immediately its brains were dashed out against a wall.[40]

> The Christians attacked them with buffets and beatings...Then they behaved with such temerity and shamelessness that the most powerful ruler of the island had to see his own wife raped by a Christian officer.[41]

> I heard one man say that he had cut a woman's private parts out, and had them for exhibition on a stick. I heard another man say that he had cut the fingers off of an Indian, to get the rings off his hand. I also heard of numerous instances in which men had cut out the private parts of females, and stretched them over their saddle-bows and some of them over their hats.[42]

The history of sexual violence and genocide among Native women illustrates how gender violence functions as a tool for racism and colonialism among women of color in general. For example, African American women were also viewed as inherently rapable. Yet where colonizers used sexual violence to eliminate Native populations, slave owners used rape to reproduce an exploitable labor force. (The children of Black slave women inherited their slave status.) And because Black women were seen as the property of their slave owners, their rape at the hands of these men did not "count." As one southern politician declared in the early twentieth century, there was no such thing as a "virtuous colored girl" over the age of 14.[43] The testimonies from slave narratives and other sources reveal the systematic abuse of slave women by white slave owners.

> For a period of four months, including the latter stages of pregnancy, delivery, and recent recovery therefrom…he beat her with clubs, iron chains and other deadly weapons time after time; burnt her; inflicted stripes over and often with scourges, which literally excoriated her whole body; forced her to work in inclement seasons, without being duly clad; provided for her insufficient food, exacted labor beyond her strength, and wantonly beat her because she could not comply with his requisitions. These enormities, besides others, too disgusting, particularly designated, the prisoner, without his heart once relenting, practiced…even up to the last hours of the victim's existence.
> [A report of a North Carolina slaveowner's abuse and eventual murder of a slave woman.][44]

> [My master] was a good man but he was pretty bad among the women. Married or not married, made no difference to him. Whoever he wanted among the slaves, he went and got her or had her meet him somewhere out in the bushes. I have known him to go to the shack and make the woman's husband sit outside while he went into his wife.….He wasn't no worse than none of the rest. They all used their women like they wanted to, and there wasn't nobody to say anything about it. Neither the woman nor the men could help themselves. They submitted to it but kept praying to God.
> [Slave testimony from South Carolina.][45]

> "Some of the troops," a white complained to their commander Rufus Saxton, "have forcibly entered the negro houses and after driving out the men (in one instance at the point of a bayonet) have attempted to ravish women." When the men protested and sought to protect "their wives and sisters," they "were cruelly beaten and

threatened with instant death." "The morals of the old plantation" Saxton feared, "seem revived in the army of occupation." [A report of the activities of Union soldiers during the Civil War.][46]

Immigrant women as well have endured a long history of sexual exploitation in the U.S. For instance, racially discriminatory employment laws forced thousands of Chinese immigrant women into prostitution. To supplement their meager incomes, impoverished Chinese families often sold their daughters into prostitution. Other women were lured to the U.S. with the promise of a stable marriage or job, only to find themselves trapped in the sex trade. By 1860, almost a quarter of the Chinese in San Francisco (all female) were employed in prostitution.[47]

Karen Warren argues that patriarchal society is a dysfunctional system that mirrors the dysfunctional nuclear family. That is, severe abuse in the family continues because the family members learn to regard it as "normal." A victim of abuse may come to see that her abuse is not "normal" when she has contact with less abusive families. Similarly, Warren argues, patriarchal society is a dysfunctional system based on domination and violence. "Dysfunctional systems are often maintained through systematic denial, a failure or inability to see the reality of a situation. This denial need not be conscious, intentional, or malicious; it only needs to be pervasive to be effective."[48]

At the time of Columbus's exploits, European society was a dysfunctional system, racked by mass poverty, disease, religious oppression, war, and institutionalized violence. For example, in the Inquisition, hundreds of thousands of Jewish people were slaughtered and their confiscated property was used to fund Columbus's voyages. David Stannard writes,

> Violence, of course, was everywhere...In Milan in 1476 a man was torn to pieces by an enraged mob and his dismembered limbs were eaten by his tormenters. In Paris and Lyon, Huguenots were killed and butchered, and their various body parts were sold openly in the streets. Other eruptions of bizarre torture, murder, and ritual cannibalism were not uncommon.[49]

Furthermore, European societies were thoroughly misogynistic. The Christian patriarchy which structured European society was inherently violent, as has been thoroughly documented.[50] For example, because English women were not allowed to express political opinions, a woman who spoke out against taxation in 1664 was condemned to having her tongue nailed to a tree near a highway, with a paper fastened to her back detailing her offense.[51] Hatred for women was most fully manifested in the witch hunts. In some English towns, as many as a third of the population were accused of witchcraft.[52] The women targeted for destruction were those most independent from patriarchal authority: single women, widows, and healers.[53]

The more peaceful and egalitarian nature of Native societies did not escape the notice of the colonizers. In the "colonial" period, it was a scandal in the colonies that a number of white people chose to live among Indian people while virtually no Indians voluntarily chose to live among the colonists. According to J. Hector St. John de Crevecoeur, the eighteenth-century author of *Letters from an American Farmer*, "Thousands of Europeans are Indians, and we have no example of even one of these Aborigines having from choice become Europeans!"[54] Colonists also noted that Native peoples rarely committed sexual violence against white prisoners, unlike the colonists. Brigadier General James Clinton of the Continental Army said to his soldiers as they were sent off to destroy the Iroquois nation in 1779: "Bad as the savages are, they never violate the chastity of any women, their prisoners."[55] William Apess, a nineteenth century Pequot, asked, "Where, in the records of Indian barbarity, can we point to a violated female?"[56] Shohat and Stam argue, the real purpose behind colonial terror "was not to force the indigenes to become Europeans, but to keep Europeans from becoming indigenes."[57]

In contrast to the deeply patriarchal nature of European societies, prior to colonization, Indian societies for the most part were not male dominated. Women served as spiritual, political, and military leaders, and many societies were matrilineal. Although there existed a division of labor between women and men, women's labor and men's labor were accorded similar status.[58] As women and men lived in balance, Native societies were consequently much less authoritarian than their European counterparts. Paul LeJeune, a Jesuit priest, remarked in the seventeenth century:

[Native peoples] imagine that they ought by right of birth, to enjoy the liberty of wild ass colts, rendering no homage to anyone whomsoever, except when they like…All the authority of their chief is in his tongue's end, for he is powerful insofar as he is eloquent; and even if he kills himself talking and haranguing, he will not be obeyed unless he pleases the savages.[59]

Furthermore, 70 percent of tribes did not practice war at all.[60] For those that did engage in war, the intent was generally not to annihilate the enemy, but to accrue honor through bravery. One accrued more honor by getting close enough to an enemy to touch him and leaving him alive than by killing him. Tom Holm writes:

Traditional Indian warfare had much more in common with Euroamerican contact sports, like football, boxing, and hockey, than with wars fought in the European manner. This, of course, is not to say that nobody was ever killed…They were—just as they are in modern contact sports—but the point of the exercise was not as a rule purposefully lethal.[61]

Of course, in discussing these trends, it is important not to overgeneralize or give the impression that Native communities were utopian prior to colonization. Certainly gender violence occurred prior to colonization. Nevertheless, both oral and written records often note its relative rarity as well as the severity of the punishment for perpetrators of violence. This record of punishment for sexual assault among the Kiowa serves as an illustration:

The Kiowas inflicted such embarrassment and ridicule on a criminal that he reportedly soon died. The man was a chronic rapist who was finally taught the error of his ways by the women; they laid an ambush and baited the trap with a beautiful young girl. When he took the bait, they suddenly appeared and overpowered him. As others held him helpless on the ground, each woman in turn raised her skirts and sat on his face. The experience was not in itself fatal, but the loss of status stemming from the derision it inspired was. The possibility of such drastic punishment was perhaps more chastening in its effect than the threat of the electric chair in more sophisticated societies.[62]

Similar practices existed among the Anishinabe:

Wife battering, as we have seen, was neither accepted nor tolerated among the Anishinabe people until after the freedom to live

Ojibwe was subdued. Wife battering emerged simultaneously with the disintegration of Ojibwe ways of life and the beginning use of alcohol. The behavior of the Ojibwe people under the influence of alcohol is often totally contrary to Anishinabe values. It is especially contrary to the self discipline previously necessary to the development of Ojibwe character.

There is no single philosophy among the people in today's society regarding the social illness of wife battering. Many have forgotten or did not receive the teachings of the social laws surrounding it. In the old Ojibwe society, society itself was responsible for what took place within it; today that is not so. What is the evidence of that statement? The harmful, destructive, traumatic cycle of domestic violence that is befalling the Anishinabe Children of the Nation.

Today we have lost a lot of the traditions, values, ways of life, laws, language, teachings of the Elders, respect, humility as Anishinabe people because of the European mentality we have accepted. For the Anishinabe people to survive as a Nation, together we must turn back the pages of time. We must face reality, do an evaluation of ourselves as a people—why we were created to live in harmony with one another as Anishinabe people and to live in harmony with the Creator's creation.[63]

European women were often surprised to find that, even in war, they went unmolested by their Indian captors. Mary Rowlandson said of her experience: "I have been in the midst of roaring Lions, and Savage Bears, that feared neither God, nor Man, nor the Devil…and yet not one of them ever offered the least abuse of unchastity to me in word or action."[64] Between 1675 and 1763, almost 40 percent of women who were taken captive by Native people in New England chose to remain with their captors.[65] In 1899, an editorial signed by Mrs. Teall appeared in the *Syracuse Herald-Journal*, discussing the status of women in Iroquois society.

They had one custom the white men are not ready, even yet, to accept. The women of the Iroquois had a public and influential position. They had a council of their own…which had the initiative in the discussion; subjects presented by them being settled in the councils of the chiefs and elders; in this latter council the women had an orator of their own (often of their own sex) to present and speak for them. There are sometimes female chiefs…The wife owned all the property...The family was hers; descent was counted through the mother.[66]

In response to her editorial, a man who signed himself as "Student" replied:

> Women among the Iroquois, Mrs. Teall says...had a council of their own, and orators and chiefs. Why does she not add what follows in explanation of why such deference was paid to women, that "in the torture of prisoners women were thought more skillful and subtle than the men" and the men of the inquisition were outdone in the refinement of cruelty practiced upon their victims by these savages. It is true also that succession was through women, not the men, in Iroquois tribes, but the explanation is that it was generally a difficult guess to tell the fatherhood of children... The Indian maiden never learned to blush. The Indians, about whom so much rhetoric has been wasted, were a savage, merciless lot who would never have developed themselves nearer to civilization than they were found by missionaries and traders....Their love was to butcher and burn, to roast their victims and eat them, to lie and rob, to live in filth, men, women, children, dogs and fleas crowded together.[67]

Thus, the demonization of Native women can be seen as a strategy of white men to maintain control over white women. This demonization was exemplified by the captivity narratives which became a popular genre in the U.S.[68] These narratives were supposedly first-person narratives of white women who were abducted by "savages" and forced to undergo untold savagery. Their tales, however, were usually written by white men who had their own agenda. For instance, in 1823 James Seaver of New York interviewed Mary Jemison, who was taken as captive by the Seneca. Jemison chose to remain among them when she was offered her freedom, but Seaver is convinced that she is protecting the Indian people by not describing their full savagery. "The vices of the Indians, she appeared disposed not to aggravate, and seemed to take pride in extolling their virtues. A kind of family pride induced her to withhold whatever would blot the character of her descendants, and perhaps induced her to keep back many things that would have been interesting."[69] Consequently, he supplements her narrative with material "from authentic sources" and Jemison's cousin, George.[70] Seaver, nevertheless, attributes these supplements to her voice in this supposed first-person narrative.

In these narratives, we can find what Carol Adams terms an "absent referent." Adams provides an example by noting how the term "battered woman" makes women the inherent victims of battering. The batterer is rendered invisible and is thus the absent referent.[71] Another example of an absent referent can be found in the Christian symbol of the crucifixion, in which Jesus is represented as one whose inherent nature and purpose is to be crucified. The individuals who put him on the cross, never depicted in representations of the cross, are erased as the perpetrators and they become the absent referent.

Andrea Dworkin argues that in a patriarchal system, "men are distinguished from women by their commitment to do violence rather than to be victimized by it. In adoring violence—from the crucifixion of Christ to the cinematic portrayal of General Patton—men seek to adore themselves."[72] June Namias argues that the point of these depictions is to instill the belief in white women that they need white men to protect them from savages.[73] Jane Caputi also suggests that in depictions of killings of women, the killer plays the alter ego to the male reader or viewer of the killing. "This convention allows the identifying viewer to gratifyingly fantasize himself in the two mutually reinforcing male roles at once. He is both...the protector and the menace."[74] According to Jane McCrea, the white man both symbolically kills the white woman through the Indians, which mirror his desires, and rushes to her rescue. The white male is absent when the violence occurs. Yet, he is the one who has created the image in which the white man is the absent referent. He glorifies his ability to brutalize white women through the Indian savage while denying his culpability.

Meanwhile, Native women are completely absent from this picture, and consequently, their actual sexual brutalization at the hands of white men escapes notice. The white man *literally* brutalizes her, while *symbolically* brutalizing the white woman through this representational practice. Native men are scapegoated for his actions so white women will see them as the enemy, while white men remain unaccountable.

Paula Gunn Allen argues that colonizers realized that in order to subjugate indigenous nations they would have to subjugate women within these nations. Native peoples needed to learn the value of hierarchy, the role of physical abuse in maintaining that hierarchy, and the importance of women remaining submissive to their men. They had to convince "both men and women that a woman's proper place was under the authority of her husband and that a man's proper place was under the authority of the priests."[75] She further argues:

> It was to the advantage of white men to mislead white women, and themselves, into believing that their treatment of women was superior to the treatment by the men of the group which they considered savage. Had white women discovered that all women were not mistreated, they might have been intolerant of their men's abusiveness.[76]

Thus in order to colonize a people whose society was not hierarchical, colonizers must first naturalize hierarchy through instituting patriarchy. Patriarchal gender violence is the process by which colonizers inscribe hierarchy and domination on the bodies of the colonized. Ironically, while enslaving women's bodies, colonizers argued that they were actually somehow freeing Native women from the "oppression" they supposedly faced in Native nations. Thomas Jefferson argued that Native women "are submitted to unjust drudgery. This I believe is the case with every barbarous people. It is civilization alone which replaces women in the enjoyment of their equality."[77] The *Mariposa Gazette* similarly noted that when Indian women were safely under the control of white men, they are "neat, and tidy, and industrious, and soon learn to discharge domestic duties properly and creditably." In 1862, a Native man in Conrow Valley was killed and scalped with his head twisted off, his killers saying, "You will not kill any more women and children."[78] Apparently, Native women can only be free while under the dominion of white men, and both Native and white women have to be protected from Indian men, rather than from white men.

A 1985 Virginia Slims ad reflected a similar notion that white patriarchy saves Native women from oppression. On the left side of the ad was a totem pole of cartoonish figures of Indian women. Their names: Princess Wash and Scrub, Little Running Water Fetcher, Keeper of the Teepee, Princess Breakfast, Lunch and Dinner Preparer, Woman Who Gathers Firewood, Princess Buffalo Robe Sewer, Little Woman Who Weaves All Day, and Woman Who Plucks Feathers for Chief's Headdress. The caption on top of the totem pole reads: "Virginia Slims remembers one of many societies where the women stood head and shoulders above the men." On the right side of the ad is a model adorned with makeup and dressed in a tight skirt, nylons, and high heels, with the familiar caption: "You've come a long way, baby." The message is that Native women, oppressed in their tribal societies, need to be liberated into a patriarchal standard of beauty, where their true freedom lies. The historical record suggests, as Paula Gunn Allen argues, that the real roots of feminism should be found in Native societies. But in this Virginia Slims ad, feminism is tied to colonial conquest — (white) women's liberation is founded upon the destruction of supposedly patriarchal Native societies.

Today we see this discourse utilized in the "war on terror." To justify the bombing of Afghanistan, Laura Bush declared, "The fight against terrorism is also a fight for the rights and dignity of women."[79] These sentiments were shared by mainstream feminists. Eleanor Smeal, former president of the National Organization for Women (NOW) and founder and president of the Fund for a Feminist Majority said, "Without 9/11, we could not get the Afghanistan tragedy in focus enough for the world powers to stop the Taliban's atrocities or to remove the Taliban. Tragically, it took a disaster for them to act definitively enough."[80]

It seems the best way to liberate women is to bomb them. Meanwhile, the Revolutionary Association of Women of Afghanistan (RAWA), whose members were the very women who were to be liberated by this war, denounced it as an imperial venture.

> RAWA has in the past repeatedly warned that the U.S. government is no friend of the people of Afghanistan, primarily because during the past two decades she did not spare any effort or expense in training and arming the most sordid, the most treacher-

ous, the most misogynic and anti-democratic indigenous Islamic fundamentalist gangs and innumerable crazed Arab fanatics in Afghanistan and in unleashing them upon our people. After the retreat of the Russian aggressors and the collapse of Najib's puppet regime in Afghanistan these fundamentalist entities became all the more wildly unbridled. They officially and wholeheartedly accepted the yoke of servitude to the interests of foreign governments, in which capacity they have perpetrated such crimes and atrocities against the people of Afghanistan that no parallel can be found in the history of any land on earth.

RAWA roundly condemns the U.S. air strikes against Afghanistan because the impoverished masses of Afghanistan — already trapped in the dog-fighting between the US's Taliban and Jihadi flunkeys — are the ones who are most hurt in the attacks, and also because the US, like the arrogant superpower she is, has violated the sovereignty of the Afghan people and the territorial integrity of the Afghan homeland.

The US is against fundamentalist terrorism to the extent and until such time as her proper interests are jeopardised; otherwise she is all too happy to be a friend and sponsor of any fundamentalist-terrorist criminal entity. If the US does not want her ridiculous bigotry to show and really wants to eliminate fundamentalist terrorism, she should draw lessons from her own past myopic policies and realise that the sources of fundamentalist terrorism are America's support to the most reactionary regimes in Arab and non-Arab countries and her military and financial largesse to Afghan fundamentalist criminals. Terrorism will be uprooted only when these two sources are dried up. [81]

So why does a group like the Fund for a Feminist Majority ignore the voice of RAWA? Again, even within feminist circles, the colonial logic prevails that women of color, indigenous women, and women from Global South countries are only victims of oppression rather than organizers in their own right.

The "assimilation" into white society, however, only increased Native women's vulnerability to violence. For instance, when the Cherokee nation was forcibly relocated to Oklahoma during the Trail of Tears in the nineteenth century, soldiers targeted for sexual violence Cherokee women who spoke English and had attended mission schools instead of those who had not taken part in these assimilation efforts. They were routinely gang-raped, causing one missionary to the Cherokee, Daniel Butrick, to regret that any Cherokee had ever been taught English.[82] Homi Bhabha and Edward Said argue that part of the colonization process involves partially assimilating the colonized in order to establish colonial rule.[83] That is, if the colonized group seems completely different from the colonists, they implicitly challenge the supremacy of colonial rule because they are refusing to adapt the ways of the colonizers. Hence, the colonized must seem to partially resemble the colonists in order to reinforce the dominant ideology, and establish that the way colonizers live is the only good way to live. However, the colonized group can never be completely assimilated — otherwise, they would be equal to the colonists, and there would be no reason to colonize them. If we use Bhabha's and Said's analysis, we can see that while Cherokee women were promised that assimilation would provide them with the benefits of the dominant society, in fact assimilation efforts made them more easily subjugated by colonial rule.

Historically, white colonizers who raped Indian women claimed that the real rapists were Indian men.[84] Today, white men who rape and murder Indian women often make this same claim. In the late 1980s, a white man, Jesse Coulter, raped, murdered, and mutilated several Indian women in Minneapolis. He claimed to be Indian, adopting the name Jesse Sittingcrow, and emblazoning an AIM tattoo on his arm.[85]

Roy Martin, a full-blooded Native man, was charged with sexual assault in Bemidji, Minnesota. The survivor identified the rapist as white, about 25 years old, with a shag haircut. Martin was 35 with hair past his shoulders.[86] In a search of major newspaper coverage of sexual assaults in Native communities from 1998 to 2004, I found coverage almost entirely limited to cases where Native man (or a white man who purports to be Native) was the suspected perpetrator and the victim was a white woman; there was virtually no coverage of Native women as victims of sexual assault. This absence is even more startling when one considers that Native women are more likely than other groups of women in the U.S. to be sexual assault victims.[87]

Similarly, after the Civil War, Black men in the U.S. were targeted for lynching for their supposed mass rapes of white women.

The racist belief was that white women needed to be protected from predatory Black men, when in fact, Black women needed protection from white men. In her investigations of lynches that occurred between 1865 and 1895, anti-lynching crusader Ida B. Wells calculated that more than 10,000 Black people had been lynched. During that same period, not one white person was lynched for raping or killing a Black person.[88] In addition, while the ostensible reason for these lynches was to protect white women from Black rapists, Wells discovered that only a third of those lynched had even been accused of rape. And most of the Black men accused of rape had been involved in obviously consensual sexual relationships with white women.[89]

Of course, Indian men do commit acts of sexual violence. After years of colonialism and boarding school experience, violence has been internalized within Indian communities. However, this view of the Indian man as the "true" rapist serves to obscure who has the real power in this racist and patriarchal society. Thus, the colonization of Native women (as well as other women of color) is part of the project of strengthening white male ownership of white women.

And while the era of Indian massacres in their more explicit form has ended in North America, the wholesale rape and mutilation of indigenous women's bodies continues. During the 1982 massacre of Mayan people in the Aldea Rio Negro (Guatemala), 177 women and children were killed. The young women were raped in front of their mothers, and the mothers were killed in front of their children. The younger children were then tied at the ankles and dashed against the rocks until their skulls were broken. This massacre, committed by the Guatemalan army, was funded by the U.S. government.[90]

In a 1997 massacre in Chiapas, Mexico, indigenous women were targeted by paramilitary forces for sexual mutilation, gang rape, and torture. Amnesty International reports that torture against indigenous peoples in Latin America is routine, including electric shocks, semi-asphyxiation with plastic bags or by submersion under water, death threats, mock executions, beatings using sharp objects, sticks, or rifle butts, rape, and sexual abuse.[91]

One wonders why the mass rapes in Guatemala, Chiapas, or elsewhere against indigenous people in Latin America does not spark the same outrage as the rapes in Bosnia in the 1990s. In fact, feminist legal scholar Catherine MacKinnon argues that in Bosnia, "The world has *never* seen sex used this consciously, this cynically, this elaborately, this openly, this systematically...as a means of destroying a whole people [emphasis mine]."[92] Here, MacKinnon seems to have forgotten that she lives on this land because millions of Native peoples were raped, sexually mutilated, and murdered. Is mass rape against European women genocide, while mass rape against indigenous women is business as usual?

The historical context of rape, racism, and colonialism continues to impact women in North America as well. This legacy is most evident in the rate of violence in American Indian communities—American Indian women are twice as likely to be victimized by violent crime as women or men of any other ethnic group. In addition, 60 percent of the perpetrators of violence against American Indian women are white.[93]

In times of crisis, sexual violence against Native women escalates. When I served as a nonviolent witness for the Chippewa spearfishers who were being harassed by white racist mobs in the 1980s, one white harasser carried a sign that read, "Save a fish; spear a pregnant squaw." During the 1990 Mohawk crisis in Quebec, Canada, a white mob surrounded an ambulance carrying a Native woman who was attempting to leave the Mohawk reservation because she was hemorrhaging after giving birth. She was forced to "spread her legs" to prove she had delivered a baby. The police at the scene refused to intervene. An Indian man was arrested for "wearing a disguise" (he was wearing jeans), and was brutally beaten at the scene, with his testicles crushed. Two women from Chicago Women of All Red Nations (WARN) went to Oka to videotape the crisis. They were arrested and held in custody for 11 hours without being charged, and were told that they could not go to the bathroom unless the male police officers could watch. The place they were held was covered with pornographic magazines.

This colonial desire to subjugate Indian women's bodies was quite apparent when, in 1982, Stuart Kasten marketed "Custer's

Revenge," a videogame in which players got points each time they, in the form of Custer, raped an Indian woman. The slogan of the game is "When you score, you score." He describes the game as "a fun sequence where the woman is enjoying a sexual act willingly." According to the promotional material:

> You are General Custer. Your dander's up, your pistol's wavin'. You've hog-tied a ravishing Indian maiden and have a chance to rewrite history and even up an old score. Now, the Indian maiden's hands may be tied, but she's not about to take it lying down, by George! Help is on the way. If you're to get revenge you'll have to rise to the challenge, dodge a tribe of flying arrows and protect your flanks against some downright mean and prickly cactus. But if you can stand pat and last past the strings and arrows—You can stand last. Remember? Revenge is sweet.[94]

Sexual violence as a tool of racism also continues against other women of color. Trafficking in women from Asian and other Global South countries continues unabated in the U.S. According to the Central Intelligence Agency, 45,000 to 50,000 women are trafficked in the U.S. each year.[95] In addition, there are over 50,000 Filipina mail-order brides in the U.S. alone.[96] White men, desiring women they presume to be submissive, procure mail-order brides who, because of their precarious legal status, are vulnerable to domestic and sexual violence. As the promotional material for mail order brides describes them, Filipinas have "exceptionally smooth skin and tight vaginas…[they are] low maintenance wives. [They] can always be returned and replaced by a younger model."[97]

Women of color are also targeted for sexual violence crossing the U.S. border. Blacks and Latinos comprise 43 percent of those searched through customs even though they comprise 24 percent of the population. The American Friends Service Committee documented over 346 reports of gender violence on the U.S.-Mexico border from 1993–1995 (and this is just the report of one agency, which does not account for the women who either do not report or report to another agency). This one case is emblematic of the kinds of abuse women face at the border: A Border Patrol agent, Larry Selders, raped several women over a period of time. Finally one of the rape victims in Nogales, Arizona had to sue the United States government for not taking action to investigate her rape. Selders demanded sex from the woman in return for her release. When she refused, Selders drove her out of town to an isolated area, raped her and threatened her not to say anything to anyone. Her defense describes in great detail the horrible trauma that she continued to suffer after the incident. Although the rape took place in 1993, it was only in October 1999 that the court finally arrived at a decision in favor of the victims. "The government guarded information about Selders' prior acts. It took more than three years of legal battles to uncover that at least three other victims were known to the government," declared the victim's attorney, Jesus Romo.[98]

Sexual Violence and Impunity

The ideology of Native women's bodies as rapable is evident in the hundreds of missing indigenous women in Mexico and Canada. Since 1993, over 500 women have been murdered in Juarez, Mexico. The majority have been sexually mutilated, raped, and tortured, including having had their nipples cut off. Poor and indigenous women have been particularly targeted. Not only have the local police made no effort to solve the cases, they appear to be complicit in the murders. Amnesty International and other human rights organizations and activists have noted their failure to seriously investigate the cases—the police have made several arrests and tortured those arrested to extract confessions, but the murders have continued unabated. Furthermore, the general response of the police to these murders is to blame the victims by arguing that they are sex workers or lesbians, and hence, inherently rapable.[99] For instance, one former state public prosecutor commented in 1999, "It's hard to go out on the street when it's raining and not get wet."[100]

Similarly, in Canada, over 500 First Nations women have gone missing or have been murdered in the past 15 years, with little police investigation. Again, it seems that their cases have been neglected because many of the women were homeless or sex workers. Ada Elaine Brown, the sister of Terri Brown, president of the Native Women's Association of Canada, was found dead in her bed in 2002. She was so badly beaten her family did not recognize her. According to Terri Brown: "The autopsy report said it was a brain aneurysm. Yeah, because she was beaten to a pulp."[101]

Within the United States, because of complex jurisdictional issues, perpetrators of sexual violence can usually commit crimes against Native women with impunity. A review of U.S. criminal justice policy in Indian country helps to clarify the current situation. In *Ex Parte Crow Dog* (1883), the Supreme Court recognized the authority of Indian tribes over criminal jurisdiction on Indian lands. In response, the U.S. passed the Major Crimes Act (1885), which mandated that certain "major crimes" committed in Indian country must be adjudicated through the federal justice system. In 1883, the Bureau of Indian Affairs (BIA) created the Court of Indian Offenses, which appointed tribal officials to impose penalties based on Anglo-American standards of law. These courts were charged with enforcing the Code of Federal Regulations (CFR), the compilation of regulations issued by federal administrative agencies, which generally stressed laws intended to assimilate Native peoples, such as laws which prohibited the practice of Indian religions.

The 1950's ushered in what is called the "termination period" in U.S. Indian policy. The government began a policy of terminating tribal status for many Indian tribes and funded relocation programs to encourage Indian peoples to relocate to urban areas and assimilate into the dominant society. During this period, the U.S. government sharply defunded the justice systems in Indian country, leaving many tribes, who did not have their traditional systems intact, with no law enforcement at all.

After obliterating tribal justice systems, the U.S. government passed Public Law 280 (PL 280) in 1953, granting states criminal and limited civil jurisdiction over tribes covered in the Major Crimes Act, without tribal consent. PL 280 is a major infringement on Native sovereignty, since tribes have generally not come under state jurisdiction. That is, while the U.S. government policy has deemed tribes under the guardianship of the federal government, tribes are supposed to be recognized as sovereign to some degree and not under state government jurisdiction.

In 1968, the U.S. made provisions for tribes to retrocede from PL 280—however, retrocession can only be undertaken with the permission of the state. However, later court decisions have found that PL 280 provides for concurrent state jurisdiction rather than state jurisdiction which supersedes tribal jurisdiction altogether. That is, while the state has the right to prosecute cases in PL 280 tribes, those tribes can prosecute the cases at the same time through tribal courts, if they have them.

However, with the advent of what is known as the period of "self-determination" in U.S. Indian policy beginning in 1968, many tribes, particularly non-PL 280 tribes, began to develop their own tribal governance. As a result, more than 140 tribes have their own court systems today. Of these, about 25 have retained CFR systems with BIA-appointed judges and others have their own tribal courts. Some tribes, operating under the radar of U.S. government surveillance, have never lost their traditional forms of governance and continue to practice them today.

But because rape falls under the Major Crimes Act, tribes are generally reliant upon the federal governments to prosecute sexual assault cases. Department of Justice representatives have informally reported that U.S. attorneys decline to prosecute about 75 percent of all cases involving any crime in Indian country. U.S. attorneys are particularly reluctant to prosecute rape cases; indeed, the Department of Justice reported in 1997 that only two U.S. attorneys regularly prosecute rape cases in Indian country.[102]

Because sexual assault is covered under the Major Crimes Act, many tribes have not developed codes to address the problem in those rape cases the federal government declines to prosecute. Those with codes are often hindered in their ability to investigate by a wait that may last more than a year before federal investigators formally turn over cases. In addition, the Indian Civil Rights Act (ICRA) of 1968 limits the punishment tribal justice systems can enforce on perpetrators.[103] For instance, the maximum time someone may be sentenced to prison through tribal courts is one year.[104] Also, Native activist Sarah Deer (Muscogee) notes that the U.S. can prohibit remedies that do not follow the same penalties of the dominant system. Thus, sentencing someone to banishment or to another traditional form of punishment can be deemed a violation of ICRA.[105] In addition, U.S. courts have conflicting rulings on whether the Major Crimes Act even allows tribes to maintain concurrent jurisdiction over certain crimes, including sexual assault.[106]

To further complicate matters, tribes covered under PL 280, which gives states criminal jurisdiction, must work with state and county law enforcement officials who may have hostile relationships with the tribe. And because tribes are often geographically isolated — reservations are sometimes over 100 miles from the closest law enforcement agency, with many homes having no phone — local officials are unable to respond to an emergency situation. Racism on the part of local police officers in surrounding border towns also contributes to a lack of responsiveness in addressing rape cases. And since the federal government does not compensate state governments for law enforcement on reservations, and tribes generally do not pay local or federal taxes, states have little vested interest in providing "protection" for Indian tribes.

Finally, American Indian tribes do not have the right to prosecute non-Indians for crimes that occur on reservations. In *Oliphant v. Suquamish Indian Tribe* (1978), the Supreme Court held that Native American tribes do not have criminal jurisdiction over non-Native peoples on reservation lands. This precedent is particularly problematic for non-PL 280 tribes, because tribal police cannot arrest non-Indians who commit offenses. Furthermore, state law enforcement does not have jurisdiction on reservation lands. So, unless state law enforcement is cross-deputized with tribal law enforcement, *no one* can arrest non-Native perpetrators of crimes on Native land.[107]

In response to these deplorable conditions, many Native peoples are calling for increased funding for criminal justice enforcement in tribal communities. (See Chapter 7 for a critique of this strategy.) It is undeniable that U.S. policy has codified the "rapability" of Native women. Indeed, the U.S. and other colonizing countries are engaged in a "permanent social war" against the bodies of women of color and indigenous women, which threaten their legitimacy.[108] Colonizers evidently recognize the wisdom of the Cheyenne saying "A nation is not conquered until the hearts of the women are on the ground."

Chapter 2

Boarding School Abuses and the Case for Reparations

The boarding school system originated in the seventeenth century, when John Eliot, a Puritan missionary in Massachusetts, erected "praying towns" for American Indians. Eliot separated Natives from their communities to receive Christian "civilizing" instruction. Colonists soon concluded that children should be targeted for these efforts, because they believed adults were too set in their ways to become Christianized. Jesuit priests began developing schools for Indian children along the St. Lawrence River in the seventeenth century.

The boarding school system became more formalized under Grant's Peace Policy in 1869. The goal of this federal policy was to turn over the administration of Indian reservations to Christian denominations, and Congress set aside funds to erect school facilities to be run by churches and missionary societies. These facilities were a combination of day and boarding schools erected on Indian reservations. They continue to exist to this day.

In 1879, the first off-reservation boarding school, Carlisle Indian School, was founded by Richard Pratt in Pennsylvania. He argued that as long as boarding schools were primarily situated on reservations, it would be too easy for children to run away from school and the efforts to assimilate Indian children into boarding schools would be reversed when children returned to their families during the summer. He proposed a policy which mandated that children be taken far from their homes at an early age and not returned until they were young adults. By 1909, twenty-five off-reservation boarding schools, 157 on-reservation boarding schools, and 307 day schools were in operation.[1] Eventually, more than 100,000 Native children were forced into attending these schools. According to Pratt, the stated rationale of the policy was to "kill the Indian and save the man."

Within the context of the white debate at the time, Richard Pratt was actually a friend of the Indians. That is, U.S. colonists, in their attempt to end Native control over their land, generally came up with two policies to address the "Indian problem." Some advocated outright physical extermination of Native peoples. Meanwhile, the "friends" of the Indians, such as Pratt, advocated cultural rather than physical genocide. Carl Schurz, a former commissioner of Indian affairs, concluded that Native peoples had "this stern alternative: extermination or civilization."[2] Henry Pancoast, a Philadelphia lawyer, advocated a similar policy in 1882: "We must either butcher them or civilize them, and what we do we must do quickly."[3]

When Pratt founded off-reservation boarding schools, he espoused a "more sensitive" attitude. "Transfer the savage-born infant to the surroundings of civilization, and he will grow to possess a civilized language and habit," he said.[4] He modeled Carlisle on a school he developed in Fort Marion Prison in Florida from 1875 to 1878, where 72 Native prisoners of war were held. There he had developed a variety of programs designed to encourage these prisoners to assimilate into white society. From this experience, Pratt developed a plan to separate children from their parents, inculcate Christianity and white cultural values, and encourage/force them to assimilate into the dominant society through off-reservation schools.

Attendance at these boarding schools was mandatory, and children from tribes across the U.S. were forcibly taken from their homes for the majority of the year. Parents who resisted were imprisoned. For instance, in 1895, 19 Hopi men were imprisoned in Alcatraz for refusing to send their children to boarding schools.[5] Indian children were forced to worship as Christians and speak English at these schools. Native traditions and languages were prohibited.[6] Around 1935, when Commissioner John Collier ushered in an era of Indian reform known as "Indian Reorganization," most of the off-reservation boarding schools closed down and those that remained became less overtly assimilationist. (Today, there are eight off-reservation boarding schools and 52 federal BIA on-reservation boarding schools still open.[7])

Of course, because of the racism in the U.S., Native peoples could never really assimilate into the dominant society. Instead, the consequence of this policy was to situate them at the bottom of the U.S. socioeconomic ladder. For the most part, schools prepared Native boys for manual labor or farming and Native girls for domestic work. Children were also involuntarily leased out to white homes as menial labor during the summers rather than sent back to their homes. Indian girls learned useful skills such as ironing, sewing, washing, serving raw oysters at cocktail parties, and making attractive flower arrangements, in order to transform them into middle-class housewives.[8] As K. Tsianina Lomawaima points out, very few Native women were ever in a position to use these skills or become housewives.

> An economic rationale of placing Indian women in domestic employment does not account for the centrality of domesticity training in their education. An ideological rationale more fully accounts for domesticity training: it was training in dispossession under the guise of domesticity, developing a habitus shaped by the messages of subservience and one's proper place.[9]

The primary role of this education for Indian girls was to inculcate patriarchal norms into Native communities so that women would lose their place of leadership in Native communities.

Some colonists supported boarding schools because they thought cultural genocide was more cost-effective than physical genocide. During his tenure as commissioner of Indian affairs, Carl Schurz concluded that it would cost only $1,200 to school an Indian child for eight years. Secretary of the Interior Henry Teller argued that it would cost $22 million to wage war against Indians over a 10-year period, but would cost less than a quarter of that amount to educate 30,000 children for a year. Administrators of these schools ran them as inexpensively as possible. Children were given inadequate food and medical care, and were over-crowded in these schools. As a result, they routinely died from starvation and disease. In addition, children were often forced to do grueling work to raise money for the schools and salaries for the teachers and administrators.

Sexual, physical, and emotional abuse has been rampant, but boarding schools have refused to investigate, even when teachers were publicly accused by their students. In 1987, the FBI found that one teacher at the BIA-run Hopi day school in Arizona, John Boone, had sexually abused at least 142 boys, but the school's principal had never investigated any allegations of abuse.[10] J.D. Todd had taught at a BIA school on the Navajo Reservation for 21 years before 12 children came forward with allegations of moles-tation against him. Paul Price taught at a North Carolina BIA school from 1971 to 1985 before he was arrested for assaulting boys. In all cases, the BIA supervisors had ignored complaints from the parents before the arrests. And in one case, Terry Hester admitted on his job application that he had been arrested for child sexual abuse. He was hired anyway at the Kaibito Boarding School on the Navajo Reservation, and was later convicted of sexual abuse against Navajo students. According to one former BIA school administrator in Arizona,

> Child molestation at BIA schools is a dirty little secret and has been for years. I can't speak for other reservations, but I have talked to a lot of other BIA administrators who make the same kind of charges.[11]

Despite the epidemic of sexual abuse in boarding schools, the BIA did not issue a policy on reporting sexual abuse until 1987 and did not issue a policy to strengthen the background checks of potential teachers until 1989.[12] The Indian Child Protection Act of 1990 was passed to provide a registry for sexual offenders in Indian country, mandate a reporting system, provide BIA and IHS rigid guidelines for doing background checks on prospective em-ployees, and provide education to parents, school officials, and law enforcement on how to recognize sexual abuse. However, this law was never sufficiently funded or implemented, and child sexual abuse rates have been dramatically increasing in Indian country while they have remained stable for the general population.[13] Sexual predators know they can abuse Indian children with impunity. According to the *American Indian Report*: "A few years ago…a patient who had worked in a South Dakota-run facility where many of his victims were Indian children…was caught and acquitted…. After [he] was released, he attacked three more kids and is now serving a 40-year sentence."[14]

On December 6, 2003, Cindy Sohappy was found dead in a holding cell in Chemawa Boarding School in Oregon, where she had been placed after she became intoxicated. She was supposed to be checked every 15 minutes, but no one checked on her for over three hours. At that point, she was found not breathing and declared dead a few minutes later. The U.S. attorney declined to charge the staff with involuntary manslaughter. Sohappy's mother is planning to sue the school. A videotape showed that no one checked on her when she started convulsing or stopped moving.[15] School administrators had been warned for 15 years by IHS officials about the dangers of holding cells, but these warnings were ignored. Particularly troubling was that she and other young women who had histories of sexual assault, abuse, and suicide attempts were put in solitary confinement.[16] The Haskell Cemetery in Lawrence, Kansas, near the Haskell Institute, a boarding school in the state, alone has 102 student graves, and at least 500 students died and were buried elsewhere.[17]

Canada developed a similar residential school system which operated from 1879 to 1986. In 1991, the Royal Commission on Aboriginal Affairs issued a report documenting abuses in residential schools. "Children were frequently beaten severely with whips, rods and fists, chained and shackled, bound hand and foot and locked in closets, basements, and bathrooms, and had their heads shaved or hair closely cropped."[18] According to students at the Mohawk Institute at Brantford, Ontario:

> I have seen Indian children having their faces rubbed in human excrement…The normal punishment for bedwetters…was to have his face rubbed in his own urine, and for those who tried to escape, nearly all were caught and brought back to face the music. They

were forced to run a gauntlet where they were struck with anything that was at hand.[19]

In 2001, a report issued by the Truth Commission on Genocide in Canada maintained that the mainline churches and the
federal government were involved in the murder of over 50,000
Native children through this system. The list of offenses committed by church officials includes murder by beating, poisoning,
hanging, starvation, strangulation, and medical experimentation.
Torture was used to punish children for speaking Aboriginal languages. Children were involuntarily sterilized. In addition, the
report found that clergy, police, and business and government officials were involved in maintaining pedophile rings using
children from residential schools.[20] Former students at boarding
schools also claim that some schoolgrounds contain unmarked
graveyards of murdered babies born to Native girls who had been
raped by priests and other church officials.[21] Since this abuse has
become public, the Royal Canadian Mounted Police has started a
task force to investigate allegations of abuse in residential schools.
By 2000, they had received 3,400 complaints against 170 suspects.
Only five people were charged. By 2001, 16,000 Native people
(which is 17 percent of living residential school alumni) had
begun legal claims against the churches or government. Liability
could run into billions of dollars, threatening some churches with
bankruptcy.[22]

While the Canadian government and some Canadian
churches have taken minimal steps to address their involvement
in this genocidal policy, the U.S government has not assumed responsibility for its policy of genocide. For instance, when noted
Native journalist, Tim Giago of Rosebud, South Dakota, wrote a
book of poetry that addressed his nine-year history of abuse in
Red Cloud Indian School, the priests expunged his records from
the school and denied that he had attended the institution for
more than six months. They completely expunged the records of
another student who had been there 12 years, denying he had ever
attended that institution.[23] Only in the past two years have U.S.
churches made any effort to address this problem. Both the United
Church of Christ and the United Methodist Church have passed
resolutions recognizing the harms resulting from boarding

schools. The reason for this lack of acknowledgment on the part of the U.S. government and churches is that these abuses are not as well documented in the U.S. as they are in Canada. Many of the books on U.S. boarding schools do not document the more extreme atrocities that I have heard of directly from boarding school survivors.[24] These include medical experimentation, sexual assaults, babies being buried behind school walls, and torture. However, some of these abuses are finally being exposed in the literature.

Indian Child Welfare

It is also important to note that the abduction of Native children from their homes has continued through the foster care system. In 1978, Congress passed the Indian Child Welfare Act (ICWA), which allows tribes to determine the placement of children taken from their homes. During the congressional hearings for this act, Congress reported that 25 percent of all Indian children were in either foster care, adopted homes, or boarding schools.[25]

In Minnesota, Indian children were 500 percent more likely to be in foster care or adoptive care than non-Indian children; in South Dakota, Indian children were 1,600 percent more likely to be in foster or adoptive care; in Washington State, 1,900 percent more likely; and in Wisconsin, 1,600 percent more likely.[26] The hearings also found that the reasons children were taken from their homes were often vague and generally ethnocentric. In North Dakota, physical violence was present in only 1 percent of the cases. Reasons that might be given for removal included ones such as children were "running wild."[27] Native families were and are often targeted because they did not fit the dominant society's nuclear family norm. For instance, when Native children reside with multiple adults and family members in their extended families, the biological parents were and are often seen as "neglecting" their children. At the time of the hearings, 85 percent of Indian children taken from their homes were put in white adoptive families or foster homes.[28]

Since ICWA was put into place, some of these problems have been alleviated. Nonetheless, ICWA is not consistently enforced since many case workers are unaware of its provisions.[29] State courts are not allowed to deny transfer of a custody proceeding to tribal court without "good cause." However, examples of "good cause" cited by states has included the distance state witnesses would have to travel to attend tribal court (which of course is the same distance tribal witnesses have to travel to attend state courts). In one case, a 15-year-old Native man was held by the court for having abandoned his son, even though the Caucasian mother's family prevented the father from having contact with the son.[30] In December 2002, Alaska tribes sued the state of Alaska for violating the ICWA by not protecting Alaska Native children or working with tribes to determine their tribal status. As of 2002, 60 percent of the children who are in Alaska foster care are Native, while Natives are only 25 percent of the population.[31]

In addition, many Christian rights groups, such as the Christian Coalition, continue to organize against ICWA, arguing that ICWA makes it more difficult for Native women to pursue adoption and hence encourages them to have more abortions. This abduction of Indian children into the foster care system is a continuation of U.S. boarding school policies designed to "civilize" Native children.

Boarding Schools and Human Rights Violations

Abuses in U.S. and Canadian boarding schools clearly violated a number of human rights legal standards, including the International Covenant on Civil and Political Rights (1976), the Draft Declaration of the Rights of Indigenous Peoples (1994), the Universal Declaration of Human Rights (1948), the Convention on the Prevention and Punishment of the Crime of Genocide (1951), and the Convention on the Rights of the Child (1990).

Allegations of human rights violations can be filed with the U.N. for events that take place after the relevant treaty entered into force. However, exceptions are made if the event occurred before the effective date of the treaty but has continuing effects after that date. In the case of boarding schools, it is clear that Native communities continue to suffer devastating effects as a result of these policies, including physical, sexual, and emotional violence in Native communities; unemployment and underemployment in Native communities; increased suicide rates; increased substance abuse; loss of language and loss of religious and cultural traditions; increased depression and post-traumatic stress disorder; and increased child abuse.

Consequently, the U.S. should be required to make reparations to address the continuing effects of these human rights violations. While not all Native people viewed their boarding school experiences as negative, after the establishment of boarding schools in Native communities, abuse seemed to become endemic within Indian families. For instance, Randy Fred (Tseshaht), a former boarding school student at Alberni Indian Residential School in Canada, says that children at his school began to mimic the abuse they were experiencing.[32] "Without parental love and without parental role models students were not adequately equipped to fit into mainstream society," he says.[33] Since Father Harold McIntee of St. Joseph's residential school on the Alkali Lake reserve in British Columbia was convicted of sexual abuse in 1989, two of his victims have been convicted of sexual abuse charges. The Royal Commission on Aboriginal Affairs made the link between residential schools and the current dysfunctionality in Native communities:

> Churches…share responsibility with government for the consequences of residential schools, which included not only individual cases of physical and sexual abuse but also the broader issue of cultural impacts:…the loss of language through forced English speaking, the loss of traditional ways of being on the land, the loss of parenting skills through the absence of four or five generations of children from Native communities, and the learned behaviour of despising Native identity.[34]

I have attended several Native wellness workshops in which participants are asked to draw a family tree that shows the generation in their family in which violence, substance abuse, and other related problems develop. Almost invariably, these problems begin with the generation that first went to boarding school. As mentioned previously, while Native peoples generally understand the relationship between the establishment of boarding schools and the onset of violence in their communities, the relationship has not been documented in the U.S. to the extent that it has been in Canada.

In 2000, the Boarding School Healing Project was founded in the U.S. in support of activists demanding reparations for boarding school abuses. This project has important implications for addressing sexual violence in communities of color, and for supporting reparations struggles internationally.

The Boarding School Healing Project

The BSHP is a coalition of several Native and allied organizations around the country, including the Tribal Policy Institute, the Indigenous Women's Network, the American Indian Law Alliance, First Nations North and South, the Seventh Generation Fund, and INCITE! Women of Color Against Violence. The BSHP seeks to document abuses so Native communities can begin healing from boarding school abuses and demand justice from the U.S. government and churches. The four components of the project are healing, education, documentation, and accountability.

Healing. The primary goal of the project is to provide healing resources for survivors of boarding school abuse and trauma. Gerry Oleman of the Provincial Residential School Project in Vancouver reports that 22 men who disclosed sexual abuse and filed suit against Canadian residential schools in 1998 have committed suicide. Armed with this information, the BSHP concluded that a healing apparatus had to be put in place first, so when the issue is publicly discussed, survivors have a place to go for support. The project has started developing support groups for survivors on reservations.

Education. An education program to encourage people to participate in the documentation/accountability process must also be developed. The BSHP holds multimedia educational events in interested communities to inform them about the project, the documentation process, and resources for healing. In addition, the BSHP is organizing the Boarding School Days of Remembrance to educate the larger public about this issue.

Documentation. The BSHP relies on a research-action model to document boarding school abuses. Researchers are recruited and trained from the community. To provide participants with time to reflect on their boarding school experiences and its impact on their lives, they are interviewed in a two-step process. This project is systematically ensuring that participants from all boarding schools and reservations in South Dakota are represented. For participants who are willing, the BSHP is video-documenting the interviews so they may be compiled into educational videos for Native communities in other areas. Through this process, the BSHP has found that many survivors often do not realize that what they have suffered was a human rights violation. For instance, some survivors who say that they were not abused often add that they saw abuse happen to other people. However, having to witness abuse is itself a human rights violation and an injury one can claim in U.S. courts as well.

At the end of the documentation process, the BSHP holds a meeting for the interviewees to discuss the results and provide a venue for them to consider how they would like to move forward. Part of the documentation process entails asking participants what types of remedies they would like to see from both churches and the U.S. government, so they can be involved in the political strategy as well.

Accountability. In 2003, a class action suit, *Zephier v. United States,* was filed against the U.S. government on behalf of all persons, or their executors and heirs, who were sexually, physically or mentally abused at Indian Boarding Schools operated under the authority and auspices of the Bureau of Indian Affairs in the years 1890 to the present.

These plaintiffs asserted breach of treaty claims on behalf of members of all nations who have entered into treaties with the U.S. government containing "Bad Man clauses,"[35] as well as a breach of fiduciary duty claim on behalf of *all* Native individuals who have suffered physical, sexual, or psychological abuse at a federal government-mandated boarding school. Unfortunately no tribal governments or attorneys were consulted before this lawsuit was filed, despite its potential impact on the legal interpretation of treaties and all survivors of boarding school abuses. The case was dismissed in 2004 by the Federal Court of Claims. The plaintiffs are now filing a complaint with the Bureau of Indian Affairs. (In Canada, accountability for boarding school abuses has taken the form of individual lawsuits against churches. This strategy has led to individualized, rather than group, struggle. The compensation, a relatively small amount per individual, does not do justice to the oppression and injury Native peoples have suffered.)

Since Native peoples are such a small percentage of the total U.S. population, they cannot be under any illusion that they can win a successful campaign on their own. And as I have argued elsewhere, Native peoples have led some of the most significant victories against multinational corporations and governments through creative coalition building, such as the successful struggles against Kerr-McGee in Oklahoma and Exxon in Wisconsin.[36] Coalition building is especially essential when considering some of the tensions indigenous peoples have had with African-descendant groups in the U.S. and abroad over reparations. Consequently, the BSHP held joint strategy sessions with activists in African American reparations struggles in 2004 to begin building relations for a stronger united front.

Boarding Schools and the Global Struggle for Reparations

> You can have the mule; but the forty acres are ours.
> — Pamela Kingfisher (Cherokee)

Pamela Kingfisher's comment, made in a dialogue between indigenous and African-descended peoples at the U.N. Conference Against Racism in 2000, encapsulates the strain between indigenous peoples and peoples of African descent over reparation issues. Although a wide variety of demands are articulated under the banner of "reparations," indigenous peoples generally oppose the demand that the U.S. government give land to African Americans and other peoples of color. From Native peoples' perspectives, it is unreasonable to petition the U.S. for land because the U.S. has no land to give — the land belongs to indigenous peoples. This disagreement was dramatically aired in March 2001 at the non-governmental Organization (NGO) preparatory meeting for the United Nations Conference on Racism in Quito, Ecuador which I participated in. At this meeting, Roma and African-descendant groups called for "self-determination over their ancestral landbases in the Americas." Of course, indigenous peoples took issue with this demand as it implicitly denied indigenous title to these same landbases.

Native activist Sherry Wilson describes similar tensions between some Native activists and the Republic of New Afrika, a group that calls for land titles in the U.S. — specifically, the states of Alabama, Georgia, Louisiana, Mississippi and South Carolina — to be transferred to African Americans. At a preparatory meeting for the U.N. Conference Against Racism in Atlanta in 2000, a representative of the Republic of New Afrika stood up and said: "Welcome to the Republic of New Afrika." This greeting did not please the Cherokee peoples attending the meeting who regard Georgia as the ancestral land of the tribe, despite the forced relocation of many Cherokee to Oklahoma in the nineteenth century. Said Wilson:

I don't think any other people of color would object to reparations [for people] who were victims of slavery. I certainly would support that. I just don't think it's going to be somebody else's land though. That's like participating in the oppression of another person.[37]

Another demand often made by reparations activists—for financial compensation to individual victims or descendants of victims of slavery or other forms of oppression—presents a barrier to indigenous peoples participating in this movement. To understand why, one must focus on the history of land-based struggles of Native peoples in the U.S.

The U.S. government has often offered financial compensation to tribes to compel them to extinguish land claims. During the 1940s and 1950s, the U.S. government pursued a policy of "termination" against Native nations, which was designed to eliminate the tribal status of Native peoples and therefore end their collective control over their lands. One policy element was compensation for outstanding land claims. In 1946, the U.S. government established the Indian Claims Commission (ICC), which was designed to adjudicate land claims. The ICC's bias was clear from the start, when it became apparent that the agency could deduct money spent by the U.S. government to massacre that tribe, or kidnap its children and put them into boarding school, from that tribe's award.

Tribes have often found that simply by the act of bringing their claims to the ICC, they have given up land title in the eyes of the U.S. government. The primary goal of the ICC was to settle land claims by providing financial compensation, thereby freeing the U.S. government from any ongoing treaty obligations with Native nations. Compensation only further consolidated U.S. government control over Native lands.

For example, in 1992 the Western Shoshone tribe in Nevada filed a claim with the ICC to have title to their lands, which was guaranteed under the 1868 Treaty of Ruby Valley, respected. At stake was the 24.5 million acres of land guaranteed to the Shoshone under this treaty. The Nevada Test Site has been located on this land since 1951. There have already been at least 650 underground nuclear explosions on Western Shoshone land, with 50 percent of these underground tests leaking radiation into the atmosphere.[38] A lawyer named Ernest Wilkinson encouraged the Shoshone to take the case before the ICC. The land is worth more than $41 billion, but the ICC settled the claim for $21 million in 1962. According to the ICC, because the Shoshone lost their land in 1872, it was appropriate to compensate the tribe at 1872 prices. Wilkinson earned $2.5 million for services rendered.

Not surprisingly, as a result of this history, Native activists are reluctant to join a movement whose common demand is financial compensation. For no matter how large the monetary settlement, ultimately compensation does not end the colonial relationship between the U.S. and indigenous nations. The struggle for native sovereignty is a struggle for control over land and resources, rather than financial compensation for past and continuing wrongs.

Despite these tensions, it is critical that indigenous peoples be part of a global movement for reparations. If we think about reparations less in terms of monetary compensation for social oppression and more in terms of a movement to transform the neocolonial economic relationships between the U.S. and people of color, indigenous peoples, and Global South countries, we see how critical this movement could be to all of us. Activists who frame the movement to cancel the Third World debt in reparations terms, for instance, help us to see how this strategy could fundamentally alter these relations. Consequently, it is important to move beyond disagreements that may exist between Native and African Americans on this issue so we can learn from the insights of our respective struggles.

As the history of neocolonialism shows us, we cannot achieve political sovereignty without economic sovereignty. And certainly one of the primary reasons why indigenous peoples in the U.S. often do not articulate sovereignty struggles in terms of political independence from the U.S. is because indigenous peoples know that without a solid economic infrastructure, which the U.S. government has systematically destroyed for most tribes (stereotypes about Indian gaming notwithstanding), political independence in and of itself could contribute to further economic devastation for Indian peoples. A successful struggle for sovereignty must incorporate a struggle for reparations.

However, for the reparations movement to be successful, national efforts must be simultaneously internationalized and pressure must be brought to bear on the U.S. The news about our efforts to struggle against U.S. policies will not reach activists in other countries unless we get that news to them ourselves. If we can expose U.S. racist policies to international activists, they'll be better positioned to challenge the U.S. claim that it is the protector of democracy abroad. As Doug McAdam documents in his study of the civil rights movement, the successes that racial justice activists have achieved have come in large part because the U.S. government wanted to avoid embarrassment in the global arena.[39]

And the reparations struggle has been globalized by African American activists such as William Patterson and Paul Robeson, who brought charges of genocide against the U.S. to the U.N. In 1951, Patterson and Robeson joined with Eslanda Goode, Harry Haywood, Mary Church Terrell, Robert Treuhaft, Jessica Mitford, and Louise Thompson to deliver a petition which charged the United States with genocide. "We Charge Genocide: The Crime of the Government Against the Negro People" exposed the government-supported conspiracy to deny Black people the right to vote, and documented hundreds of cases of murder, bombing, and torture. For instance, the petitioners provided evidence of the lynching murders of at least 10,000 black people since abolition. As reparations activists, we should continue the legacy of these pioneers, remembering that white supremacy is a global problem that requires a global response.

We should also frame reparations as a human rights issue rather than as a civil rights issue; human rights are recognized under international law to be inalienable and independent on any particular government structure. Furthermore, to rely solely on a constitutional framework reifies the legitimacy of the U.S. government, which is founded on the gross human rights violations of people of color and the continuing genocide of indigenous peoples. As anti-violence activists, this is precisely the struggle—forcing the U.S. to be accountable to international law rather than its own claims to power—we must be engaged in. And while we may use a variety of rhetorical and organizing tools, our overall strategy should not be premised on the notion that the U.S.

should or will always continue to exist. (For more on this topic, see Chapter 8.)

The BSHP contributes a feminist perspective to reparations struggles. That is, the sexual violence perpetrated by slave masters and by boarding school officials constitutes, in effect, state-sanctioned human rights violations. As a result of this systematic and long-term abuse, sexual and other forms of gender violence have been internalized *within* African American and Native American communities. Thus, our challenge as reparations activists is to create a strategy that addresses an insidious colonial legacy — violence within our communities. We must also generate an analysis that frames gender violence as a continuing effect of state-sanctioned human rights violations so we can, in turn, challenge the mainstream antiviolence movement to confront the role of the state. (See Chapter 7 for fuller discussion.)

The issue of boarding school abuses forces us to see the connections between state violence and interpersonal violence. Violence in our communities was introduced through boarding schools. We continue to perpetuate that violence through violence against women, child abuse, and homophobia. Similarly, much of the sexual violence in African American communities is the colonial legacy of slavery. That is, under the slavery system, Black women were deemed inherently rapable by slave masters who could violate them with impunity. Black men were also often forced by their masters to rape Black women. As scholar Traci West documents, the colonial ideology that Black women are inherently rapable is evidenced in popular culture, public support for Clarence Thomas and Mike Tyson and public scorn for their victims, and the astronomical rates of violence that Black women continue to face.[40]

No amount or type of reparations will "decolonize" us if we do not address oppressive behaviors that we have internalized. Women of color have for too long been presented with the choice of prioritizing either racial justice or gender justice. Activists should ask what would reparations *really look like* for women of color who suffer the continuing effects of slavery and colonialism through interpersonal gender violence.

This project also highlights the importance of analyzing the interrelatedness of white supremacy and Christian imperialism. While many political liberals fight for the "separation of church and state" and complain about the George W. Bush administration's support for faith-based initiatives, the reality has been that, for Native peoples in particular, there has never been a separation of church and state. Grant's Peace Policy of 1869 turned Indian reservations over to church denominations for administrative control. Native religious traditions were banned. Even today, Native peoples still do not have constitutional protection for their spiritual practices.[41]

Colonialists saw the cultural assimilation and missionization processes as part of the same project. From their point of view, Indians not only lacked the Scripture, they lacked the language that would allow them to comprehend God. Complained Jonathan Edwards: "The Indian languages are extremely barbarous and barren, and very ill fitted for communicating things moral and divine, or even things speculative and abstract. In short, they are wholly unfit for a people possessed of civilization, knowledge, and refinement."[42] Missionaries also complained that indigenous languages were unable to communicate the concepts of "Lord, Saviour, salvation, sinner, justice, condemnation, faith, repentance, justification, adoption, sanctification, grace, glory, and heaven."[43] It is not sufficient, therefore, simply to have scriptures; the scriptures must be in a suitable language—and that language happens to be English. In the colonial imagination, to truly be Christian is to be white and vice versa. Thus, any struggle to dismantle white supremacy needs to incorporate a critique of Christian imperialism in its analysis.

Today, the effects of boarding school abuses continue to play out throughout indigenous communities, largely because these abuses have not been acknowledged or addressed by the larger society. As a result, silence continues within Native communities, preventing Native peoples from seeking support and healing as a result of the intergenerational trauma. Native peoples individualize the trauma they have suffered, thus contributing to increased shame and self-blame. If boarding school policies and the impact of these policies were recognized as human rights violations, some of the shame attached to talking about these issues would be removed, and communities could begin to heal. We are already seeing the results of such work in Canada, but Native peoples in the U.S. have yet to benefit from this movement.

Conclusion

Articulating boarding school abuses from a reparations framework can be beneficial for all peoples, not just indigenous peoples. Many African American activists have expressed reluctance to work in coalition with other oppressed groups over the struggle for reparations because of the fear that the specific demands of African Americans will diminish in importance. Native people in turn have not organized to support the struggle for reparations for slavery and the vestiges of slavery. This lack of coalition-building only keeps white supremacy and colonialism in place.

The issue at stake is whether we want to formulate reparations as a reformist, and even potentially reactionary, demand, or as a radical demand for social transformation. A variety of platforms have been developed under the rubric of "reparations," and many of these demands can actually serve to *strengthen* the demands of white supremacy. Those demands that simply call for individual payments for human rights abuses under slavery do not fundamentally challenge the economic structures that keep people of color oppressed. In fact, they suggest that by simply paying a lump sum for the injustices it has perpetrated and continues to perpetrate, the U.S. can absolve itself of any responsibility to transform these institutionalized structures of white supremacy.

Radical African Americans and Native activists, however, are formulating demands that require us to fundamentally challenge the global economic system. For example, the BSHP is asking: Can we ask for land rather than monies? Can we call for the repeal of repressive legislation that undermines the sovereignty of Native nations?

By holding the U.S. government and U.S. churches account-able for boarding school abuses, Native peoples have an opportunity to demand adequate funding for healing services. Survivors should make their demands now, because the U.S. government is cutting tribally controlled education and social services programs and state governments are increasingly supporting "English-only" laws, which threaten the survival of indigenous languages.

We could also use a reparations framework to demonstrate that "services" provided by the U.S. government (health care, public assistance, education, etc.) are not services to be taken away in times of economic crisis or otherwise. Rather, these are reparations owed to communities of color for human rights violations on the part of the U.S. To make such radical demands effectively, it is clear that we need a global reparations movement that unites all colonized peoples.

Chapter 3

Rape of the Land

As discussed in Chapter 1, Native peoples have become marked as inherently violable through a process of sexual colonization. By extension, their lands and territories have become marked as violable as well. The connection between the colonization of Native people's bodies—particularly Native women's bodies—and Native lands is not simply metaphorical. Many feminist theorists have argued that there is a connection between patriarchy's disregard for nature, women, and indigenous peoples. The colonial/patriarchal mind that seeks to control the sexuality of women and indigenous peoples also seeks to control nature. Jane Caputi states:

> Violence against women remains protected by custom, indifference, glamorization, and denial. Concomitantly, the culture, language, traditions, myths, social organizations, and members of gynocentric cultures, such as those of North American Indians, have been slashed and trashed. Moreover, as I will demonstrate, the basic myths, motivations, and methods behind genocide—the wasting of the organic and elemental worlds and the attempted

annihilation of the planet — are rooted in gynocidal and misogynist paradigms.[1]

A common complaint among colonizers was that indigenous peoples did not properly subdue the natural environment. This reasoning became the colonizer's legal basis for appropriating land from Native peoples. For instance, Governor John Winthrop of the Massachusetts Bay colony declared that "America fell under the legal rubric of *vacuum domicilium* because the Indians had not 'subdued' it and therefore had only a 'natural' and not a 'civil' right to it."[2] George E. Ellis said that the Indians "simply wasted everything within their reach....They required enormous spaces of wilderness for their mode of existence."[3] Walter Prescott Webb reasoned that free land was "land free to be taken."[4] This notion that Native peoples did not properly use land and hence had no title to it forms the basis of the "doctrine of discovery" which is the foundation of much U.S. case law relating to Indian land claims.

This principle as articulated in *Johnson and Graham's Lessee v. William McIntosh* (1823) held that the U.S. federal government holds "exclusive right to extinguish the Indian title of occupancy, either by purchase or conquest" by right of discovery. According to the Supreme Court, "The title by conquest is acquired and maintained by force. The conqueror prescribes its limits."[5] The justification for conquest was that "the tribes of Indians inhabiting this country were fierce savages, whose occupation was war, and whose subsistence was drawn chiefly from the forest. To leave them in possession of their country, was to leave the country a wilderness."[6]

The courts did not rule that Native peoples had no claim to land at all; rather, they had no right to transfer land to another party. "It has never been contended, that Indian title amounted to nothing...Indian inhabitants are to be considered merely as occupants, to be protected, indeed while in peace, in the possession of their lands, but to be deemed incapable of transferring the absolute title to others."[7]

And certainly, even today, colonizers justify the theft of Native lands on the grounds that Native peoples did not or do not properly control or subdue nature. For instance, among the

Christian Right, John Eidsmoe contends that Christians never stole Indian land. He argues that since Native people did not privatize land, and since these communities had not been "established by God," Europeans had a right to seize the land from them.[8] And furthermore, while Christianity may have been forced on Native people, "millions of people are in heaven today as a result."[9] And as Pat Robertson writes,

> These tribes are…in an arrested state of social development. They are not less valuable as human beings because of that, but they offer scant wisdom or learning or philosophical vision that can be instructive to a society that can feed the entire population of the earth in a single harvest and send spacecraft to the moon….Except for our crimes, our wars and our frantic pace of life, what we have is superior to the ways of primitive peoples…Which life do you think people would prefer: freedom in an enlightened Christian civilization or the suffering of subsistence living and superstition in a jungle? You choose.[10]

Controlling Nature?

Unfortunately for the colonizers, nature is not so easy to subdue and control. As we find ourselves in the midst of environmental disaster, it is clear that no one can escape the repercussions of environmental damage. Yet colonizers attempt to deny this reality by forcing those people who have already been rendered dirty, impure, and hence expendable to face the most immediate consequences of environmental destruction.

Marginalized communities suffer the primary brunt of environmental destruction so that other communities can remain in denial about the effects of environmental degradation. The United Church of Christ's landmark study on environmental racism, *Toxic Wastes and Race*, found that race is consistently the most statistically significant variable in the location of commercial hazardous waste facilities. Three out of every five African Americans and Latino North Americans live in communities with toxic waste sites. Half of all Asians, Pacific Islanders, and American

Indians live in communities with uncontrolled toxic waste sites.[11] People of color are also disproportionately affected by workplace hazards. For instance, pesticide exposure among primarily Latino farmworkers causes more than 300,000 pesticide-related illnesses each year.[12]

American Indian lands are a particular focal point in the struggle for environmental justice. It is not an accident that virtually all uranium production takes place on or near Indian land.[13] Nor is it a coincidence that to date, more than 50 reservations have been targeted for waste dumps.[14] Military and nuclear testing also takes place almost exclusively on Native lands. For instance, there have been at least 928 nuclear explosions on Western Shoshone land at the Nevada test site. Fifty percent of these underground tests have leaked radiation into the atmosphere.[15] Native peoples, the expendable ones, are situated to suffer the brunt of environmental destruction so that colonizers can continue to be in denial about the fact that they will also eventually be affected.

As a case in point, Native Americans for Clean Environment (NACE) was one of the organizers of the campaign to stop the Kerr-McGee Sequoyah Fuel Facility (a uranium conversion facility) in Oklahoma. In its campaign, NACE discovered that Kerr-McGee was using radioactive wastes to make fertilizer. Kerr-McGee was eventually closed down, although it has not cleaned up its nuclear waste at this plant. The Nuclear Regulatory Commission also allowed Kerr-McGee to use this fertilizer on 15,000 acres of hay fields in Oklahoma, where cattle are grazed before being sold on the open market. The only health study conducted on the cattle revealed that 10 percent of the cattle had resulting cancerous growths. A frog with nine legs was discovered in a nearby pond.[16] These effects were deemed "normal" by Kerr-McGee. Clearly, non-Native peoples are affected by radiation poisoning.[17]

Another example of environmental racism is the plan to relocate all U.S. nuclear wastes into a permanent high-level nuclear waste repository in Yucca Mountain, which is on Shoshone land and located on an active volcanic zone, increasing the risk of radioactive leakage.[18] To encourage the opening of these facilities, George W. Bush pushed for this plan to fuel the "war on terror," and in 2002, Congress approved the repository at an estimated cost of $3.25 billion. Waste storage is scheduled to begin by 2010. While Indians are once again on the frontlines, the Shoshone are not the only people affected by the creation of this repository; it will also impact the people who reside near freeways where the waste will be transported. (The repository on Yucca Mountain will receive nuclear wastes from throughout the U.S. — only five states would not be affected by the transportation of high-level radioactive wastes.)

Furthermore, the effects of environmental contamination are global. "Depleted" uranium is the byproduct that results when enriched uranium is separated from natural uranium in order to produce fuel for nuclear reactors. Chemically toxic, depleted uranium is used by the nuclear industry to produce deadly weapons that have been used on peoples around the world. It is an extremely dense, hard metal and can cause chemical poisoning to the body in the same way as lead or any other heavy metal. Depleted uranium is also radioactive, and it spontaneously burns on impact, creating tiny glass particles which are small enough to be inhaled. With a half-life of 4.5 billion years, it poses a long-term threat to human health and the environment. [19]

Depleted uranium was used against the peoples of Bosnia, Afghanistan, and Iraq. During the Persian Gulf War, the U.S. blasted Iraqis retreating from Kuwait with depleted uranium. The area where it was used is now known as the "Highway of Death." People who live in the area continue to suffer increased birth defect and cancer rates. Depleted uranium has also been linked to the "Gulf War Syndrome" suffered by U.S. soldiers.[20]

Sovereignty and Environmentalists

Because the environmental issues that impact Native peoples eventually impact everyone, it would seem logical that mainstream environmental organizations would naturally find themselves allied with Native peoples. But while there have certainly been important alliances, environmentalists have actively opposed Native treaty rights in many cases. For instance, environmental groups, like the Sierra Club, Audubon and Earth Action, formed the Alaska Coalition in 1970 to protect Alaska's national parks and refuges. In the 1980s, it organized primarily to stop the drilling for oil in the Arctic National Wildlife Refuge, home to the Gwich'in people in northeast Alaska. The drilling in the proposed 1991 Johnson-Wallup bill would have destroyed 40 percent of the caribou that the Gwich'in depended on for subsistence. As part of their strategy to prevent drilling in the refuge, the Alaska Coalition backed a compromise bill that would provide incentives for oil drilling in the lower 48 states. Since a large percentage of oil reserves in the lower 48 are on Indian land, this legislation would have continued to jeopardize Native people.

When activists confronted Sierra Club president Michael Fischer on this position at the People of Color Environmental Summit in October 1991, he denied that the Sierra Club supported the bill, even though his support for the bill had been widely reported. Then later, he contradicted this denial in his correspondence with Chicago Women of All Red Nations (WARN). The rationale for this support was that "we had to take a little of the bad with...all of the good" and "on sovereign Indian lands only Indians themselves have the authority and responsibility to make the decision [to drill for oil]."[21]

Unfortunately, indigenous peoples do not have full authority to decide because, under U.S. law, as decided in *Lonewolf v. Hitchcock* (1903), it is the U.S. Congress that has full "plenary power" to decide the fate of indigenous peoples and lands. In fact, from the perspective of the U.S. government, the term "reservation" indicates that the U.S. owns title to these lands but "reserves" them for use by Indian peoples. There is no reason to believe that decisions made about oil drilling will ever be solely in the hands of Native peoples. Fortunately, neither bill passed, although the threats against the Arctic National Wildlife Refuge continue today.

Tension between Native peoples and mainstream environmentalists was also generated by the spearfishing struggle in northern Wisconsin in the late 1980s and early 1990s.[22] In 1989, the federal courts recognized the right of the Chippewa to spearfish in ceded territory. As a result, a number of anti-Indian hate groups, such as Stop Treaty Abuse (STA) and Protect America's Rights and Resources (PARR), were formed. When the Chippewa attempted to spearfish, these groups would mobilize white people to flock to the boat landings and physically and verbally harass the spearfishers and their allies. Some local environmental and animal rights groups sided with the harassers, and even disallowed a Native speaker from speaking on Earth Day in Wisconsin. They agreed with the assertion made by the hate groups that the Chippewa were "overfishing."

These activists failed to see the bigger picture. Around the same time as the spearfishing fights, corporations had begun mining for natural resources in northern Wisconsin. Their first efforts in the early 1980s had been derailed by a united Indian and non-Indian opposition. Clearly, the courts' recognition of the Chippewa's right to hunt, fish, and gather posed an additional threat to these companies and should have bolstered the hopes of the environmentalists. If their mining operations degraded the environment so the Chippewa could not use it, then the tribe could argue that their operations violated treaty rights.

By not defending treaty rights, these groups risked losing an important legal weapon that could be used to prevent mining companies from coming in and polluting the area. As Native activist Justine Smith argues,

> Animal rights and environmental organizations played right into these divide-and-conquer techniques of mining companies. Through their narrow definition of animal rights, they did not pick up on the fact that the treaties retaining the Chippewa's right to hunt, fish, and gather in the ceded territory in Wisconsin was (and is) one of the best protections against potential widespread environmental degradation....What happens to Native peoples and Native nations will eventually happen to everyone. *Defending and protecting Native rights and sovereignty is a first step toward preservation of the global community* (emphasis added).[23]

Fortunately, as other scholars have documented, the Chippewa were able to create coalitions with sport fishers by demonstrating that mining companies were the real threat to Wisconsin. They then mobilized these coalitions to pressure the governor of Wisconsin into supporting a moratorium on mining.[24]

Similar politics erupted over the Makah whaling controversy in Washington State beginning in the late 1990s. The Coalition for Human Dignity documents how animal and environmental rights groups, such as the Sea Shepherd Conservation Society (SSCS) and the Progressive Animal Welfare Society, collaborated with far-right Republican legislator Jack Metcalf to oppose the Makah. Metcalf has openly spoken at the meetings of overtly racist and anti-Semitic organizations and has called for the abrogation of Indian treaty rights. These groups, instead of developing strategies to negotiate their differences with the Makah that respected Native sovereignty, advocated for the U.S. to abrogate its 1855 treaty with the Makah that guarantees their right to whale hunt. What these "environmentalists" did not consider is that if they had been successful in legitimizing the abrogation of one treaty, it would have the effect of delegitimizing all treaties. They would be destroying the efforts of Native peoples across the country who are opposing corporate control through the use of treaties. Many of the leaders of these organizations, such as Dave Forman, Farley Mowat, and Paul Watson of SSCS, are also promoting an anti-immigration platform in environmental groups such as the Sierra Club (as I will discuss later in this chapter). Also collaborating with SSCS is Brigitte Bardot, ally of the leading neofascist political party in France, the National Front. She is also overtly anti-immigrant, particularly anti-Arab and anti-Muslim. In *Le Figaro*, she stated: "Now my country, France, my homeland, my land, is with the blessing of successive government again invaded by a foreign, especially Muslim, overpopulation to which we pay allegiance."[25]

Humans Versus Nature

One reason for tensions between Native and mainstream environmental activists is the environmentalists' use of rhetoric—usually concern for the well-being of the earth—that obfuscates colonialism and racism. For instance, in his discussion of deep ecology,[26]

Michael Zimmerman argues in favor of eradicating the dualism between humans and nature: "Only by recognizing that humanity is no more, but also no less, important than all other things on Earth can we learn to dwell on the planet within limits that would allow other species to flourish."[27]

Yet some deep ecologists and other environmental theorists apply this theory inconsistently. For instance, writers in *Earth First!* journals have said that "the AIDS virus may be Gaia's tailor-made answer to human overpopulation" and that famine should take its course in Africa to stem overpopulation.[28] And as the platform for Deep Ecology states: "The flourishing of nonhuman life requires...a decrease [in human population].[29]

Such sentiments reinforce, rather than negate, the duality between humans and nature. They imply that humans are not a part of nature, and that their destruction would not also mean environmental destruction. In addition, it is noteworthy that the people who are targeted as expendable (people with AIDS and Africans in the foregoing examples) are people of color or Global South people who have the least institutional power or access to resources in society. Once again, the notion that certain populations are inherently "dirty" or "polluting" prevails, even within environmental discourse.

While these may be extreme examples, I often hear pro-population control environmentalists say that the world would be much better off if people just died or that the world needs to cleanse itself of people. Again, this sentiment assumes that people are not part of the world. This sentiment also assumes that all people, not just those with wealth and institutional power, are equally responsible for massive environmental destruction. It is racist and imperialist to look at the people who are dying now from environmental degradation (generally people of color and poor people) and say that it is a good thing that the earth is cleansing itself. As Native activist Marie Wilson, a Gitksan-Wet'suwet'en tribal councilor, says,

> I have to say that the Indian attitude toward the natural world is different from environmentalists. I have had the awful feeling that when we are finished dealing with the courts and our land claims, we will then have to battle the environmentalists and they will not

understand why. I feel quite sick at this prospect because the environmentalists want these beautiful places kept in a state of perfection: to not touch it, rather to keep it pure. So that we can leave our jobs and for two weeks we can venture into the wilderness and enjoy this ship in a bottle. In a way this is like denying that life is happening constantly in these wild places, that change is always occurring. Human life must be there too. Humans have requirements and they are going to have to use some of the life in these places.[30]

Native Women and Environmental Destruction

Katsi Cook, a Mohawk midwife, argues that attacks on nature are also attacks on Native women's bodies, and by extension, attacks on the bodies of Native children.[31] Toxins are generally stored in fat, and during pregnancy and lactation, women's fat is metabolized, exposing fetuses and newborns, at their most vulnerable stages of development, to these chemicals.[32] According to the National Wildlife Federation, most people receive up to 12 percent of their lifetime dose of toxic chemicals in the first year of their life.[33]

In a similar vein, a 1996 University of Minnesota study found that the children of farmers who rely on pesticides have a higher rate of birth defects than the children of those who do not. The highest rates were among children conceived in spring, when crops were most intensely sprayed.[34] A Michigan study found that 11-year-olds whose mothers had consumed Lake Michigan fish during pregnancy scored six points lower than their peers on IQ tests.[35]

Unlike adults, children cannot excrete or store contaminants, so they are more vulnerable to toxins. Some studies are underway to determine if environmental toxins, such as DDT, PCBs, dioxins, mercury, lead, benzene, and toluene, disrupt the endocrine system. It is believed that these chemicals mimic naturally occurring hormones secreted by the endocrine system, which regulates immunity, reproduction, behavior, metabolism, and growth, disrupting it and having an effect like DES (diethylstilbestrol)[36] on pregnant women. This theory may explain why certain toxins are correlated with lower IQs in children, reduced fertility, genital deformities, and abnormalities within the immune system.[37] In addition, certain toxins bioaccumulate, becoming more concentrated as they move along the food chain.[38]

Indigenous peoples living near the Arctic, such as the Inuit, are at particular risk because the region lacks the soil and vegetation that absorb pollution elsewhere. In addition, the cold temperatures prevent the toxins, emitted from industries largely in the U.S., from breaking down. These toxins make their way into the fat of whales, walruses, and seals, which form the diet of indigenous peoples in the Arctic, who have few other food options. Notably, there have been a number of reports of animals with abnormalities, including seals without hair, and polar bears with reproductive organs of both sexes.[39]

This combination of a high-fat diet and toxins in the fat that have bioaccumulated seems to have contributed to disproportionate reproductive health problems among indigenous women in the Arctic. For instance, in Nunavut, Inuit mothers' breast milk has twice the level of dioxin as does women's breast milk in southern Quebec, even though there are no sources of dioxin within 300 miles of Quebec. The major source of this dioxin pollution is the U.S.[40]

In 2002, a Centers for Disease Control study found that the U.S. government had underestimated the impact of another environmental toxin—radiation poisoning—on Native communities because researchers did not factor in the large amount of fish consumed by some communities. (During fishing seasons, fish may be all that some families eat.) Radiation poisoning may be linked to the astronomical rates of lupus, an immune system disorder, among Nez Perce women living near the Columbia River in Washington State. Wastes from the Hanford Nuclear Reactor, which began production of weapons-grade plutonium in 1943, were improperly disposed of in the river. And while most of Hanford's reactors were closed down in the 1960s, nuclear wastes will likely remain in the area until 2030.[41] Today, the incidence of lupus among Nez Perce women is five times greater than among other Native women.

One tribal member, Justine Miles, reports that she has suffered lupus, several miscarriages, broken bones, endometriosis, life-threatening infections, and meningitis.[42] Jane Caputi writes of the devastating impact of the Hanford Nuclear Reactor on nearby residents, including this narrative by Tom Baile:

> As "downwinders," born and raised downwind of the Hanford Nuclear Reservation in Washington, we learned several years ago that the government decided—with cold deliberation—to use us as guinea pigs by releasing radioactivity into our food, water, milk and air without our consent. Now, we've learned that we can expect continuing cancer cases from our exposure in their "experiment." Is this what it feels like to be raped?[43]

Baile's narrative illustrates how environmental racism is another form of sexual violence, as it violates the bodies of Native and other marginalized peoples. As mentioned in Chapter 1, a patriarchal system based on violence operates by appearing "normal" and attacking alternative systems that might challenge its legitimacy. Similarly, the effects of environmental degradation are often not questioned because they are termed "normal." Comments Baile: "Unknowingly, we had been seeing the effects for a long time. For us, the unusual was the usual!" The effects he perceived to be "normal" included the following:

> I was born a year after my stillborn brother. I struggled to breathe through underdeveloped lungs, and suffered to overcome numerous birth defects. I underwent multiple surgeries, endured paralysis, endured thyroid medication, a stint in an iron lung, loss of hair, sores all over my body, fevers, dizziness, poor hearing, asthma, teeth rotting out and, at age 18, a diagnosis of sterility.[44]

In areas where uranium is mined, such as the Four Corners (where the Utah, Arizona, New Mexico, and Nevada borders meet) and the Black Hills in South Dakota, Indian people face skyrocketing rates of cancer, miscarriages, and birth defects. Men and women who grew up in Four Corners develop ovarian and testicular cancers at 15 times the national average.[45] Meanwhile, Indian women on Pine Ridge in the Black Hills experience a miscarriage rate six times higher than the national average.[46] And on the Akwesasne Mohawk reserve in New York, one of the most polluted areas in the country, the PCBs, DDT, Mirex, and HCBs that are dumped into their waters are stored in women's breast milk.[47] Through the rape of the earth, Native women's bodies are raped once again.

Perhaps the indigenous women who have suffered the most devastating effects of environmental racism are the women from the Marshall Islands in the Pacific. After World War II, the U.S. exploded a bomb that was 1,300 times more destructive than the bombs dropped on Hiroshima and Nagasaki; this test was the first of 66 nuclear tests conducted in the Marshall Islands. The people from one of the islands, Rongelap, were directly in the fallout and have continued to suffer cancer and major birth defects (including "jelly fish babies" — babies born without bones), and from the contamination of their food sources since the first explosions. Residents were told that the effects of the radiation were not serious until 1982, when a study by the U.S. government found that the island was too unsafe to live on. With the help of Greenpeace, the residents of Rongelap relocated to another island. One midwife of the islands describes the islanders' rage:

> We are very angry at the U.S. and I'll tell you why. Have you ever seen a jelly fish baby born looking like a bunch of grapes, so the only reason we knew it was a baby was because we could see the brain? We've had these babies—they died soon after they were born.[48]

Between 1954 and 1958, one in three births in the Marshall Islands resulted in fetal death.[49] Neal Palafox, associate professor of family practice at the University of Hawaii in Honolulu and an advocate for Pacific Islander health, points out that the rate of hepatitis B, a risk factor for liver cancer, is approximately 30 times higher in the Marshall Islands than in the mainland U.S. In women of the Marshall Islands, cervical cancer mortality is 60 times greater than in the mainland U.S., breast cancer and gastrointestinal cancer rates are five times greater, and lung cancer rates are three times greater.[50] Among men, the lung cancer mortality rate is nearly four times greater than overall U.S. rates, while oral cancer rates are 10 times greater. Lijon Eknilang of the Marshall Islands provided this testimony of the impact of nuclear testing:

> Not long after the light from Bravo, it began to snow in Rongelap. We had heard about snow from the missionaries and other Westerners who had come to our islands, but this was the first time we saw white particles fall from the sky and cover our village.
>
> Of course, in 1951, Marshallese children and their parents did not know that the snow was radioactive fallout. My own health has suffered very much as a result of radiation poisoning. I cannot have children. I have had miscarriages on seven occasions. On one of those occasions, the child I miscarried was severely deformed — it had only one eye. I have also had thyroid surgery to remove nodules. I have lumps in my breasts.
>
> Marshallese women suffer silently and differently from the men who were exposed to radiation. Our culture and religion teaches us that reproductive abnormalities are a sign that women have been unfaithful. For this reason, many of my friends keep quiet about the strange births they have had. In privacy, they give birth, not to children as we like to think of them, but to things we could only describe as "octopuses," "apples," "turtles" and other things in our experience. We do not have Marshallese words for these kinds of babies, because they were never born before the radiation came.
>
> Women on Rongelap, Likiep, Ailuk and other atolls in the Marshall Islands have given birth to these "monster babies." Many of these women are from atolls that foreign officials have told us were not affected by radiation. We know otherwise, because the health problems are similar to ours. One woman on Likiep gave birth to a child with two heads. Her cat also gave birth to a kitten with two heads. There is a young girl on Ailuk today with no knees, three toes on each foot and a missing arm.
>
> The most common birth defects on Rongelap and nearby islands have been "jellyfish" babies. These babies are born with no bones in their bodies and with transparent skin. We can see their brains and hearts beating. The babies usually live for a day or two before they stop breathing. Many women die from abnormal pregnancies, and those who survive give birth to what looks like purple grapes that we quickly bury.[51]

Native Hawai'ian activist Haunani-Kay Trask reports that the life expectancy on the Marshall Islands has sharply declined to what it is now — only 40 years.[52] Mililani Trask notes that the people of the Marshall Islands have been genetically altered as a result of these tests. Some communities have decided to stop reproducing and go extinct.[53] Some area activists believe that the testing was a planned effort by the U.S. government to examine the effects of nuclear radiation on humans.

Many Marshall Islanders have complained that many of the studies that have "proven" that they are not suffering from radiation fallout are studies funded by the Department of Energy.[54] Medical research often conveniently overlooks the environmental causes of disease, placing the blame on Native peoples themselves. Governments and multinational corporations are then left unaccountable for their policies of environmental contamination. Native bodies will continue to be seen as expendable and inherently violable as long as they continue to stand in the way of the theft of Native lands.

Environmental Racism and Sexism

In 1991, environmental justice activists converged in Washington, D.C. to formulate the principles of environmental justice at the People of Color Environmental Justice Summit. This summit was called because activists felt that mainstream environmental groups were divorcing environmental issues from larger social justice issues. Participants adopted the Principles of Environmental Justice, which called for environmental protection within the context of "political, cultural and economic liberation."[55]A follow-up summit was held in 2002 in Washington, D.C. to assess the work of the environmental justice movement and forge strategies for future work.

While the analysis and organizing of the environmental justice movement is exemplary, it often marginalizes women of color. That is, women of color are suffering from not only environmental racism but environmental sexism. This intersectionality is advanced in what Betsy Hartmann calls "the greening of hate." The greening of hate describes the phenomenon of people who acknowledge the importance of environmental destruction, but place the blame on the Global South, immigrants, and people of color (primarily women of color) for this destruction.

Drawing on Malthusian logic, some population alarmists assert that "overpopulation" is the primary cause of poverty and environmental destruction in the world: population grows geometrically, they claim, while food production grows arithmetically. According to this logic, eventually the number of people on the earth must outstrip the earth's "carrying capacity." In much of the populationist literature, overpopulation is "the single greatest threat to the health of the planet."[56] Even the more moderate populationists, such as the Sierra Club, blame population growth for,

> profound consequences for the global environment, including species extinction, deforestation, desertification, climate change, and the destruction of natural ecosystems. These global environmental impacts pose a significant threat to the earth's sustainability and impact our quality of life.[57]

Since the fertility rates of the industrialized world are stable at replacement levels, population control advocates can devote their time and energy to the burgeoning growth rates in the Global South and immigration issues in the U.S. In effect, women of color, immigrant women, and women from the Global South then become the perpetrators, rather than the victims, of environmental degradation.

One flaw of the Malthusian argument is the underlying assumption that "natural fertility rates" are always high and checked only by the vicissitudes of famine, war, and disease. To the contrary, women have always had means of controlling reproduction. Ironically, colonial powers often tried to stamp out traditional means of birth control to ensure a large supply of cheap labor and a captive market for their finished goods.[58] In recent years, Nestle has discouraged breast-feeding, a natural birth spacer, in order to increase sales of its infant formula among Global South women: more babies means more formula, more formula means more babies. As Maria Mies and Vandana Shiva note, the population of India was stable until the advent of British colonialism.[59]

Poverty, starvation, environmental degradation, and over-population are the direct result of specific colonial practices. When colonization forced women into cash economies, it became neces-sary for them to have more children in order to raise more cash crops. Also, increased mortality rates that have resulted from the effects of colonialism and structural adjustment programs moti-vate women to have more children in hopes that some will survive. Over the last 25 to 30 years, structural adjustment pro-grams have cut social services in the Global South, making children necessary for old age security and for helping with womens' increased workloads. In fact, by the age of 15, children in the Global South have repaid their parents' investment in their upbringing.[60]

Some populationists say population growth contributes to starvation. Yet there is actually enough food produced in the world to sustain every person at a 3,000-calorie-per-day diet.[61] However, land is used inefficiently in order to support livestock for environmentally unsustainable Western meat-based diets. The same land that is used to maintain livestock for 250 days worth of food could be used to cultivate soybeans for 2,200 days.[62] By cycling our grain through livestock, we end up with only 10 percent of the calories for human consumption as would be avail-able if we ate the grain directly. In addition, food produced in the Global South is often exported to pay off debts to the World Bank rather than used to meet local needs. Consequently, even coun-tries that are stricken by famine export food.[63] Unfortunately, rather than look at the root causes of environmental destruction, poverty, and rapid population growth, population alarmists scapegoat "overpopulation" as the primary cause of all these problems, allowing corporations and governments to remain unaccountable.

This "greening of hate" particularly victimizes women of color. A glaring example is the work of Center for Research on Population and Security, headed by Stephen Mumford and Elton Kessel. Mumford and Kessel have been involved with a number of mainstream environmental organizations to form a National Optimum Population Commission, which would determine how many people should live in the U.S. to promote ecological sustainability. These same individuals are involved with the Federation of American Immigration Reform (FAIR), and have stated on the BBC's *Human Laboratory* that immigration is a threat to the national security of the U.S. To forestall this national security risk, Mumford and Kessel globally distribute a drug for sterilization, Quinacrine.

Quinacrine is a drug that is used to treat malaria. It can also be inserted into the uterus, where it dissolves, causing the fallopian tubes to scar and rendering the woman irreversibly sterile. Family Health International conducted four in-vitro studies and found Quinacrine to be mutagenic in three of them. As a result, Family Health International and the World Health Organization recommended against further trials for female sterilization, and no regulatory body supports Quinacrine for sterilization. However, the North Carolina–based Center for Research on Population and Security has circumvented these bodies through private funding from such organizations as the Turner Foundation and the Leland Fykes Organization, which has been distributing it for free to researchers and government health agencies. Field trials are underway in 11 countries, with over 70,000 women sterilized. In Vietnam, 100 female rubber plant workers were given routine pelvic exams during which the doctor inserted the Quinacrine without their consent.

Thus far, the side effects linked with the drug include ectopic pregnancy, puncturing of the uterus during insertion, pelvic inflammatory disease, and severe abdominal pain. Other possible concerns include heart and liver damage, and the exacerbation of preexisting viral conditions. In one of the trials in Vietnam, a large number of cases in which women had serious side effects were excluded from the data.[64] Yet Mumford and Kessel publicly stated at the Beijing U.N. Conference on Women that they plan to supply Quinacrine to clinicians in the U.S. for female sterilization. Other physicians seem to be following suit. For example, a clinical trial on Quinacrine is currently underway at the Children's Hospital of Buffalo under the supervision of Jack Lippes, M.D. And in its July 2002 newsletter, the Women's Global Network for Reproductive Rights reported that Quinacrine sterilizations were advertised and offered at Family Planning Inc., a private clinic run by Randall B. Switney, M.D., in Daytona Beach.

Despite the attacks they've made on womens' reproductive rights, mainstream environmental organizations cooperate with Mumford and Kessel in campaigning for an optimum-population commission. Yet in their efforts to further population control, many environmentalists argue that the need to control population takes precedence over women's reproductive freedom. Lester Brown of the Worldwatch Institute favors China's one-child policy, as did the late Garrett Hardin, activist and author of *Tragedy of the Commons*. Hardin, former vice president of the American Eugenics Society, was a popular thinker in the environmental movement, and sat on the board of Washington D.C.-based Population Environment Balance. In a 1997 interview with the *Wall Street Journal*, Hardin argued that the problem is not simply that there are too many people in the world, but there are too many of *the wrong kind of people*. "It would be better to encourage the breeding of more intelligent people rather than the less intelligent," he said. In fact, Hardin argued that the one-child policy was not strict enough, and that he supported infanticide as another viable component of population control.[65] Similarly, at an ecofeminist conference, Population-Environment Balance, an anti-immigration environmentalist group, advocated that "at risk" teenagers be subjected to mandatory Norplant.[66]

The Population Paradigm

Rather than being caused by overpopulation, significant environmental damage is actually caused by the environmentally destructive Western development projects, such as hydroelectric dams, uranium development, militarism, and livestock production. These projects ultimately benefit the wealthy living in industrialized countries, which are responsible for producing over 75 percent of the world's pollution.[67] Development projects also cause unparalleled environmental damage, such as damming programs that flood entire biosystems or projects that rely on massive deforestation. More than one third of World Bank projects completed in 1993 were judged failures by its own staff, with some countries experiencing a success rate of less then 50 percent.[68] Any damage done by indigenous people, peasants, and Global South farmers cannot compare to the damage done by multinationals and the World Bank, so the claim that stopping the "overpopulation" of peasants and indigenous peoples in Global South countries will "save the environment" is baseless. Furthermore, Fatima Mello of FASE (Federation of Educational and Social Assistance Organizations — a Brazilian environmental and development NGO), notes that in Brazil, a higher density of population in certain areas of the Amazon often helps to *stop* encroachment by the World Bank or multinational corporations and their environmentally disastrous projects.[69]

Related to these neocolonial policies is the resulting immigration to the U.S. from poor countries/the Global South. As the U.S. extracts resources from the Global South, people naturally follow these resources to the U.S. Yet, some mainstream environmentalists complain that the U.S. is now "overpopulated" by immigrants. Immigrants, Garrett Hardin claims, cause "global warming, species extinction, acid rain, and deforestation. …Immigration…is threatening the carrying capacity limits of the natural environment." Because of "their excessive reproductive rates," immigrants cause mass environmental damage, "compete with our poor for jobs," and burden the taxpayer through "increased funding obligations in AFDC, Medicare, Food Stamps, School Lunch, Unemployment Compensation, [etc.]."[70] The Garrett Hardin Society links concerns about the environment to concerns about terrorism on its Web site:

> The fact is that the huge annual legal immigrant flow (1.5 million in 2001), coupled with hundreds of thousands of illegal crossings, not only provides opportunities for terrorism, but also causes population growth, which increasingly stresses our overburdened environment. The threats to our national security from massive legal and illegal immigration are immediate and increasing daily. Are we prepared for another 9-11?[71]

Anti-immigration forces also lead a campaign in 1998 to get Sierra Club members to pass an anti-immigration platform under the rationale that immigration was destroying the environment. Fortunately, this campaign was defeated through the leadership of a San Francisco–based environmental justice organization, the Political Ecology Group.[72] Then, in 2004, anti-immigration activists tried to take control of the organization by running for five open seats on the board of directors. However, all of the anti-immigration candidates were defeated by a landslide. Board members have agreed to ask members again if the Sierra Club should take a position on immigration.[73]

Again, anti-immigrant environmentalists presume that all people consume equally. But the impact of an immigrant family living in a one-bedroom apartment and taking mass transit pales in comparison to that of a wealthy family living in a single family home with a swimming pool and two cars. Much of the environmental decline in this country has nothing to do with population growth or individual consumer choices. For example, in the 1930s and the 1940s, General Motors, Firestone, and Standard Oil (or Chevron) bought out and dismantled the electric trolley systems in Los Angeles and 75 other cities to create demand for their products.[74]

Such organizations ignore the consumption patterns of the more well-to-do, the role of U.S. businesses, and the role of the U.S. military in causing environmental degradation. Despite these facts, increasingly, right-wing environmental organizations, such as Carrying Capacity Network (CCN), Population-Environment Balance and Negative Population Growth, are urging a closing of the borders in order to "save the environment." Underlying these politics is an ideology implicitly based on eugenics. Virginia Abernathy of CCN and Population Environment Balance has advocated withholding aid to poor countries because, she incorrectly argues, poor people have more children.[75] CCN has argued, "The Anglo-Saxon civil culture of the nation must continue to reign supreme in the interest of stability and prosperity for everyone."[76]

Unfortunately, some of these groups have used the rhetoric of "women's liberation" to support their white supremacist population control ideology. CCN argues that true feminists must restrict the immigration of non-European cultures into the U.S. because they are too sexist. "There's a choice to be made between feminism and multiculturalism....[The West] is the only civilization that made an effort to overcome its sexist traditions."[77] The influence of the eugenics movement is also evident in the work of the Pioneer Fund, a eugenics organization started in 1987 by a millionaire, Ron May, who advocated sending African Americans back to Africa. The Pioneer Fund has also supported Nazi eugenicist work and eugenicist research in the U.S., including Charles Murray's "bell curve" studies, and it funds FAIR, the anti-immigration organization, which was very active in organizing around the anti-immigration ballot in the Sierra Club in 1997–1998.

Notably, many members of the Sierra Club, including Allan Weeden, belong to FAIR. Weeden controls the multimillion-dollar Frank Weeden Foundation, which funds environmental and population/immigration groups, including FAIR. It's been estimated that Weeden spent over a million dollars to pressure Sierra Club members to vote for the anti-immigration platform on the Sierra Club ballot in 1998.[78] Popular population alarmist/environmentalist Paul Ehrlich of CCN also sits on the executive board of FAIR.

Another initiative on the part of the anti-immigrant sector of the environmental movement is the campaign to pressure George W. Bush to create the previously described National Optimum Population Commission. The NOPC would determine an "ideal" population size for the U.S. and answer the following question: "How many people can we support in perpetuity under the most favorable circumstances with the highest quality of life?" The commission would determine an "optimum" population based "upon an assessment of the nation's climate, geography, renewable resource base, cultural preferences and other factors." NOPC recommendations would likely include drastic reductions in legal immigration and sharp decreases in birthrates, particularly among poor women and women of color.

Some environmentalists have also espoused immigration restrictions, opposed family reunification, and advocated coercive contraceptive policies for immigrant women. For instance, Bill

DeValle, a leader in the deep ecology movement, has said that he will support immigration into his "bioregion" only if immigrants promise to have no children, if they do not bring their families with them, and if they devote their lives to preserving the environment.[79] Anti-immigration activism also negatively affects immigrant women's reproductive health because it drives women underground and makes it more difficult for them to organize and access health care.

Not surprisingly, many far-right organizations are finding the xenophobic and racist agendas of these organizations attractive. The Aryan Women's League has described their strategy for gaining public legitimacy:

> The way to do this is to make ourselves known as environmentalists and wildlife advocates. There are many groups out there helping wildlife and the environment. They are not necessarily white power advocates like ourselves, but if we make contributions to these groups, we achieve two things, 1) we break out of our media stereotype and 2) we gain recognition.[80]

One of the reasons why this racist ideology is so popular is because it is the continuing legacy of sexual violence against Native peoples and peoples of color that has rendered them inherently impure and dirty in the U.S. psyche. The images proffered by the environmental movement are ones in which Native peoples are depicted as "ruining *our* environment." "They" are crowding "us" out. Women of color, who have the ability to reproduce the next generations, are a particular threat, and consequently their fertility must be monitored and controlled.

For instance, Paul Ehrlich describes his conversion to population politics:

> I have understood the population explosion intellectually for a long time. I came to understand it emotionally one stinking hot night in Delhi a few years ago. The streets seemed alive with people. People eating, people washing, people sleeping. People defecating and urinating. People clinging to buses. People herding animals. People, people, people...Since that night I've known the feel of overpopulation.[81]

As another example, I was giving a talk at a population conference. I asked everyone to tell me what word came up when they thought of India. Almost everyone said "dirty," "polluted," "crowded."

In 1990, I spoke to a largely white audience in Illinois on the issues of mining in northern Wisconsin. After explaining the devastating impact mining companies might have on Native peoples and non-Native peoples in the area, the response I received was, "But don't you think the *real* reason Native peoples have environmental problems is because they're having too many children?"

The racism in the population movement, as well as in society at large, is usually more subtle. Consequently, racist ideology is often framed by "race-neutral" language. For instance, anti-immigration activists may argue that they support immigration restrictions, regardless of race. Nevertheless, when mainstream (and far-right) activists are pushing immigration restrictions, they are thinking about protecting "the border." When they talk about population reduction, they usually have Global South women in mind, since the First World is at replacement-level fertility rates.

Often, in my experience, population control groups will assert that they are concerned with eradicating economic inequality, racism, and colonialism. However, since these organizations address these issues through a population paradigm, inevitably their efforts are directed toward reducing population growth of all peoples in theory and of people of color in reality. In 1998, I gave a presentation about population control at the Environmental Law Conference in Eugene, Oregon. Several audience members contended that their groups, while concerned about population growth, were equally concerned about eradicating racism, colonialism, and sexism. So I asked them what percentage of their organizing was actually devoted to working on those issues. Every single person answered "none." With allies like this, it is no wonder that the statement made on this issue at the first People of Color Environmental Justice summit was, "We're not interested in controlling our population for the sake of your population."

Chapter 4

"Better Dead Than Pregnant"
The Colonization of Native Women's Reproductive Health

The notion that communities of color, including Native communities, pollute the body politic continues to inform the contemporary population control movement. People of color are scapegoated for environmental destruction, poverty, and war. Women of color are particularly threatening, as they have the ability to reproduce the next generations of communities of color. Consequently, it is not surprising that control over the reproductive abilities of women of color has come to be seen as a "national security" issue for the U.S.

In particular, Native women, whose ability to reproduce continues to stand in the way of the continuing conquest of Native lands, endangering the continued success of colonization. As Ines Hernandez-Avila notes, "it is because of a Native American woman's sex that she is hunted down and slaughtered, in fact, singled out, because she has the potential through childbirth to assure the continuance of the people."[1] David Stannard points out that control over women's reproductive abilities and destruction of women and children is necessary to destroy a people. If the women of a nation are not disproportionately killed, then that

nation's population will not be severely affected. He argues that
Native women and children have been historically targeted for
wholesale killing in order to destroy the Indian nations.[2] Indeed,
colonizers such as Andrew Jackson recommended that troops systematically kill Indian women and children after massacres in order
to complete the extermination. Similarly, in the nineteenth century,
Methodist minister Colonel John Chivington's policy was to "kill
and scalp all little and big" because "nits make lice."[3] Under colonialism, Native women and women of color have not had any
guarantees to bodily integrity; it seems that any form of dangerous
contraception is appropriate, so long as it stops them from reproducing. Or, as Chicago-based reproductive rights activist Sharon
Powell describes it, women of color are "better dead than
pregnant."

Sterilization Abuse

As many Global South countries began to resist the neocolonial
economic policies imposed by the World Bank and International
Monetary Fund (IMF), U.S. government and business interests
blamed the unrest on an "overpopulation problem." In 1977, R. T.
Ravenholt of the U.S. Agency for International Development
(USAID) announced the plan to sterilize a quarter of the world's
women because, as he put it,

> Population control is necessary to maintain the normal operation
> of U.S. commercial interests around the world. Without our trying
> to help these countries with their economic and social develop-
> ment, the world would rebel against the strong U.S. commercial
> presence.[4]

Not surprisingly, during the 1970s the population growth of non-
whites in the Global South and the U.S. was viewed by elites as a
"national security risk." One recently declassified federal document, the National Security Study Memorandum 2000, includes a
1976 memo authored by former Secretary of State Henry
Kissinger outlining the nature of this threat:

It seems well understood that the impact of population factors on the subjects already considered — development, food requirements, resources, environment — adversely affects the welfare and progress of countries in which we have a friendly interest and thus indirectly adversely affects broad U.S. interests as well....

Population factors contribute to socio-economic variables including breakdowns in social structures, underemployment and unemployment, poverty, deprived people in city slums, lowered opportunities for education for the masses, few job opportunities for those who do obtain education, interracial, religious, and regional rivalries, and sharply increased financial, planning, and administrative burdens on governmental systems at all levels. These adverse conditions appear to contribute frequently to harmful developments of a political nature: Juvenile delinquency, thievery and other crimes, organized brigandry, kidnapping and terrorism, food riots, other outbreaks of violence; guerilla warfare, communal violence, separatist movements, revolutionary movements and counter-revolutionary coups. All of these bear upon the weakening or collapse of local, state, or national government functions. Beyond national boundaries, population factors appear to have had operative roles in some past politically disturbing legal or illegal mass migrations, border incidents, and wars. If current increased population pressures continue they may have greater potential for future disruption in foreign relations.[5]

In the U.S., the Department of Health, Education, and Welfare (HEW) accelerated programs in 1970 that paid for the majority of costs to sterilize Medicaid recipients.[6] In 1979, 7 in 10 U.S. hospitals performing voluntary sterilizations for Medicaid recipients had violated federal guidelines by disregarding informed consent procedures and sterilizing women through "elective" hysterectomies.[7]

Thus, it is not surprising that Native women became targets of the population craze when Indian Health Services (IHS) initiated a fully federally funded sterilization campaign in 1970.[8] Connie Uri, a Cherokee/Choctaw medical doctor, was one of the first people to uncover this mass sterilization of Native women in the 1970s after a young Indian woman entered her office in Los Angeles in 1972 and requested a "womb transplant." Upon further investigation, Uri discovered that the woman had been given a complete hysterectomy for birth control purposes when she was 20 years old and had not been informed that the operation was irreversible. The woman was otherwise completely healthy. Initially, Uri thought she had encountered an isolated incidence of malpractice but she continued to hear from Indian women who had been sterilized under duress, or without being informed that the procedure was irreversible. She and other activists pressured Congress to investigate, and eventually Senator James Abourezk, a Democrat from South Dakota, requested a study of IHS sterilization policies.[9]

As a result, in 1976 the General Accounting Office (GAO) released a report studying 4 of the 12 areas serviced by IHS (Albuquerque, Phoenix, Aberdeen, and Oklahoma City). According to this report, 3,001 Native women of childbearing age, or approximately 5 percent of all Native women of childbearing age in these areas, were sterilized between 1973 to 1976.[10] Of these sterilizations, the GAO reported that 36 were performed on women under the age of 21, despite a court-ordered moratorium on such procedures.[11]

Native activists have argued that the percentage of Native women sterilized is much higher. Dr. Uri conducted an investigation of sterilization policies in Claremore, Oklahoma, and charged that the Claremore facility was sterilizing one woman for every seven births that occurred in the hospital. She claimed that 132 women had been sterilized in 1973, 100 of them nontherapeutic. And in July 1974, Uri found 48 Native women, most of them in their twenties, who had been sterilized.

Unlike the GAO report, her investigation did not rely only on hospital records, but on interviews with women who had been sterilized. Consequently, her numbers are much higher than the GAO's report of Native women in the Oklahoma City IHS area.[12] Her investigations led her to conclude that 25 percent of Native women had been sterilized in that same area without their informed consent.[13] She also charged that "all the pureblood women of the Kaw tribe of Oklahoma have now been sterilized."[14] Other activists have reported even higher numbers. Women of All Red Nations (WARN) issued an alert stating that close to 50 percent of Indian women had been sterilized in the 1970s. Native rights activist Lehman Brightman asserts that 40 percent of Native women and 10 percent of Native men were sterilized during the decade.[15] Pat Bellanger of WARN contends that sterilization rates were as high as 80 percent on some reservations.[16]

One study of sterilization rates in Montana, which focused on the Blackfeet Reservation and the urban Indian population of Great Falls, found that Indian women were twice as likely to be sterilized as were white women.[17] Another study of sterilization rates on the Navajo reservation found that tubal ligations increased by approximately 61 percent from 1972 to 1977.[18]

Most of these numbers, such as Dr. Uri's, are based on sterilizations at one or two IHS hospitals, from which activists extrapolate sterilization rates. It is also difficult to come up with accurate data, because IHS did not have uniform protocols for sterilization procedures until after the uproar over sterilization abuses forced the agency to adopt one. As a result, sterilization policies fluctuated greatly from region to region, varying due to philosophies of the particular administrators in IHS areas.

Given that the population of Native peoples did increase in this period, it might seem unlikely that 50 percent of Native women of childbearing age had been sterilized. However, a study of sterilization rates in Montana found that on average Native women who were sterilized already had three or four children, which might explain how high sterilization rates might not lead to a population decrease in Native communities.[19] And some data strongly suggests that Indian women were targeted for sterilization without their informed consent. For example, Uri discovered that many of the women sterilized in Claremore were sterilized within a day or two after having given birth, which means physicians may have violated federal regulations requiring a 72-hour waiting period between consenting to the operation and having it performed. One woman informed Dr. Uri that she was advised to be sterilized for headaches. "The doctor told the woman her head hurt because she was afraid of becoming pregnant, and advised sterilization. The woman agreed, but the headaches persisted. She later learned she had a brain tumor."[20] Another woman went to a doctor for stomach problems. The doctor assumed she was ill because she was pregnant and yelled, "Why the hell don't you get your tubes tied so you won't get sick anymore?"[21]

Maria Sanchez, former chief tribal judge of the Northern Cheyenne, reported that two 15-year-old girls were sterilized during what they were told were tonsillectomy operations.[22] In another story, Norma Jean Serena (Creek/Shawnee) was pressured by welfare caseworkers to undergo a tubal ligation after the birth of her third child. These caseworkers also removed all her children into foster care because she was an "unfit mother." Three years later, she sued Armstrong County for damages from the sterilization and to have her children returned to her. The jury found that the children had been taken away under false pretenses, but the jury did not support her claim that her civil rights had been violated through the sterilization procedure. During the court proceedings, the major complaint against Serena was that she was "dirty and unkempt" and that she had Black friends who, in the minds of the social workers, were also inherently polluting to the body politic.[23]

Interestingly, the 1976 GAO report sidesteps the issue of informed consent because "we believe such an effort would not be productive."[24] But the GAO did note that IHS was "generally not in compliance with IHS regulations. Although there were consent forms in the medical files, most of these forms did not comply with IHS requirements."[25] These consent forms did *not*

> (1) indicate that the basic elements of informed consent had been presented orally to the patient; (2) contain written summaries of the oral presentation; and (3) contain a statement at the top of the form notifying subjects of their right to withdraw consent. One consent form document did meet the Indian Health Service requirements, but when used was filled out incorrectly.[26]

IHS was also out of compliance with specific HEW regulations, and these regulations were also problematic. By the time of the report (1976) HEW had eliminated a requirement mandating that "individuals seeking sterilization be orally informed at the outset that no Federal benefits can be withdrawn because of failure to accept sterilizations."[27] Further, HEW did not require that the signature of the patient appear on the consent forms, so we must rely upon the word of the doctors that informed consent was given.[28] In addition, the informed consent sheet is highly technical and would not necessarily be understandable to someone who was not fluent in English. Further complicating matters, over half of the sterilizations were performed by contract facilities, which do not have to abide by federal procedures regarding informed consent.[29]

Eventually, IHS strengthened its sterilization policies. Today sterilization procedures must meet "the standard set forth in Sub-section F of Section 3-13.12 of the IHS Manual and regulatory policy and legal requirements for informed consent and performance of sterilization procedures."[30] Additionally, "the area/program director must dispatch all data and statistics to headquarters on time."[31] The current IHS policy regarding sterilization is as follows:

> IHS will neither promote nor discourage sterilization or fertility of the population it serves. Its overall policy is geared to the enhancement of life through assuring the availability of legally, ethically and medically acceptable information and services that afford families and individuals the opportunity to assure that each child is a wanted one. In addition, before discharge following delivery the mother will be offered an opportunity for counseling, guidance and/or services for family planning.[32]

Sterilization abuse, while curbed, is certainly not dead, either in IHS or society at large. One woman I know went into IHS in the 1990s for back surgery and came out with a hysterectomy. In Peru, the Health Ministry recently issued a public apology for sterilizing 200,000 indigenous people (primarily Quechua and Aymara) without consent during the presidency of Alberto Fujimori. One witness reported that a group of doctors visited her Andean village promising its residents a new era of well-being and improved health. "Later, they threatened us and practically forced us to [accept sterilization]," she said. "They shut me up in a room and forced me to get undressed. Everything that happened was because they used force. I didn't want to go through with it."[33] Several women died during sterilization operations, which were carried out under non-hygienic conditions. The majority of operations were undertaken without anesthesia and without aftercare. Some experts estimate that only 10 percent of the sterilizations conducted from 1996 to 2000 in Peru were voluntary. The number of sterilizations during this period were three times higher than during the previous four-year period, and sterilizations increased each year to meet Fujimori's "family planning" targets. The rural villages that were targeted now face a shortage of young people that threatens their future.[34]

In 1997, Barbara Harris started an organization called CRACK (Children Requiring a Caring Kommunity, sic) in Anaheim, California, which gave women money to have sterilizations.[35] Harris's mission is to "save our welfare system and the world from the exorbitant cost to the taxpayer for each drug-addicted birth by offering effective preventative measures to reduce the tragedy of numerous drug-affected pregnancies."[36] Some of CRACK's initial billboards read, "Don't let a pregnancy ruin your drug habit."[37]

Over the last decade, CRACK has opened offices in several cities around the country, and changed its name to Project Prevention to present a less inflammatory image. Nonetheless, its basic message is the same: poor women who are substance abusers are the cause of social ills, and that the conditions that give rise to poor women becoming substance abusers do not need to be addressed. It further trades on a racist image of women of color in particular being the cause of social ills, as CRACK/Project Prevention primarily advertises in communities of color. Yet Barbara Harris defends herself against charges of bias by arguing that she cannot be racist because her husband is a Black man. Says Harris, "people don't know anything about me. I'm the only white person in my house."[38]

CRACK/Project Prevention also conveys the message that women who are substance abusers should be criminalized, not treated, for their addiction. As race and reproductive scholar Dorothy Roberts notes, women of color are more likely to be criminalized for their drug use because they are more likely to be in contact with government agencies where their drug use can be detected. While white pregnant women are more likely to engage in substance abuse than Black pregnant women, public health facilities and private doctors are more likely to report Black women to criminal justice authorities.[39]

The Seattle-based group Communities Against Rape and Abuse, (CARA), a leading organization that opposes the politics of CRACK/Project Prevention, notes how such efforts disproportionately impact survivors of sexual violence since survivors are more than 10 times more likely to abuse alcohol and drugs.[40] Finally, as community organizer and CARA staffer Joelle Brouner notes, the organization's message is based on an able-bodied supremacist notion of "value," which asserts that babies born to women who are substance abusers are "damaged" because they are "burdens to society." The assumption behind these claims, asserts Brouner, is that lives are of value to the extent that they meet capitalist expectations of self-sufficiency and productivity.[41]

Meanwhile, pregnant women who would like treatment for their addiction can seldom get it because treatment centers do not meet their needs. One study found that two thirds of drug treatment centers would not treat pregnant women.[42] Furthermore, the criminalization approach is more likely to prevent pregnant women who are substance abusers from seeking health care for fear of being reported to the authorities.[43] Roberts critiques communities of color for often supporting the criminalization of women of color addicts; she sees this criminalization as a strategy that elides the effects of poverty and racism and supports white supremacy.

Similarly, Native scholar Elizabeth Cook-Lynn (Crow Creek Sioux) critiques Native communities for supporting the criminalization of pregnancy. She says that at the same time Native peoples were rallying around Leonard Peltier, no one stood beside Marie Big Pipe in South Dakota when she was incarcerated on a felony charge of assault with intent to commit serious bodily harm because she breast-fed her child while under the influence of alcohol. Big Pipe was denied substance abuse services and access to abortion services when she became pregnant. Nevertheless, her community supported her incarceration. In doing so, Cook-Lynn argues, the community supported the encroachment of U.S. federal jurisdiction on tribal lands for an issue that would normally be under tribal jurisdiction.[44] Meanwhile, the federal government, which is supposed to prosecute "major crimes" on Indian land, prosecutes virtually no cases of rape committed against Indian women.

Cook-Lynn also charges that this demonization of Native women was assisted by the publication of Michael Dorris's *Broken Cord*, which narrates his adoption of a Native child who suffered from fetal alcohol syndrome.[45] While this book has been crucial in sensitizing many communities to the realities of fetal alcohol syndrome, it also portrays the mother of the child unsympathetically and advocates repressive legislative solutions targeted against women substance abusers. As Cook-Lynn notes,

> Dorris directs his frustrated wrath toward some of the least powerful among us: young childbearing Indian women. He says they must pay the price for the health crisis and family disintegration that can be observed not only on Indian reservations but in cities and rural areas throughout the country. Forcing these young women, as much the victims as their martyred children, into detention centers is presented as a solution to failed health care systems, inadequate education, poverty, and neglect.[46]

Within Native communities, the growing demonization of Native women substance abusers has prompted tribes to collude with the federal government in whittling away their own sovereignty.

Abuse of Long-Acting Hormonal Contraceptives

While sterilization abuse in the U.S. has ebbed since the 1970s, state control over reproductive freedom continues through the promotion of unsafe, long-acting hormonal contraceptives like Depo-Provera and Norplant for women of color, women on federal assistance, and women with disabilities. As the population scare and the demonization of poverty moved to the mainstream of the dominant culture in the U.S., Norplant and Depo-Provera became frontline weapons in the war against the poor and populations of color.

For instance, state legislatures considered bills that would give women on public assistance bonuses if they used Norplant.[47] In California, a Black single mother convicted of child abuse was given the "choice" of using Norplant or being sentenced to four years in prison.[48] In 1991, the *Philadelphia Inquirer* ran an editorial suggesting that Norplant could be a useful tool in reducing the underclass.[49] Over 87 percent of Norplant implants were paid for by government programs, indicating that poor women have been targeted for Norplant.[50]

Depo-Provera and Norplant were approved for contraceptive use, in 1992 and 1990 respectively, by the Food and Drug Administration (FDA). However, as the National Women's Health Network points out, FDA approval does not necessarily guarantee the safety of a drug.[51] The FDA relies upon the manufacturer's data regarding animal and human testing and does not routinely double-check the manufacturer's data. The agency also does not permit consumer groups to double-check research studies; data are prepared by researchers who are often funded directly or indirectly by manufacturers. FDA advisory committees are not composed of experts who are knowledgeable about the wide variety of drug side effects. Instead, the FDA relies upon the manufacturer for information on adverse effects. Physicians are not required to report adverse drug reactions to the FDA, and the FDA seldom follows up on adverse-reaction reports from consumers.[52] In fact, FDA commissioner Jaime Goddard estimates that "one percent or less" of the adverse reactions to any drug are ever reported to the FDA by the doctors.[53]

Depo-Provera is a long-acting injectable contraceptive made by the Upjohn Company. This injection prevents pregnancy by stopping the production of progesterone and estrogen, which in turn inhibits ovulation and prevents the lining of the uterus from being prepared to accept a fertilized egg. Also, the drug can cause a mucus plug to form in the cervix, preventing contact between the sperm and ovum.[54]

Side effects that have been linked to Depo-Provera include irregular bleeding, depression, weight gain, osteoporosis, loss of sex drive, breast cancer, sterility, cervical cancer, and headaches.[55] Upjohn, not surprisingly, denies the link between the more extreme conditions and Depo-Provera. The National Women's Health Network maintained a registry of reported Depo-Provera side effects and recorded over 100 related symptoms.[56] The *Ultimate Test Animal*, a documentary on Depo-Provera, interviewed several women who suffered from blood clots in the lungs, extreme bleeding (one woman eventually had to undergo a hysterectomy to address this symptom), and cervical cancer after using the drug.

In tests on animals in 1968, Depo-Provera was linked to increased risk for breast and uterine cancer.[57] The FDA Public Board of Inquiry stated in 1982 that "never has a drug whose target population is entirely healthy people been shown to be so pervasively carcinogenic in animals as has Depo-Provera."[58] Many health-care activists have argued that Upjohn has suppressed much of the information from these animal tests, and that these tests indicate that Depo is even more carcinogenic than reported.[59] Upjohn argued that beagles were not an appropriate test subject for Depo-Provera because beagles are very susceptible to breast cancer. Dr. Solomon Sobel of the FDA, however, testified that there are no other contraceptives which are carcinogenic in beagles which have reached the U.S. market.[60]

The largest test on humans was conducted for 11 years beginning in 1967, through the Grady Clinic, affiliated with Emory University in Atlanta. The *Ultimate Test Animal* documents the widespread abuses in this clinical trial. Robert Hatcher, who directed the study, admits that there was no established protocol for the study. In 1978, FDA sent investigators to Grady. They found that many women were not told they were part of an experiment or that there were side effects associated with Depo. Several women developed cancer during the trial, but these cases were not reported to the FDA as was required. Women with medically contraindicated conditions, such as cancer, were still given the shot. And record keeping was sloppy; over half of the 13,000 women in the trial were lost to followup. Hatcher's response to the critiques of his clinical trial was that these mistakes "did not have any detrimental impact on patients."[61]

The Black Women's Health Project tracked some of the women who had been lost in the trials, and found that they were suffering from extremely adverse effects. Many young women had uterine, cervical or breast cancer, or had undergone hysterectomies as a result of hemorrhaging.[62] Several women had also became clinically depressed from Depo, and had attempted suicide as a result.[63] Upjohn's response to this side effect was, "headaches, depression and loss of libido mostly require reassurance from a trusted and respected friend or counselor."[64]

Sobel concluded that the Grady study was "not a carefully controlled trial, but rather... a treatment program in which the drug was dispensed without the usual care and monitoring that we associate with a controlled clinical trial. The patient followup was not good, and the FDA could not really accept this as a study of the quality that we require in the drug approval process."[65] And because of the side effects, several national women's health organizations, including the National Women's Health Network, the Native American Women's Health Education Resource Center, the National Latina Health Organization, and the Black Women's Health Project, have condemned the drug and urged women not to use it. In 1978 the FDA denied approval for Depo-Provera as contraception on the grounds that animal studies confirmed an elevated rate of breast cancer; there appeared to be an increased risk of birth defects in human fetuses exposed to the drug; and there was no pressing need shown for use of the drug as a contraceptive.[66]

Yet in 1987, the FDA changed its regulations and began to require cancer testing in rats and mice instead of dogs and monkeys, and Depo-Provera did not cause cancer in these animals.[67] The World Health Organization added its endorsement in 1991, concluding that there was "no evidence for increased risk of breast cancer with long duration of use" after a nine-year study.[68] It is important to note, however, that nine years does not necessarily constitute a "long duration," and no other tests proving the long-term safety of Norplant or Depo-Provera exists. Furthermore, as the Women's Health Education Project points out, all of these studies were conducted by Upjohn. And as with animal studies and the Grady study, it was reported that women with extreme side effects were eliminated from the data, and some of the trials were conducted on sample sizes too small to be statistically significant.[69] In spite of all of this, Depo-Provera was approved by the FDA for contraceptive use in 1992.

Before Depo was approved in 1992, it was routinely used on Native women by IHS, particularly on Native women with disabilities. According to area director Burton Attico, the Phoenix IHS had already begun to substitute Depo for sterilization on patients with mental disabilities in the 1980s because by then sterilization had been prohibited. Said Attico, "We use it to stop their periods. There is nothing else that will do it. To have to change a pad on someone developmentally disabled, you've got major problems. The fact they become infertile while on it is a side benefit."[70] Raymond Jannett of the Phoenix IHS suggested that Depo-Provera aided young women dealing with PMS-like symptoms."Depo-Provera turned them back into their sweet, poor, handicapped selves. I take some pride in being a pioneer in that regard," he said.[71] But, while Jannett did not have any reservations about using it on Indian women, he said he did not plan to use it "on attractive 16-year-old girls who one day hope to be mothers."[72] Patrick Gideon, with the IHS in Oklahoma City, said it would be appropriate to prescribe the drug to "women who are unable to care for themselves. For hygienic reasons, we will go ahead and give it."[73] Apparently, keeping Native women "clean" by sterilizing them is more important than protecting Native women's health; in this way, Native womens bodies are viewed as inherently dirty, in need of cleansing and purification *at any cost.*

Often, the IHS distributed Depo-Provera without the informed consent of patients or their caretakers. Attic claimed that doctors obtained oral consent but admitted they did not use written consent forms. Jannett similarly said that he never offered consent forms to his patients or explained the potential risks or side effects of Depo-Provera. "I don't tell them that rhesus monkeys did strange things, no...Most parents don't have rhesus-monkey children...I don't go into a great deal that it's carcinogenic...Instead, I tell them it's a drug that helps combat cancer."[74] Cecile Balone, executive director of "A School for Me," a Navajo reservation facility, reports that Depo-Provera was used for two years in the community before written consent forms were developed. And Balone says even after they were developed that they were not circulated to parents or guardians of the girls on Depo-Provera.[75]

Norplant, another long-acting contraceptive, was approved for distribution in the U.S. in 1990. Norplant is implanted through five rods into a woman's arm and prevents pregnancy for five years by maintaining low-level doses of progesterone in the system, suppressing ovulation and thickening the cervical mucus so that it is impervious to sperm. As with Depo-Provera, there are no studies which demonstrate Norplant's long-term safety. Instead, use of Norplant has been correlated with several side effects, with constant bleeding—sometimes for more than 90 days—being the most common. About 82 percent of Norplant users experience irregular, usually heavy, bleeding during the first year of use.[76] This side effect is particularly problematic for Native women, since women are often excluded from ceremonies while they are bleeding. And as irregular bleeding is a symptom of endometrial and cervical cancer, Norplant use can mask those symptoms. Other reported side effects include blindness, hair loss, dizziness, nausea, headaches, strokes, heart attacks, tumors, and sterility.[77]

Prior to its approval, Norplant had been tested in several Global South countries. The BBC video *The Human Laboratory* (1995) documented how women receiving Norplant in Bangladesh without their informed consent were not able to have it removed when they developed side effects. (Distribution of the drug in Bangladesh began in 1985.) Furthermore, when they attempted to report side effects, doctors scolded them and refused to record the information. One woman attempting to get it removed told her doctor, "I'm dying, please help me get it out." Her doctor responded "OK, when you die you inform us, we'll get it out of your dead body."[78] Similar stories have been reported in Haiti, India, and many other Global South countries.[79] Nevertheless, Wyeth-Ayerst continued to report that "Norplant is a highly effective, safe and acceptable method among Bangladeshi women."[80]

Because of the extreme side effects, approximately 30 percent of women on Norplant wanted it removed within one year,[81] and the majority wanted it out within three years.[82] While Norplant is still being used in IHS, Wyeth-Ayerst withdrew the drug from the market in 2000, after paying a reported $54 million to more than

36,000 women in 1999. These women had sued the company claiming that their health had been damaged by the drug. But Wyeth-Ayerst refuses to discontinue its promotion of the drug, or warn women of the risks associated with it. The U.S. Food and Drug Administration (FDA) continues to carry Norplant on its list of approved drugs and devices, as a substance for regulating pregnancy. Moreover, many doctors know how to insert Norplant but they do not know how to remove it. (Medicaid typically paid for Norplant insertion, but not its removal.)[83]

Yet despite the evidence indicating that Depo-Provera and Norplant are dangerous, when the Native American Women's Health Education Resource Center (NAWHERC) conducted a study of IHS policies regarding the drugs in 1993, it found that IHS was aggressively promoting them in many Native communities. NAWHERC concluded that IHS policies regarding Norplant and Depo-Provera are similar to its sterilization policies in the 1970s, before uniform policies and procedures were instituted. For example, prior to FDA approval of Depo-Provera in 1992, IHS maintained a registry of women using it. This practice was discontinued after its approval, and now women on Depo-Provera or Norplant are not monitored or tracked in a systematic manner.[84] Given the high turnover within IHS and the periodic monitoring required by Norplant (it must be removed after five years to avoid life-threatening ectopic pregnancies) and Depo-Provera (it must be administered quarterly to be effective), these practices are highly problematic. Women in India were not tracked during clinical trials of Norplant, and encountered great difficulty in having it removed after the five year period. Native women may face similar circumstances.[85]

NAWHERC found that not all IHS areas were lax in their protocol regarding Norplant and Depo-Provera distribution. It applauds the Crow service unit for its detailed protocol which ensures that "the more complex tasks of counseling and documentation are extensively supervised, and that the counseling is performed by each provider in a standardized, acceptable fashion."[86] However, NAWHERC suggests that IHS adopt a uniform policy on Depo-Provera that ensures all women using the contraceptive receive informed consent and are monitored to ensure that any side effects they suffer from are addressed promptly.

While NAWHERC's study is useful, the organization questioned the providers of Norplant and Depo-Provera, not the recipients. A study which focuses on the recipients might reveal different information about IHS policies regarding informed consent. When I worked with WARN in Chicago, which provided much educational material on these contraceptives to the Native community, I routinely heard from women who said they were pressured by either their welfare case workers or IHS doctors to take Norplant. They also informed me that were not told of its side effects.

In 1996, I attended NAWHERC conference on reproductive rights in Rapid City, South Dakota. At the workshop on Depo-Provera, the room was filled with distraught Native women who were hearing for the first time about the side effects of the Depo-Provera injections they had been receiving. The documentary *Under Her Skin* reports how Native women in one IHS area were told that Norplant has no side effects, and yet women receiving Norplant were suffering from hair loss, tumors, depression, and constant bleeding. In the film *Ultimate Test Animal*, a woman enters an urban clinic with a hidden camera pretending to seek contraceptive counseling. Following is a transcription of the information she received:

> Your body gets mixed up when it's on Depo-Provera so your monthly period may not return right away. Another thing you need to know about this shot is that it is not approved for birth control by the FDA, which we think is stupid…There was this one study that was done on beagle dogs and they gave a bunch of beagle dogs this medicine, though in much higher dosages than you will be getting, and some of the dogs developed breast cancer. Now, this study was not a good one because beagles are susceptible to breast cancer anyway. You're obviously not a beagle dog; you're obviously not going to get as high dosage, but we're obligated to tell you this anyway.[87]

This transcript demonstrates that it is possible for health-care providers to provide information that conveys a misleading and incomplete sense of the issues involved with these contraceptives.

Furthermore, even when women receive information on the side effects of contraceptives, they assume that their doctors will not provide them with drugs that could be unsafe. As one victim of the Grady clinical trial stated in *The Ultimate Test Animal*: "I felt anything Grady would give me would be for my better, and not experimental."[88]

Abortion and Sterilization

Government policies couple the promotion of sterilization or dangerous contraceptives with restrictive abortion policies. As a result of the Hyde Amendment, which eliminated federal funding for abortion services in 1976, IHS cannot provide abortions unless the mother's life is in danger or the pregnancy is the result of incest or rape. Because most Native women rely almost exclusively on IHS for their healthcare, and IHS does not provide abortion services except under these limited circumstances, it is clear that the Hyde Amendment discriminates on the basis of race. Thus, all racial justice groups should be opposing the Hyde Amendment as a racial justice issue.

Unfortunately, this issue has not been addressed by either racial justice or pro-choice organizations. In fact, in the early 1990s, pro-choice organizations such as NARAL (National Abortion Rights Action League) and Planned Parenthood made the conscious choice to sell out the interests of Native women, poor women, and women of color when they supported the Freedom of Choice Act, which retained Hyde Amendment provisions. In fact, one of NARAL's petitions stated, "The Freedom of Choice Act (FOCA) will secure the original vision of Roe v. Wade, giving *all* women reproductive freedom and securing that right for future generations [emphasis added]."[89] Apparently, poor women and indigenous women do not qualify as "women."

Furthermore, when NAWHERC studied IHS abortion policies in 2002, it found that 85 percent of surveyed IHS service units were not compliant with official IHS abortion policy. Sixty-two percent of the units did not provide abortion services when the mother's life was in danger. In fact, only 5 percent of service units performed abortion procedures at their facilities.[90]

Unfortunately, racial justice groups have generally not addressed racism in reproductive rights policies, marginalizing them as "women's" issues. For example, these issues were almost completely absent at the 2001 United Nations World Conference on Racism, where a variety of issues related to racism—including reparations, the colonization of Palestine, and caste discrimination—were addressed. And as Dorothy Roberts notes, some activists refuse to address racism in abortion policies, arguing that abortion access represents "genocide" for communities of color. These advocates fail to consider that restrictions to abortion can become another strategy to coerce Native women or women of color to pursue sterilization or long-acting hormonal contraceptives. The strategy of coupling restrictive abortion with sterilization policies is evident within a bill considered but eventually defeated by the North Carolina legislature in 1993: "The Department of Human Resources shall ensure that all women who receive an abortion funded through the State Abortion Fund receive Norplant implantation and do not remove it unless the procedure is medically contraindicated."[91] This legislation sought to target women during a vulnerable period, while facing an unwanted pregnancy, to pressure them into accepting long-acting hormonal contraceptives.

In the Northwest Territories of Canada, the Status of Women Council uncovered similar punitive abortion policies at the Stanton Yellowknife Hospital, which services Inuit women. Women were denied anesthesia during abortion services as punishment for seeking abortions. One woman was told by her doctor: "This really hurt, didn't it? But let that be a lesson before you get yourself in this situation again."[92] This controversy was uncovered when a rape victim, Ellen Hamilton, went to the media saying that her abortion had been worse than the rape: she was given no counseling, pinned down, and given no anesthesia during the procedure.

Hamilton's experience was publicized in the Northwest Territories, prompting a flood of responses from women who had suffered a similar fate. The hospital responded that it had provided all the women with aspirin, making them the only hospital in Canada to provide only aspirin for pain relief during abortion procedures.[93] The Canadian government ordered an inquiry into the hospital's procedures, forcing the hospital to issue a statement that it had developed a new plan "for providing patients with choices in pain control during abortion procedures."[94]

These policies appear to punish the women for having abortions. One woman who went in for an abortion and a tubal ligation the same day reported that she was told,"The anesthesiologist does not believe in abortions, we will administer the anesthetic following the abortion, for the tubal ligation."[95] By increasing the pain and trauma associated with abortion, or by making it inaccessible, the health care establishment exerts even more pressure on Native women to agree to sterilizations or dangerous contraceptives.

Beyond Choice

The history of Native women and colonial reproductive policies demonstrates the political bankruptcy of the "choice" paradigm for articulating a reproductive rights agenda. As Native activist Justine Smith states,

> The reproductive rights movement frames the issues around individual "choice" —does the woman have the choice to have or not to have an abortion. This analysis obscures all the social conditions that prevent women from having and making real choices—lack of health care, poverty, lack of social services, etc....In the Native context, where women often find the only contraceptives available to them are dangerous...where they live in communities in which unemployment rates can run as high as 80 percent, and where their life expectancy can be as low as 47 years, reproductive "choice" defined so narrowly is a meaningless concept. Instead, Native women and men must fight for community self-determination and sovereignty over their health care.[96]

A variety of scholars and activists have critiqued the choice paradigm because it rests on essentially individualist, consumerist notions of "free" choice that do not take into consideration all the social, economic, and political conditions that frame the so-called choices that women are forced to make.[97] Historian Rickie Solinger contends that in the 1960s and 1970s, abortion rights advocates initially used the term "rights" rather than "choice," rights understood as those benefits owed to all those who are human regardless of access to special resources. By contrast, argues Solinger, the concept of "choice" is connected to possession of resources, thus creating a hierarchy among women based on who is capable of making legitimate choices.[98] As Solinger writes,

> "Choice" also became a symbol of middle-class women's arrival as independent consumers. Middle-class women could afford to choose. They had earned the right to choose motherhood, if they liked. According to many Americans, however, when choice was associated with poor women, it became a symbol of illegitimacy. Poor women had not earned the right to choose.[99]

What her analysis suggests is that, ironically, while the pro-choice camp contends that the pro-life position diminishes the rights of women in favor of "fetal" rights, the pro-choice position actually does not ascribe inherent rights to women either. Rather, women are ascribed reproductive choices if they can afford them or if they are deemed legitimate choice-makers. Building on this analysis, I would argue that while there is certainly a sustained critique of the "choice" paradigm, particularly among women of color reproductive rights groups, the choice paradigm continues to govern much of the policies of mainstream groups in a manner which continues the marginalization of women of color, poor women, and women with disabilities.

One example of this marginalization is how pro-choice organizations narrow their advocacy to legislation that affects the right to choose to have an abortion—without addressing the conditions that put women in the position of having to make the decision in the first place. Consequently, politicians, such as former president Bill Clinton are heralded as "pro-choice" as long as they do not support legislative restrictions on abortion regardless of their stance on other issues that may equally affect the reproductive choices women make. Clinton's approval of federal welfare reforms that place poor women in the position of possibly being forced to have an abortion because of cuts in social services, for instance, while often criticized, was not criticized as an "anti-choice" position. On the Web sites for Planned Parenthood and NARAL, there is little mention of welfare policies in their pro-choice legislation alerts.

The consequence of the "choice" paradigm is that its advocates often take positions that are oppressive to women from marginalized communities. For instance, this paradigm often makes it difficult to develop nuanced positions on the use of abortion when the fetus is determined to have abnormalities. Focusing solely on the woman's choice to have or not have this child does not address the larger context of a society that sees children with disabilities as having lives not worth living and that provides inadequate resources to women who may otherwise want to have them. As Martha Saxton notes, "Our society profoundly limits the 'choice' to love and care for a baby with a disability."[100] If our response to disability is to simply facilitate the process by which women can abort fetuses that may have disabilities, we never actually focus on changing economic and social policies that make raising children with disabilities difficult. Rashmi Luthra notes, by contrast, that reproductive advocates from other countries such as India, who do not operate from this same "choice" paradigm, are often able to take more complicated political positions on issues such as this one.[101]

Another example is the difficulty pro-choice groups have in maintaining a critical perspective on dangerous or potentially dangerous contraceptives, arguing that women should have the "choice" of contraceptives. Mainstream pro-choice organizations have not generally taken on the issue of informed consent as part of their agenda.[102] One reason these groups have not taken a position on informed consent on potentially dangerous contraceptives is because they are invested in population control. Yet, as Betsy Hartmann has argued, while contraceptives are often articulated as an issue of "choice" for white women in the First World, they are articulated as an instrument of population control for women of color and women in the Global South.[103] Indeed, in her book *The War on Choice*, Gloria Feldt, president of Planned Parenthood, equates opposition to Norplant and Depo-Provera as opposition to "choice."[104] Planned Parenthood and NARAL opposed restrictions against sterilization abuse, despite the thousands of women of color who were being sterilized without their consent, because such policies would interfere with women's "right to choose."[105]

Some of these organizations have been supported by the Center for Research on Population and Security, the purveyor of Quinacrine. The Fund for a Feminist Majority featured this organization at its 1996 Feminist Expo because, I was informed by the organizers, they promoted "choice" for women. Then in 1999, Planned Parenthood nearly sponsored a Quinacrine trial in the U.S., until pressure from groups such as the Committee on Women, Population and the Environment and the Boston Women's Health Book Collective forced it to change its position.[106]

The prevalent ideology within the mainstream pro-choice movement is that women should have the "choice" to use whatever contraception they want. Yet mainstream activists often do not consider that a choice among dangerous contraceptives is not much of a choice. In a study commissioned in 1960, Planned Parenthood concluded that poor people "have too many children,"[107] and something must be done to stop this trend in order to "disarm the population bomb."[108] Today, Planned Parenthood is particularly implicated in this movement, as can be seen by the groups it lists as its allies on its Web site: Population Action International, the Population Institute, Zero Population Growth, and the Population Council. A central campaign of Planned Parenthood is to restore U.S. funding to the United Nations Population Fund (UNFPA). In addition it asserts its commitment to addressing "rapid population growth." As Hartmann documents, the UNFPA has long been involved in coercive contraceptive policies throughout the world. The Population Council assisted in Norplant trials which were conducted without informed consent of participants in Bangladesh and other countries.[109] In fact, trial administrators often refused to remove Norplant when requested.[110] All of these population organizations generally share the goal of promoting long-acting hormonal contraceptives of dubious safety around the world.[111]

Of course Planned Parenthood does provide valuable family planning resources to women around the world as well, but it does so through a population framework that inevitably shifts a focus from family planning as right in and of itself to family planning as an instrument of population control. Groups that advocate population control, such as Planned Parenthood, have become increasingly more sophisticated in their rhetoric and often talk about ensuring social, political, and economic opportunity. However, the "population" focus of this model still results in its advocates focusing their work on reducing population rather than in actually providing social, political and economic opportunity.

Another unfortunate consequence of uncritically adopting the "choice" paradigm is the tendency of reproductive rights advocates to make simplistic analyses of who our political friends and enemies are in the area of reproductive rights. That is, all those who call themselves "pro-choice" are our political allies while all those who call themselves pro-life are our political enemies. An example of this rhetoric is Gloria Feldt's description of anyone who is pro-life as a "right-wing extremist."[112] As I have argued elsewhere, this simplistic analysis does not actually do justice to the complex political positions people inhabit.[113] As a result, we often engage uncritically in coalitions with groups who, as antiviolence activist Beth Richie states, "do not pay us back."[114] Meanwhile, we often lose opportunities to work with people with whom we may have sharp disagreements, but who may, with different political framings and organizing strategies, shift their positions.

To illustrate: Planned Parenthood is often championed as an organization that supports women's right to choose, and one with whom women of color should ally. Yet, the roots of the organization are in the eugenics movement. Its founder, Margaret Sanger, collaborated with eugenics organizations during her career, and linked the need for birth control to the need to reduce the number of those in the "lower classes."[115]Today Planned Parenthood is heavily invested in the population establishment, and continues to support population control policies in the Global South.

In contrast, the North Baton Rouge Women's Help Center in Louisiana, a crisis pregnancy center, articulates its pro-life position from an antiracist perspective. It argues that Planned Parenthood has advocated population control, particularly in communities of color. It critiques the Black Church Initiative and the Religious Coalition for Reproductive Choice for contending that charges of racism against Sanger are "scare tactics."[116] It also attempts to provide its services from a holistic perspective — it provides educational and vocational training, GED classes, literacy programs, primary health care and pregnancy services, and child placement services. Says one of the Help Center's leaders, "We cannot encourage women to have babies and then continue their dependency on the system. We can't leave them without the resources to care for their children and then say, 'Praise the Lord, we saved a baby.'"[117]

While both groups support some positions that are beneficial to women of color, they both support positions that are detrimental to women of color. So, if we are truly committed to reproductive justice, why should we presume that we should necessarily work with Planned Parenthood and reject the Women's Help Center? Why would we not instead position ourselves independently from both of these approaches and work to shift both of their positions to a stance that is truly liberating for all women?

To develop an independent position, it is necessary to reject the "pro-choice" framework. Such a strategy would enable us to fight for reproductive justice as a part of a larger social justice strategy. It would also free us to think more creatively about whom we could work in coalition with while simultaneously allowing us to hold those who claim to be our allies more accountable for the positions they take. To be successful in this venture, it is not sufficient to simply articulate a women of color reproductive justice agenda — we must focus on developing a nationally coordinated women of color movement. There are many women of color reproductive rights organizations, relatively few actually focus on bringing new women of color into the movement and training them to organize on their own behalf. And such groups that do exist are not generally coordinated into national mobilization efforts. Rather, national work is generally done on an advocacy level, with heads of women of color organizations advocating for policy changes but often working without a solid base to back their demands.[118] Consequently, women of color organizations are not always in the strongest position to negotiate with power brokers and mainstream pro-choice organizations or to hold them accountable.

As an example, many women of color groups mobilized to attend the 2004 March for Women's Lives in Washington, D.C. to push the march beyond a narrow pro-choice abortion rights agenda to a broad-based reproductive rights agenda. While this broader agenda was reflected in the march, it became co-opted by the pro-choice paradigm in the media coverage of the march. My survey of major newspaper coverage of the march indicates that virtually no newspaper described the march as anything other than a pro-choice, abortion rights march.[119] To quote New Orleans health activist Barbara Major, "When you go to power without a base, your demand becomes a request."[120] Such base-building work, which many women of color organizations are beginning to focus on, is very slow work, which may not show results for a long time. But maybe one day, we will have a march for women's lives in which the main issues addressed and reported on include repealing the Hyde Amendment; stopping the promotion of dangerous contraceptives; decriminalizing women who are pregnant and who have addictions; and ending welfare policies that punish women, in addition to other such issues that speak to the intersections of gender, race, and class in reproductive rights policies.

In 1991, I attended a meeting of the United Council of Tribes in Chicago, and representatives came from the Chicago Pro-Choice Alliance to inform us that we should join the struggle to keep abortion legal or we would lose our reproductive rights.[121] A woman in the audience responded, "Who cares about reproductive rights? We don't have any rights period." Her response suggests that a reproductive justice agenda must make the dismantling of capitalism, white supremacy, and colonialism *central* to its agenda, and not just principles added to organizations' promotional material designed to appeal to women of color, with no budget behind making these principles a reality. We must reject single-issue, pro-choice politics of the mainstream reproductive rights movement as an agenda that not only does not serve women of color but actually promotes the structures of oppression which keep women of color from having real choices or healthy lives.

Today, Native women have organized under a more holistic analysis of reproductive justice. A leading organization in this area is NAWHERC, based on the Yankton Sioux reservation in South Dakota. It provides comprehensive services and advocacy to Native women in the areas of reproductive health, including contraceptive information, environmental advocacy, violence against women, and advocacy around abortion policies. It has also organized a number of Native women's reproductive rights round tables, through which it articulated a reproductive rights platform. The principles include:

1. The right to knowledge and education for all family members, concerning sexuality and reproduction that is age, culture, and gender appropriate.
2. The right to all reproductive alternatives, and the right to choose the size of our families.
3. The right to affordable health care, including safe deliveries within our communities.
4. The right to access safe, free, and/or affordable abortions, regardless of age, with confidentiality and free pre- and post-counseling.
5. The right to active involvement in the development and implementation of policies concerning reproductive issues, including, but not limited to, pharmaceuticals and testing.
6. The right to include domestic violence, sexual assault, and AIDS as reproductive rights issues.
7. The right to programs which meet the nutritional needs of women and families.
8. The right to programs to reduce the rate of infant mortality and high-risk pregnancies.
9. The right to culturally specific, comprehensive chemical dependency prenatal programs including, but not limited to, prevention of fetal alcohol syndrome and its effects.
10. The right to stop coerced sterilization.

11. The right to a forum for cultural/spiritual development, culturally-oriented health care, and the right to live as Native women.
12. The right to be fully informed about, and to consent to, any forms of medical treatment.
13. The right to determine who are members of our Nations.
14. The right to continuous, consistent, and quality health care for Native peoples.
15. The right to reproductive rights and support for women with disabilities, including emotional disabilities.
16. The right to parent our children in a non-sexist, non-racist environment.
17. The right of Two Spirited women, their partners, and their families to live free from persecution or discrimination based on their sexuality and/or gender, and the right to enjoy the same human, political, social, legal, economic, religious, tribal, and governmental rights and benefits afforded all other indigenous women.
18. The right to give birth and be attended to in the setting most appropriate, be it home, community, clinic, or hospital, and to be able to choose the support system for our births, including, but not limited to, traditional midwives, families, and community members.
19. The right to education and support for breastfeeding that includes, but is not limited to, individuals and communities that allow for regrowth of traditional nurturing and parenting of our children.[122]

Conclusion

The attacks on the reproductive rights of Native women are frontline strategies in the continuing wars against Native nations. These attacks metaphorically transform Native people into pollution or dirt from which the body politic, to ensure its growth, must constantly purify itself. Herbert Aptheker describes the logical consequences of population control movements:

> The ultimate logic of this is crematoria; if people are themselves constituting the pollution and inferior people in particular, then

crematoria becomes really vast sewerage projects. So only may one understand those who attended the ovens and concocted and conducted the entire enterprise; those "wasted" — to use U.S. army jargon reserved for colonial hostilities — are not really, not fully people.[123]

Patricia Hill Collins observes that the state's interest in limiting Black population growth coincided with the expansion of post-World War II welfare provisions that allowed many African Americans to leave exploitative jobs. As a result, the growing numbers of unemployed people of color were no longer simply a resource of cheap and convenient labor for white America; now these people of color are considered "surplus" populations.[124]

While Native people constitute a relatively small workforce, it is important to remember that the majority of the energy resources in this country are on Indian lands, so the continued existence of Indian people is a threat to American capitalism. Senate testimony by Utah politician Scott M. Matheson in 1989 opposing the protection of Indian sacred sites, on behalf of the mining industry, offers evidence of this fact. "Much of the country's natural resources are located on federal land. For example, federal lands contain 85 percent of the nation's crude oil, 40 percent of the natural gas, 40 percent of the uranium, 85 percent of the coal reserves, and 47 percent of the standing soft wood timber," said Matheson. "Thus it is obvious that [federal protection of sacred sites] by creating a Native American veto over federal land use decisions, will …severely interfere with the orderly use and development of the country's natural resources."[125]

As the ability of Native women to reproduce the next generations of Native people continues to stand in the way of government and corporate takeovers of Indian land, Native women become seen as little more than pollutants which may threaten the well-being of the colonial body. In the colonial imagination, Native women are indeed "better dead than pregnant."

Chapter 5

"Natural Laboratories"
Medical Experimentation in Native Communities

In 1929, we were removed from under the Catholic Church into the Indian Bureau. When we got into the Indian Bureau we were also used as guinea pigs. They gave us vaccinations. Needles broke in some of the people's arms. They were not removed.

Then they came into the reservation for dental work. They drilled from under our jaws into our mouths, and caused infections. They put black stuff into our teeth as experiments. This was very painful. We were used by the government to test a new material as fillings for teeth. Today, the dentists look at our mouths and tell us there was never anything wrong with our teeth in the first place.

Our eyes were scraped. They told us we had acoma [sic] which the eye specialist now says we never had. Now our eyes are gone, our teeth are gone.

They used us to make drugs for other people. They gave us many vaccinations and after the vaccinations many people became sick with tuberculosis. Most of our people died of tuberculosis and small pox that were given to us by the government.

This was forced on us. We had no choice. They put vaccinations in our arms. Then some of our people died. Some

lived. They would not allow us to go to school because they said
we had acoma.

I will answer to anyone that this is what happened to us in Big
Valley in California, 1931–1933.

—Theresa Brown, letter dated March 24, 1993

*I*n her letter, Theresa Brown of Clear Lake, California, testifies to
her history of medical experimentation to Mary Ann Mills and
Bernadine Atcheson, Alaska Native health activists. One of the
common demands of many mainstream feminist organizations is
increased funding for medical research on women's health, such
as breast cancer. What is generally not considered in the making of
these demands, however, is who will this research be done on and
under what circumstances? As the previous chapter indicates,
much contraceptive research has been conducted on women in
the Global South or on indigenous women and other women of
color in the U.S. with little regard to their safety. However, unethical medical experimentation programs have not been limited to
contraceptives.

One example is the controversial 1982 hepatitis B trial vaccine
program conducted among Alaska Native children.[1] Mary Ann
Mills and Bernadine Atcheson (Traditional Dena'ina) began to investigate this program when a mother came to them inquiring
about the vaccine that had been given to her child without her permission. They soon discovered that this vaccine was Heptavax B,
a trial vaccine for hepatitis B, that was being administered without
parental consent. The rationale for the experiment was that Alaska
Natives were at particularly high risk for hepatitis B. However, in
checking the statistics, Mills and Atcheson found that hepatitis B
was on a sharp decline among Alaska Natives before the immunizations, with a 0–0 .5 percent prevalence rate.[2] Interestingly, they
argue that Native people are in fact not at high risk for hepatitis B.

Mills and Atcheson began to question the benefits of vaccines
in general. First, they concluded that vaccines are often given
credit for eradicating disease when the illness is often already on
the decline because of other environmental factors. Vaccines also
expose the body to germs which may negatively impact one's
immune system. In addition, people can contract the disease for

which they are being vaccinated. For instance, in 1985, the Center for Disease Control reported that 87 percent of the cases of polio in the U.S. between 1973 and 1983 were caused by the vaccine and later declared that all but a few imported cases since were caused by the vaccine—and most of the imported cases occurred in fully immunized individuals. Jonas Salk, inventor of the polio vaccine, testified before a Senate subcommittee that nearly all polio outbreaks since 1961 were caused by the oral polio vaccine.[3] And according to Mills and Atcheson, in 1988, William Jordan, former Director of the Infectious Diseases Division at the National Institutes of Health (NIH) stated at an infectious disease conference in New Zealand that virtually all field trials of new vaccines in the U.S. are done amongst indigenous tribes in Alaska, and most do nothing to prevent disease.[4]

Mills and Atcheson argue that a proliferation of "mystery illnesses" seemed to occur soon after vaccination programs were introduced in the Yukon Delta. Merck, Sharp & Dohme, the producers of Heptavax B, as well as other medical professionals involved in the study, sharply contest these claims, arguing that Mills and Atcheson are using "scare tactics" to discourage people from taking the vaccines. However, when members of WARN talked to some of these professionals, they did not deny that the program was done without true informed consent. In Manitoba, concerns also arose over Merck's hepatitis B vaccine. Dr. Byron Hyde, who is generally pro-vaccine, reported an unusually high number of cases with severe side effects, including chronic fatigue syndrome and fibromyalgia. "We have sent 65 cases to the government (Health Canada), two died, some went blind, one could no longer use an arm. I've never seen anything like this in any immunization." Several months later, the government issued a report stating that it had investigated the cases, and discovered no problems. Yet when Dr. Hyde contacted 45 of these patients, he found that none had been medically examined, and only two had been contacted by phone.[5]

Native peoples have every right to be concerned about trial vaccine programs because of the evidence that vaccination programs can cause illness. For instance, hepatitis B outbreaks started in 1945, when soldiers were given yellow fever vaccines that had been tainted with the virus.[6] Vaccination programs are not always about promoting health; vaccines are big business, and some doctors even receive benefits for the number of children they vaccinate. In addition, side effects ranging from fever to even death, are common. For instance, the United Kingdom is considering withdrawing the MMR (Mumps, Measles, and Rubella) vaccine because over 2,000 claims have been filed against the government on behalf of children injured or killed as a result of the vaccine.[7] There is also a lawsuit filed in 2001 in the U.S. against pharmaceutical companies which distributed vaccines that contained poisonous mercury. According to the law firm litigating the case,

> on July 7, 1999, the American Academy of Pediatrics (AAP) issued with the US Public Health Service (USPHS) a joint statement alerting clinicians and the public of concern about thimerosal, a mercury-containing preservative used in some vaccines. The reason for the warning is that thimerosal contains a related mercury compound called methyl mercury. Mercury is a toxic metal that can cause immune, sensory, neurological, motor, and behavioral dysfunctions. The Food and Drug Administration suggested that some infants, depending on which vaccines they receive and the timing of those vaccines, may be exposed to levels of methyl mercury that could build up to exceed one of the federal guidelines established for the intake of methyl mercury. Symptoms of mercury toxicity in young children are extremely similar to those of autism. This can explain the recent increase in the numbers of children diagnosed with autism since the early 1990s. The numerous amount of children diagnosed with autism seems to directly correlate with the recommendation of both the hepatitis B and HIB vaccine to infants in the early 1990s.[8]

Vaccination programs should not be assumed to be safe; rather, Native communities (and all communities) deserve to have full information on vaccination programs before participating in them.

Caution about vaccine programs is also warranted because indigenous peoples have been regarded as expendable by the dominant society. For instance, the Interagency Arctic Research Policy Committee (which includes agencies such as the National Science Foundation, the Department of Defense, and numerous U.S. government agencies) states that because Alaska Native villages are covered under IHS, they constitute a comprehensive "extensive data base" which "provides a resource for studying health problems which will benefit *other* populations [emphasis mine]."[9] Furthermore, according to this policy committee, Alaska is "a natural laboratory and as such a region where health research may have broad implications and applications."[10]

Another hepatitis trial vaccine program was established in South Dakota in 1991, with participating children given an experimental hepatitis A vaccine. In this case, the control group was not given a placebo, but a hepatitis B vaccine.[11] But shortly after the trials began, the producers of this hepatitis A vaccine, Smith Kline, resigned from the Australian Pharmaceutical Manufacturer's Association after complaints about unethical school promotions and misleading advertising were lodged against the company.[12] Smith Kline also claimed to be procuring informed consent, but children were offered candy and parents were promised free diapers if they participated in the South Dakota program.[13]

Disturbingly, Mills and Atcheson point out that the consent forms for the vaccine trial in Alaska were startlingly similar to the forms used in the Tuskegee syphilis study that started in the 1930s and ran into the 1970s. In this infamous case, African Americans with syphilis were told by the U.S. Public Health Service that they were being treated for the disease, but they were actually not treated so researchers could chart the trajectory of the disease. In a letter sent to Tuskegee patients, they were told,

> ...some time ago you were given a thorough examination and since that time you have gotten a great deal of treatment for bad blood. You will now be given your last chance to get a second examination...Remember, this is your last chance for special free treatment.[14]

From the letter to Alaska Native patients,

> Hepatitis B vaccinations are available to you at the Dena'ina Health Clinic. Because you qualify for ANS benefits you can be screened and immunized at no cost to you. This service is scheduled for this year only. Without this program, the cost of the vaccination will cost $100. We urge you to take advantage of this program now![15]

Besides the sociomedical questions they have about trial programs, Mills and Atcheson also note that less invasive remedies are not widely funded or studied. For instance, hepatitis A could be eradicated through improved plumbing and sanitation; seventy-three percent of hepatitis A cases among Alaska Natives are in villages with no flush toilets.[16] However, financial support goes to areas that are most likely to be profitable for pharmaceutical companies. This limited research agenda not only benefits pharmaceutical firms, but those corporations linked to pollution and environmental degradation that result in disease.

These vaccine trials represent the tip of the iceberg with regards to the medical experimentation that has been conducted in Native communities. For instance, a GAO report on sterilization abuses in IHS also found that there were 36 medical experimentation programs conducted by IHS during 1974 and 1975.[17] The GAO denied that any of the programs resulted in negative medical consequences for Native peoples, but the report indicates serious lapses in informed consent procedures. The Children's Defense Fund reported that Indian children in boarding schools were subjected to a trachoma experiment during the years 1967–68 and 1972–73 without parental consent. The Proctor Foundation, which conducted the research, maintained that informed consent was not necessary because "Indian Health Services acts as legal guardian for the children while they attend boarding schools."[18] Several other programs were assessed in this report, including one study of pulmonary disease among White Mountain Apache children which consisted of painful tests that were conducted without consent.[19] Furthermore, the GAO also found that the IHS did not have standardized procedures to ensure that researchers were actually following the protocol approved by IHS research committees.[20]

While the GAO concludes that for many of the programs, consent was documented, the GAO relied solely on records provided by IHS and did not interview patients themselves. As with the report on sterilization abuses, GAO states:

> We did not interview patients to determine if they were adequately informed of the risks, discomforts, and benefits of the project. We believe that such an effort would not be productive

because (1) no serious hazard existed for the patients and (2) recently published research noted a high level of inaccuracy in the recollection of patients 4 to 6 months after giving informed consent.[21]

Again, how informed can the consent be if one cannot remember giving it? In addition, the report claims that "no serious hazards existed" while stating in other sections that some of the experimentation programs, particularly those involving trial vaccines, had to be terminated because "the reaction rate was too high to risk any more immunizations."[22]

As anti-prison activist Luana Ross writes, Native women in prison are particularly subjected to medical experimentation programs in order to "cure" them of the ailment that supposedly led to their incarceration.[23] Former prisoner Stormy Ogden described her ordeal with the medical industry while in prison:

> I was given a combination of 300 milligrams of Elavil, Mellaril, Thorazine and Chlorohydrate, to keep me calm. What it did was make you stop talking. I still stutter and still have problems getting my words out because too much medication has gone through my body. I had to take this. There was no way I could get around taking it; they make sure. And a lot of Indian women are being given Thorazine, to keep us calm, because we are the savages.[24]

Meanwhile, despite these programs intended to improve community health, Native peoples still have little in the way of actual and effective health care. In 1976, Congress passed the Indian Health Care Improvement Act, which affirmed its "special responsibilities and legal obligations to the American Indian people, to meet the national goal of providing the best possible health status to Indians and to provide existing Indian health services with all resources necessary to effect that policy." In *White v. Califano* (1978), the U.S. Court of Appeals for the Eighth Circuit affirmed that the U.S. was obliged to provide health care in Native communities: "We do not refer to a relationship that exists only in the abstract but rather a congressionally recognized duty to provide services for a particular category of human needs." Yet since 1997, 16 of the 49 IHS hospitals did not meet the minimum standards in one or more areas set by the Joint Commission on Accreditation of Healthcare Organizations, which monitors national quality standards for hospitals. By contrast, less than 1 percent of hospitals nationwide ranked as poorly. And between January 1997 and September 2000, patients or relatives filed 342 formal malpractice complaints against IHS. (This equals more than one complaint for every three doctors.) Although most of these claims were denied, in the last four years IHS has paid at least $23.6 million in malpractice settlements and judgments.[25]

Because Native peoples are among the poorest in the country, they generally cannot afford alternative health care services. In addition, Native peoples are often entangled by various bureaucratic requirements that prevents them from accessing health care. For instance, it is not uncommon for IHS to require Native peoples to access services through Medicaid. Then, Medicaid will require that Native peoples first access care through IHS. The result is that American Indians suffer from the most serious health problems in the U.S. On reservations, American Indians have a life expectancy of 47 years. The tuberculosis rate for Natives is 533 percent higher than the national average; the accident mortality rate 425 percent higher; the infant mortality rate 81 percent higher; the sudden infant death syndrome rate 310 percent higher; the alcoholism rate 579 percent higher; the diabetes rate 249 percent higher; and the suicide rate 190 percent higher than the national average.[26]

Conclusion

The biocolonial ideology that casts Native people as guinea pigs, instead of as people who deserve quality health care, was summed up by an IHS administrator who, during a 1992 meeting with WARN activists, said she encouraged Native people to participate in medical experiments because they provided the only access to health care for Native people. She added that once drugs are proven "safe," they are generally no longer available to Indian Health Services.[27]

These attitudes have a long history in the U.S. During the colonial massacres of Indian peoples, colonizers attempted to defeat

Indian people *and* to eradicate their identity and humanity. They attempted to transform Indian people into tobacco pouches, bridle reins or souvenirs—objects for the consumption of white people. This history reflects a disrespect not only for Native people's bodies, but a disrespect for the integrity of all creation, the two being integrally related.

Unlike Native people, who see animals as beings deserving of bodily integrity and, furthermore, view their identities as inseparable from the rest of creation, colonizers see animals as rapable and expendable. By extension, because colonizers viewed Indian identity as inextricably linked to animal and plant life, Native people have been seen as rapable, and deserving of destruction and mutilation. This equation between animals and Native people continues. In the 1992 edition of the Physicians' Desk Research Manual, it is noted that Merck, Sharp & Dohme experimented on "chimpanzees and... Alaska Native children."[28]

Mills and Atcheson question the precepts of Western medicine, which senselessly dissects, vivisects and experiments on both animals and human beings, when there are much more effective preventative and holistic forms of medicine. States Mills, "Today we rely on our elders and our traditional healers. We have asked them if they were ever as sick as their grandchildren or great-grandchildren are today. Their reply was no; they were much healthier than their children are today."[29]

Chapter 6

Spiritual Appropriation as Sexual Violence

In analyzing spiritual appropriation as a form of sexual violence, I start with what may seem a strange source: the Bible. The Hebrew word *YDH*, which translates as "*to know a person*, carnally, of sexual intercourse," is used frequently in the Hebrew scriptures to connote sexual relations. For instance, Genesis 4:1 states: "now the man *knew* his wife Eve, and she conceived and bore Cain saying, 'I have produced' a man with the help of the Lord" (NRSV). *YDH* colloquially refers to engagement in sexual relations. Inherent in this definition of "to know" is the sense that sexual intimacy conveys a profound knowledge of a person, but also that knowing a person intimately conveys a sense of sexual relatedness.

Consensual sexual relationships require the loosening of the boundaries of one's physical and psychic space — they involve not only allowing another person to become close to you physically, but allowing her or him to know more about you. Sexual violence then suggests that the violation of these boundaries operates not only on the physical but on spiritual and psychic levels as well. In addition, sexual violence is ultimately structured around power relations—it entails establishing the power to control someone's life. Similarly, "knowledge" about someone also gives one power over that person. Withholding knowledge, then, is an act of resistance against those who desire to know you in order to better control you.

It is with this understanding of sexual violence that I wish to explore how the "New Age" movement and other forms of indigenous spiritual/cultural appropriation constitute a form of sexual violence. While there have been endless critiques of spiritual/cultural appropriation, I want to focus particularly on how it can be analytically understood as a form of sexual violence. I also wish to extend my discussion beyond the most obvious forms of appropriation as found in the New Age movement to explore its problematics in seemingly more innocuous forms, such as that found in academic religion classes.

Using this analytical framework, I would suggest that much of the energy directed toward "knowing" more about Native peoples can also be understood as concerns about what Mary Douglas terms, "matter out of place."[1] That is, Native peoples as well as other people of color who continue to survive centuries of genocide are a constant threat to the dominant culture's confidence that it will remain triumphant. Native peoples who continue to exist pollute the colonial body from the colonizer's perspective—they are matter out of place. To fully understand, to "know" Native peoples is the manner in which the dominant society gains a sense of mastery and control over them.

Consequently, Indian communities are flooded with people who want to know more about them—New Agers looking for quick spiritual enlightenment, anthropologists eager to capture "an authentic culture thought to be rapidly and inevitably disappearing,"[2] and Christians eager to engage in interreligious dialogue. How one evaluates these attempts to understand and "know" Indians revolves in large part around how one analyzes the primary causes of the oppression of Native peoples. Many people believe that the primary problem Native peoples face is ignorance. That is, non-Indians oppress Indians because they are ignorant about the value of Native cultures. Under this paradigm, if only non-Indians knew more about Indians, they would be nicer to them. This approach is typical of many books on Native religions. For instance, Dennis and Barbara Tedlock note in their *Teachings From the American Earth: Indian Religion and Philosophy* that "the American Indian has already taught us a great deal…[but now we must learn] his more difficult lessons about the mind and spirit…We have to recognize that some of what he has to teach transcends cultural and historical boundaries."[3] Thus, even if one's attempts to "know" more about Indians are problematic, we can assume that at least these attempts are a step in the right direction.

Without wanting to fashion too simplistic a dualism, I would suggest that the primary reason for the continuing genocide of Native peoples has less to do with ignorance and more to do with material conditions. Non-Indians continue to oppress Indians because Indians occupy land resources that the dominant society wants. The majority of energy resources in this country are on Indian land.[4] The U.S. could not stop oppressing Indian people without fundamentally challenging its hegemonic position or multinational capitalist operations. If we frame Native genocide from a materialist perspective, then we have to rethink our analysis of ignorance about Native cultures on the part of non-Natives. This ignorance becomes a willful ignorance. The larger society will never become educated about non-Indians because it is not in their economic interest to do so. Thus, these efforts to "know" Indians seem less benevolent in their intent and in their effects.

Native spiritualities are land based — they are tied to the landbase from which they originate.[5] When Native peoples fight for cultural/spiritual preservation, they are ultimately fighting for the landbase which grounds their spirituality and culture. For this reason, Native religions are generally not proselytizing. They are typically seen by Native peoples as relevant only to the particular landbase from which they originate; they are not necessarily applicable to peoples coming from different landbases. In addition, as many scholars have noted, Native religions are practice centered rather than belief centered. That is, Christianity is defined by belief in a certain set of doctrinal principles about Jesus, the Bible, etc. Evangelical Christianity holds that one is "saved" when one professes belief in Jesus Christ as one's Lord and Savior. But what is of primary importance in Native religions is not being able to articulate belief in a certain set of doctrines, but being able to take part in the spiritual practice of one's community. In fact, it may be more important that a ceremony be done correctly than it is for everyone in that ceremony to know exactly *why* everything must be done in a certain way. As Vine Deloria (Dakota) notes, from a Native context, religion is "a way of life" rather than "a matter of the proper exposition of doctrines."[6] Even if Christians do not have access to church, they continue to be Christians as long as they believe in Jesus. Native spiritualities, by contrast, may die if the people do not practice the ceremonies, even if the people continue to believe in their power.

Native communities argue that Native peoples cannot be alienated from their land without committing cultural genocide. This argument underpins many sacred sites cases, although usually to no avail, before the courts. Most of the court rulings on sacred sites do not recognize this difference between belief-centered and practice-centered traditions or the significance of land-based spiritualities. For instance, in *Fools Crow v. Gullet* (1983), the Supreme Court ruled against the Lakota who were trying to halt the development of additional tourist facilities in the Black Hills. The Court ruled that this tourism was not an infringement on Indian religious freedom because, although it would hinder the ability of the Lakota to *practice* their beliefs, it did not force them to relinquish their beliefs. For the Lakota, however, stopping the *practice* of traditional beliefs destroys the belief systems themselves. Consequently, for the Lakota and Native nations in general, cultural genocide is the result when Native landbases are not protected.[7]

When the dominant society disconnects Native spiritual practices from their landbases, it undermines Native peoples' claim that the protection of the landbase is integral to the survival of Native peoples and hence undermines their claims to sovereignty. Such appropriation is prevalent in a wide variety of cultural and spiritual practices — from New Agers claiming to be Indians in former lives to Christians adopting Native spiritual forms to further their missionizing efforts. The message is that anyone can practice Indian spirituality anywhere, so there is no need to protect the specific Native communities and their lands that are the basis of these spiritual practices.

The assumption that Native knowledge is for the taking is also evident in multinational corporations' continued assault on indigenous knowledge. Current intellectual property rights law only respects individual ownership and not community ownership over intellectual or cultural property. Nonindigenous entrepreneurs have been able to gather knowledge about indigenous plants, medicines, music, or other cultural knowledge and take it because it is understood as "public" property. By obtaining an individual patent or copyright for it, they effectively seize control over this knowledge and can profit from it. As Laurie Whitt describes in the case of indigenous music,

> While others are free to copy the original indigenous song with impunity, were someone to attempt to copy the "original" copy (now transformed into the legally protected individual property of a composer who has "borrowed" it from the indigenous "public domain"), he or she would be subject to prosecution for copyright infringement. This includes any members of the indigenous community of the song's origin who cannot meet the requirement of "fair use."[8]

Thus, in this society, white people have clear legal boundaries over their knowledge, while indigenous communities have none. Native communities and their practices can be known to all; their boundaries are inherently violable.

As Rayna Green suggests, spiritual appropriation is a practice that is based on genocide. Non-Natives feel justified in appropriating Native spirituality and Native identity because they do not believe existing Native communities are capable of independently preserving Native cultural practices. Rather, the common belief is that Native peoples are vanishing, and white people must preserve indigenous cultural practices since Native peoples are unable to do so. Through cultural appropriation, white people establish themselves as the true inheritors of Indianness. As a result, they can lay legitimate claim to Indian lands. Green argues,

> For I would insist now, the living performance of "playing Indian" by non-Indian peoples depends on the physical and psychological removal, even the death, of real Indians. In that sense, the

performance, purportedly often done out of a stated and implicit love for Indians, is really the obverse of another well-known cultural phenomenon, "Indian hating," as most often expressed in another deadly performance genre called "genocide."[9]

Exemplifying this ideology is the Improved Order of the Red Men, a white fraternal organization that has been in existence since 1765 in which participants, supposedly patterningthemselves on the Iroquois Confederacy, wear "Native" regalia and take part in other "Indian" cultural practices. According to the group's Web site, www.redmen.org:

> The Improved Order of Red Men is a national fraternal organization that believes in
>
> - Love of and Respect for the American Flag.
> - Preserving our Nation by defending and upholding the principle of free Government.
> - America and the democratic way of life.
> - Preserving the traditions and history of this great Country.
> - Creating and inspiring a greater love for the United States of America.
> - Helping our fellow men through organized charitable programs.
> - Linking our members together in a common bond of Brotherhood and Friendship.
> - Perpetuating the beautiful legends and traditions of a once-vanishing race and the keeping alive of its customs, ceremonies, and philosophies.

These people see themselves as preserving the "traditions of a once-vanishing race" for the purpose of preserving "America," which is built on the genocide of Native peoples.

Furthermore, the colonial relations that mark the relationship between indigenous communities and the dominant society that wants to "know" more about them are themselves structured by sexual violence. Haunani-Kay Trask, Native Hawaiian activist, argues that colonizers destroy the cultural base from which indigenous people resist colonization by commodifying it to meet Western consumerist needs. She terms the phenomenon "cultural prostitution."

"Prostitution" in this context refers to the entire institution which defines a woman (and by extension the "female") as an object of degraded and victimized sexual value for use and exchange through the medium of money... .My purpose is not to exactly detail or fashion a model but to convey the utter degradation of our culture and our people under corporate tourism by employing "prostitution" as an analytical category... .The point, of course, is that everything in Hawaii can be yours, that is, you the tourist, the non-native, the visitor. The place, the people, the culture, even our identity as a "Native" people is for sale. Thus, Hawaii, like a lovely woman, is there for the taking.[10]

In Trask's model, the exchange between Native and non-Native cultures is governed by the interests of non-Natives; that is, Natives exist to meet the needs of non-Native peoples, regardless of the impact on indigenous communities. Trask's exploitation model can also be applied to the first Re-Imagining Conference, held by the National Council of Churches in Minneapolis, Minnesota in 1993. The conference was explicitly called so women could reimagine a non-patriarchal Christianity, yet Native women and Native practices were marginalized and disrespected. A group of women was invited to dance in traditional costumes, but Native women were not invited to speak on any struggles at any time during the conference. Native women had offered medicine bundles, which are to be treated with great respect, but the primarily white audience unceremoniously threw themon the floor. The women were to be voiceless objects of consumption, "there for the taking." They were, as Trask writes, "transformed to [be] complicitous in their own commodification."[11]

It is particularly troubling when this colonial practice — which is structured by sexual violence — is adopted by white feminists in their efforts to heal from patriarchal violence. For this kind of appropriation hinders Native women in *their* healing and recovery, not only from personal abuse, but from the patterned history of abuse against their families, their nation, and the environment.[12] When white women appropriate Indian spirituality for their own benefit, they are participating in this pattern of abuse against Indian peoples' cultures.

Still, many non-Native peoples argue that they have a "right" to access Native spiritual knowledge. I taught a class where we discussed the issue of spiritual appropriation. The white students told me about how beneficial Native spirituality was to them, and that they felt they had to take part in certain New Age practices because there were no other suitable substitutes. So I asked, "Even if the New Age movement is as beneficial to you as you say, do you have any responsibility to Native communities when you take part in these practices?" What struck me was that none of the students had even considered this issue before. This practice of taking without asking, and the assumption that the needs of the taker are paramount and the needs of others are irrelevant, mirrors the rape culture of the dominant society.

Healing spiritual practices have not only been appropriated by the dominant society, but they have been sexually colonized as well. As Will Roscoe notes, colonizers have a long history of "documenting" what they see as sexual perversity in Native ceremonies in order to suppress them. Roscoe, a radical historian, points to the efforts to undermine John Collier, a white man who helped to establish the All-Pueblo Council in 1922 and served as executive secretary of the American Indian Defense Association in 1923. (Collier was later appointed Commissioner of Indian Affairs by President Franklin Roosevelt.)

Collier attempted to protect Native religious freedom in the southwest despite widespread rumors that "Zuni men and women imitated sodomy in a dance, that boys and girls were put together 'for unrestricted sexual intercourse,' that the Taos Indians sacrificed two boys per year."[13] According to Roscoe, William Johnson, a one-time special officer of the Indian Office, desired to spread this "knowledge" about Indians to as widely as possible and wrote a 1924 letter to the *New York Times* that attacked Collier and charged that:

> [B]oys and girls returned from Government schools are stripped naked and herded together entirely nude and encouraged to do that very worst that vileness can suggest; that at Zuni little girls were debauched in these dances; that Indian mothers, wives and daughters [are] ravished before hundreds of yelling, naked savages; and that little girls, too young and tender to be ravished,

have been whipped naked until their little bodies were bruised and covered with purple welts...and Indian boys were being withdrawn from government schools for a two years' course in sodomy under pagan instructors.[14]

This historical correlation between Native spirituality and sexual exploitation can be found in contemporary attitudes about Native people. For example, journalist Andy Rooney depicts Native spiritual traditions as involving "ritualistic dances with strong sexual overtones [which are] demeaning to Indian women and degrading to Indian children."[15] Along similar lines, Mark and Dan Jury produced a film, *Dances: Sacred and Profane* (1994), and advertised it as "climax[ing] with the first-ever filming of the Indian Sundance ceremony." This so-called ceremony consisted of a white man, hanging from meat hooks from a tree, praying to the "Great White Spirit." Then C.C. Sadist, a group that performs sadomasochistic acts for entertainment, appears in the film.[16]

Self-described Cherokee porn star Hyapatia Lee directed a pornographic film framed as a documentary titled *Native Tongue* (1999). The film begins with the statement, "Each of the girls is of Cherokee ancestry with teachings offered to all people." Each scene depicts one of these "Cherokee" girls copulating with a white man. Hyapatia prefaces these scenes with, "I'm mostly Cherokee Indian. I was taught to worship nature and honor my traditional religion. They knew [past tense] how connected everything is." As Rayna Green argues in "The Tribe Called Wannabee," playing Indian is part of an ongoing genocidal project where white people become the inheritors of all that Indians "knew." In this case, this inherited knowledge is limited to how Indians supposedly engaged in various sexual acts.[17]

The film then attempts to turn Native cultural/spiritual traditions into pornography. For instance, one scene begins with "Because we don't see ourselves as superior to animals, we can learn from them," which is followed by a couple having sex "doggy-style." Other scenes depict couples smudging each other or smoking a pipe before engaging in sex. Finally, one scene begins, "The Indian culture teaches us the medicine path." Viewers are then called to "honor the four directions, more commonly known as sixty-nine."

Further trivializing women's status in Native communities, one scene begins with a talk about how Native communities respected women and men equally. "Father Sky wraps around Mother Earth." Christians, Lee continues, don't understand women's power. She proceeds to perform oral sex on a white man. Thus, symbolically the equality of men and women in Native societies is subordinated to the dominance of white men.

Finally, after repeated scenes of various pornographic acts, the "documentary" ends with "We hope this will be helpful for all our Anglo brothers. The teachings are meant for all. They are meant to keep us on the sacred path." In this conclusion, we can see how "knowledge" about Native communities is explicitly tied to sexual exploitation. Native communities have no boundaries, psychic or physical, that the dominant society is bound to respect. What Native peoples have and know are not under their control; it must be shared with all, particularly our "Anglo brothers."

Another "self-described Cherokee," Harley Swiftdeer, markets sex orgies as Cherokee ceremonies. He promotes "fire breath orgasms," which he contends are a regular part of Cherokee ceremonies and have been passed down through the "Twisted Hairs Metis Medicine Society Council of Elders." According to the promotional material:

> Originally established in 1250 B.C. as the Rattlesnake School of Turtle Island, the Twisted Hairs Metis Medicine Society Council of Elders is a body of shamans, medicine men and women, sorcerers and magicians from many tribes throughout North, Central and South America, who have traveled and studied beyond their traditional tribal boundaries and evolved to levels of great learning, wisdom, power and knowledge. Turtle Island is called the Southwest Power, one of the Eight Great Powers of knowledge and wisdom on the planet. At times throughout history the magical mystery schools were forced to take their teachings and knowledge "underground" for safekeeping because they were being misused by others for personal power and domination or perverted by religious hierarchies. This happened here on Turtle Island following the Spanish conquest by Cortes, Pizarro, and others, as well as the invasion of Europeans onto the North American continent.

> In 1975, hearing the call of Grandmother Earth and seeing both the need and the readiness within the collective, the Elders of the Council decided to again release the first of many Wheels and Keys of this Sweet Medicine SunDance Path so that these teachings would be available to anyone seeking personal growth and spiritual awakening. The Council designated SwiftDeer as one of the Carriers of the Shields of Knowledge of this Path... .
>
> In July of 1992, SwiftDeer was seated and sealed as a Twisted Hairs elder on the Council.[18]

Swiftdeer's "Cherokee" sex teachings have been integrated into a variety of seminars including the "Spiritual Sexuality" workshops conducted by the GoldenWind Dreamers Lodge based in Phoenix, Arizona.[19] This sexual colonization of Native spirituality cloaks itself in the rhetoric of resistance to colonization.

In these sites of sexual exploitation, Native peoples are constantly equated with nature, which is in turn equated with unbridled sexuality. The various instructive scenes in *Native Tongue* are all interspersed with nature scenes. As Lee states, it was because her people "worshiped" nature that they learned to engage in wild sex. Similarly, the handbook *Indian Love Signs* (1999) purports to show how "Native American astrology can help you find someone to love."[20] This pan-Indian astrological system appears to be based on Sun Bear's medicine wheel. It is virtually indistinguishable from the traditional zodiac except that it is "directly related to nature," and is concerned only with giving the reader information on her/his love life.

Similarly, Jack Glover's *Sex Life of the American Indian* (1973) purports to describe the mating patterns of Native peoples, presuming the Native world is homogenous in its practices. "The material I obtained I kept factual for the historian, I kept spicy for the casual reader and above all, the material in this volume is for the reader interested in the Sex Life of the American Indian." What distinguishes the sex life of the American Indian is that "the Indian had an animal-like nature because a lot of them patterned themselves after the wildlife in the forest." He then describes how Indians like to show off because they hung around wolves. According to Glover, when Native peoples intermarry with Black people, who are perhaps even more "animal-like," this "mixture of Negro and Indian blood produced some of the worst outlaws the Indian nation ever knew."[21]

The Mending the Sacred Hoop Stop Violence Against Indian Women Technical Assistance Project in Duluth, Minnesota notes that one difficulty in organizing against sexual violence in Native communities is that many community members believe that it is "traditional," despite the historical evidence which suggests sexual violence was rare in Native communities prior to colonization. One can see how these books and videos promote the internalization of violence in Native communities. For instance, Glover's account of Native communities suggests that Native women were nothing more than commodities. Rape was unheard of in many tribes, he argues, not because Native women were respected, but because it was just commonly understood that Indian women had to be sexually available whenever men wanted them to be. Fathers are described as having sex with their daughters. "The daughters didn't mind as they seemed happy and satisfied." If a man rapes a woman besides his wife, his wife "might welcome it, to keep him off her for awhile." Men had complete license to kill their wives: "The Indian man had the final say about anything that went on in camp and elsewhere. When he wanted he could kill his wife."[22]

Native communities, where violence against women was relatively rare, are depicted as hotbeds of abuse and violence. This reversal becomes internalized within Native communities themselves, evident in the proliferation of "plastic medicine men" who are often notorious for sexually abusing their clients in fake Indian ceremonies. After Jeffrey Wall was sentenced for sexually abusing three girls, he claimed the abuse was part of American Indian spiritual rituals he conducted as an Indian medicine man.[23] David "Two Wolves" Smith and Alan Campnhey "Spotted Wolfe" were also charged for sexually abusing girls during supposed "cleansing" ceremonies.[24] In 1998 an Omaha priest, Daniel Herek, was convicted for using Catholic and "Native American ceremonies" as a pretext for sexually abusing a boy for five years. Herek and this boy formed their own "tribe" called the "Pondering People." The boy called himself "Pondering Raven" and the priest called himself "Wolf Hawk." Herek then repeatedly asked him to take part in "Native American" rituals involving the boy removing his clothing so Herek could fondle him.[25] Michael Rea in Larimer County, Colorado, posed as a Lakota Medicine Man and offered to teach the children in his apartment Native spiritual practices. He was later charged with sexually abusing children in these sessions.[26]

Bonnie Clairmont, a Ho-Chunk based in St. Paul, Minnesota, is doing groundbreaking work by exposing sexual exploiters who claim to be spiritual leaders. Unfortunately, not all these spiritual leaders are obvious "wannabes". Some are Native men who are respected in their community. Because she has not been afraid to address this abuse, Clairmont has been widely criticized. But she continues to hold conferences and speak out on these kinds of abuses. At one of Clairmont's conferences, one elder suggested that the New Age movement has helped to create conditions ripe for sexual exploitation within "traditional" spiritual ceremonies. That is, New Age spirituality promises quick-fix solutions by "powerful" shamans who know all. As a result, people seeking guidance learn to surrender their authority to so-called leaders and disregard warning signs when their boundaries are violated. This leader concluded, "I am no one special. When you come to see me, do not leave behind your common sense."

Spiritual Appropriation Is Hazardous to Your Health

Because Native spiritual traditions are practice centered, it is critical that ceremonies be performed correctly in order for the well-being of their participants to be ensured. Otherwise, the effects can be detrimental. I have heard many elders express concern about the non-Native practitioners who dabble in Native spiritual practices, because they do not fully comprehend the possible consequences of their actions, and it is likely that something bad will happen if ceremonies are not performed correctly.

The dangers of appropriation are evident in several recent inci-
dences involving non-Indian practitioners. As one example, Kirsten
Dana Babcock, 34, of Redding, California, and David Thomas
Hawker, 36, of Union City, California, were participating in a ritual
resembling a sweat lodge when they died of asphyxiation in 2002.
They completely sealed the "sweat lodge" in plastic for a
four-hour cleansing ritual, chanting amid the vapors of herbs and
water poured over the hot rocks. The sweat lodge was made of a
wooden frame shaped in a near-circle, about 10 feet in diameter,
and covered with plastic sheeting. The sheeting was buried in the
ground around the lower edge to make it airtight, and the plastic
was covered with sleeping bags and blankets to keep in the heat.
The surviving participants told officers that they were seeking
spiritual enlightenment by sitting in the steam in the sealed environment.[27]

As Tony Incashola, director of the Flathead Reservation cultural committee, states in the Native Voices Public Television film,
White Shamen, Plastic Medicine Men (1995):

> In my culture, it has always been taught that when you don't
> respect, you don't show respect, you don't treat things properly, in
> the end it comes back on you. In the end, it will hurt and destroy you
> in some way. And I believe the punishment, whether it be today, to-
> morrow, or somewhere down the line will come back on you.

New Age and the Academic Study of Religion

In academic circles, I have noticed that academicians often criti-
cize New Agers and others who exploit Native spirituality and
culture. However, in this analysis, I also want to point to how the
academic study of Native religious traditions can unwittingly
support this paradigm of sexual violence that undergirds the
manner in which non-Indians attempt to "know" Indians. Just as
those who sexually dominate others often contend that if they
enjoyed the act, then "she must have wanted it," some academics
assume that if they want to study Native communities, the com-

munities must want that as well. A link between the ethnographic imperative that guides the study of Native peoples and sexual violence can be seen in the Greek translation of the Hebrew words (YDH) which can be found in the Septugaint. It translates into "to know by seeing through the mind's eye, " and is the perfect form of the word which means "to see." The forceful act of gazing at the other, gaining knowledge and control over her by seeing her, is likened to sexual intimacy. Thus, the ethnographic gaze can be understood as the act of sexually possessing a people.

The assumption that this pursuit is inherently positive undergirds academic treatments of Native religious tradition. As Cree historian Winona (Stevenson) Wheeler notes, Western-based academics place a high value on procuring "knowledge" or the "truth" as a goal in and of itself. By contrast, knowledge does not confer the right to communicate that knowledge to outsiders in Native communities:

> One of the major tenets of Western erudition is the belief that all knowledge is knowable. In the Cree world all knowledge is not knowable because knowledge is property in the sense that it is owned and can only be transmitted by the legitimate owner.... You can't just go and take it, or even go and ask for it. Access to knowledge requires long-term commitment, apprenticeship and payment. As a student of oral history, in the traditional sense, there is so much I have heard and learned yet so little I can speak or write about, because I have not earned the right to do so. I cannot tell anyone or write about most things because it has not been given to me. If I did it would be theft. So I'll probably be an Old Lady before I am allowed to pass it on. By then, I'll have learned all those rules of transmission and will probably feel impelled to keep it in the oral tradition and not write it down.[28]

Often, researchers have not asked "Do Native people want others to know about them?" or "Do Native communities find this research helpful to them?" As a result, tribal communities are beginning to place restrictions on what kinds of information should be provided to outsiders; many are developing additional protocols or taking other proactive steps regarding research that is done in their communities. For example, at a 1998 conference on biopiracy held at the Salish/Kootenai College in Montana, representatives from a tribal community reported that a researcher visited their reservation reporting that he had been given a grant to study them, even though he had not shared his research proposal with the community before he received funding. The tribal council contacted the agency that funded the researcher and convinced the organization to retract the funding and redirect it to the tribe to conduct its own research.

I would suggest that most people studying Native religions do so to support Native communities. However, we have inherited a colonial model of teaching, researching, and learning that undermines this approach. Not surprisingly, there is often a very sharp disjuncture between how Native people learn spiritual knowledge in their communities and the learning models we use in teaching college classes. Within the community, I always hear elders say, if you want to learn, be quiet and pay attention. Only through being part of the community over a period of time and developing trust does the knowledge come to you — very slowly. Meanwhile, in the classroom setting, we are encouraged to present the information very quickly and completely so that students can learn it for the final. Consequently, we promote the misperception that Native traditions are easily learned, can be learned quickly, and can be learned outside of a community context. I have lost count of the number of students who have informed me that they know all about Indians because they took one class on Indian religions in college. They also seem to learn from classes that they are entitled to learn whatever they want from Native communities; again, that Native communities have no boundaries that non-Natives need to respect. It is interesting to think about alternative models that might resemble indigenous methodologies of learning. A story set in an Ojibwe community that my sister shared with me hints at such an alternative approach:

> In this community, there was a respected elder who knew all about cliff drawings and rock paintings as well as where they were located on the reservation. A young man who was interested in learning about traditional ways went to the elder and asked if the elder would teach him. So the elder agreed to teach him. He would take this young man on long walks to where the rock paintings

were and take great care in uncovering them. He would then tell him a little about the paintings. Then, he would take great care to cover them up again before they took a long walk home. This went on for some time before the young man said, "We could save a lot of time if we just stayed here and you told me what the paintings all mean." To this, the elder replied that walking to the paintings and taking care of them was as important to understanding the traditions as was hearing about what they meant. Simply knowing facts was not enough; Native traditions are a way of life, and you have to know everything about the way of life. It wasn't just about information, it was about a way of being. Whatever comes easy, you do not value. He concluded: "It is not enough for you to understand the traditions, you must learn how to respect them."

Chapter 7

Anticolonial Responses to Gender Violence

*B*ecause sexual violence has served as a tool of colonialism and white supremacy, the struggle for sovereignty and the struggle against sexual violence cannot be separated. Some people have argued that we must prioritize sovereignty. If we successfully decolonize, so the argument goes, we will necessarily end sexism because Native societies were not male dominated prior to colonization.[1] The flaw with this argument is that, regardless of its origins in Native communities, sexism operates with full force today and requires strategies that directly address it. Before Native peoples fight for the future of their nations, they must ask themselves, who is included in the nation? It is often the case that gender justice is articulated as being a separate issue from issues of survival for indigenous peoples. Such an understanding presupposes that we could actually decolonize without addressing sexism, which ignores the fact that it has been precisely through gender violence that we have lost our lands in the first place. In my activist work, I have often heard the sentiment expressed in Indian country: We do not have time to address sexual/domestic violence in our communities because we have to work on "survival" issues first. However, according to U.S. Department of Justice statistics, Indian women suffer death rates twice as high as any other women in this country from domestic violence.[2] We are clearly not surviving as long as issues of gender violence go unaddressed. Scholarly analyses of the impact of colonization on Native communities often minimize the histories of oppression of Native women. In fact, some scholars argue that men were disproportionately affected by colonization because the economic systems imposed on Native nations deprived men of their economic roles in the communities.[3] By narrowing analysis solely to the economic realm, they fail to account for the multiple ways women have disproportionately suffered under colonization—from sexual violence to forced sterilization. As Paula Gunn Allen argues,

> Many people believe that Indian men have suffered more damage to their traditional status than have Indian women, but I think that belief is more a reflection of colonial attitudes toward the primacy of male experience than of historical fact. While women still play the traditional role of housekeeper, childbearer, and nurturer, they no longer enjoy the unquestioned positions of power, respect, and decision making on local and international levels that were not so long ago their accustomed functions.[4]

Rather than adopt the strategy of fighting for sovereignty first and improving Native women's status second, as many activists argue, we must understand that attacks on Native women's status are themselves attacks on Native sovereignty. Lee Maracle illustrates the relationship between colonization and gender violence in Native communities in her groundbreaking work, *I Am Woman*:

> If the State won't kill us
> we will have to kill ourselves.
> It is no longer good etiquette to head hunt savages.
> We'll just have to do it ourselves.
> It's not polite to violate "squaws"
> We'll have to find an Indian to oblige us.
> It's poor form to starve an Indian
> We'll have to deprive our young ourselves
> Blinded by niceties and polite liberality
> We can't see our enemy,
> so, we'll just have to kill each other.[5]

It has been through sexual violence and through the imposition of European gender relationships on Native communities that Europeans were able to colonize Native peoples in the first place. If we maintain these patriarchal gender systems, we will be unable to decolonize and fully assert our sovereignty.

In addition, conceptualizing sexual violence as a tool of genocide and colonialism fundamentally alters the strategies for combating it. We must develop anticolonial strategies for addressing interpersonal violence that also address state violence.

Native Peoples and the Criminal Justice System

For many years, activists in the rape crisis and domestic violence movements have promoted strengthening the criminal justice system as the primary means to reduce sexual and domestic violence. Particularly since the passage of the Violence Against Women Act in 1994, antiviolence centers have been able to receive a considerable amount of funding from the state, to the point where most agencies are dependent on the state for their continued existence. Consequently, their strategies tend to be state friendly: hire more police, give longer sentences to rapists, pass mandatory arrest laws, etc. There is a contradiction, however, in relying upon the state to solve problems it is responsible for creating. Native people are per capita the most arrested, most incarcerated, and most victimized by police brutality of any ethnic group in the country.[6] Given the oppression Native people face within the criminal justice system, many communities are developing their own programs for addressing criminal behavior, which often draw on some of the principles of "restorative justice."

"Restorative justice" is an umbrella term that describes a wide range of programs which attempt to address crime from a restorative and reconciliatory rather than a punitive framework. As opposed to the U.S. criminal justice system, which focuses solely on punishing the perpetrator and removing him (or her) from society through incarceration, restorative justice attempts to involve all

parties (perpetrators, victims, and community members) in deter-
mining the appropriate response to a crime in an effort to restore
the community to wholeness.

These models have been particularly well developed by many
Native communities, especially in Canada, where the sovereign
status of Native nations allows them an opportunity to develop
community-based justice programs.[7] In one program reported by
Rupert Ross's study, for example, when a crime is reported, the
working team that deals with sexual/domestic violence talks to
the perpetrator and gives him the option of participating in the
program. The perpetrator must first confess his guilt and then
follow a healing contract, or go to jail. The perpetrator is free to
decline to participate in the program and go through normal
routes in the criminal justice system. If s/he pursues the restorative justice model, however, everyone (victim, perpetrator,
family, friends, and the working team) is involved in developing
the healing contract. Each participant is also assigned an advocate
through the process. Everyone also shares the responsibility of
holding the perpetrator accountable to his contract. One Tlingit
man noted that this approach was often more difficult than going
to jail:

> First one must deal with the shock and then the dismay on your
> neighbors' faces. One must live with the daily humiliation, and at
> the same time seek forgiveness not just from victims, but from the
> community as a whole.... [A prison sentence] removes the of-
> fender from the daily accountability, and may not do anything
> towards rehabilitation, and for many may actually be an easier dis-
> position than staying in the community.[8]

Along similar lines, scholar and prison educator Elizabeth
Barker asserts that the problem with the criminal justice system is
that it diverts accountability to the criminal justice system instead
of the community. By removing perpetrators from their community, they are further disabled from developing ethical
relationships within a community context.[9] "In reality, rather than
making the community a safer place, the threat of jail places the
community more at risk."[10] During the time that the Hollow Lake
reserve in Canada used a community approach (from approximately 1984 to 1996) 48 offenders were identified. Only five chose

to go to jail, and only two who entered the program have committed crimes since.

However, as James and Elsie B. Zion note, Native domestic violence advocates are often reluctant to pursue alternatives to incarceration for addressing violence against women.[11] Survivors of domestic and sexual violence programs are often pressured to "forgive and forget" in tribal mediation programs that focus more on maintaining family and tribal unity than on providing justice and safety for women. Rupert Ross's study of traditional approaches for addressing sexual/domestic violence on First Nations reserves in Canada notes that they are often very successful in addressing child sexual abuse, as communities are less likely to blame the victim for the assault. In these cases, the community makes a proactive effort in holding perpetrators accountable so that incarceration is often unnecessary. However, Ross notes that these approaches often break down in cases involving an adult woman victim because community members are more likely to blame her instead of the perpetrator for the assault. He also notes that they are most successful in small, geographically isolated areas where it is more difficult for the perpetrator to simply move to another area.[12]

Many Native domestic violence advocates I have interviewed have observed similar problems in applying traditional methods of justice in cases of sexual assault and domestic violence. T., an advocate from a tribally based program in the Plains area, contends that traditional approaches are important for addressing violence against women, but they are insufficient. To be effective, she argues, they must be backed up by the threat of incarceration. T. notes that medicine men have come to her program saying, "We have worked with this offender and we have not been successful in changing him. He needs to join your batterers' program." Traditional approaches toward justice presume that the community will hold a perpetrator accountable for his crime. However, community members often do not regard sexual violence as a crime when cases involve adult women, and they will not hold the offender accountable. Before such approaches can be effective, T. contends, we must implement community education programs that will sufficiently change community attitudes about these issues.

Another advocate, D., who lives on a reservation in the Midwest, argues that traditional alternatives to incarceration were actually more harsh than incarceration. While many Native people presume that traditional modes of justice focused on conflict resolution, she argues that penalties for societal infractions were not lenient, entailing banishment, shaming, reparations, and sometimes death. D. became involved in an attempt to revise tribal codes by reincorporating traditional practices, but she found it difficult to determine what these practices were and how they could be made useful today. For example, some punishments, such as banishment, would not have the same impact today. Prior to colonization, Native communities were so close-knit and interdependent that banishment was often the equivalent of a death sentence. Today, however, Native peoples can simply leave home and move to an urban area. In addition, the elders with whom she consulted admitted that their memories of traditional penal systems were tainted by their own boarding school experiences. As a result of her research, D. believes that incarceration is the most appropriate way to confront sexual violence. She argues that if a Native man rapes someone, he subscribes to white values rather than Native values, because rape is not an Indian tradition. Thus, if he follows white values, he should suffer the white way of punishment.

However, Native antiviolence advocates also struggle with a number of difficulties in using incarceration as the primary strategy to solve the problem of sexual violence. First, so few rapes are reported that the criminal justice system rarely has the opportunity to address the problem. Among five tribal programs I reviewed in 1998, only six rapes were reported to law enforcement officials in that year. Complicating matters, cases involving rapes on tribal land were generally handed to the local U.S. attorney, who then declined to prosecute the vast majority of cases.[13] By the time tribal law enforcement programs even see rape cases, a year may have passed since the assault, making if difficult for these programs to prosecute. Furthermore, because rape is covered under the Major Crimes Act (see Chapter 1), many tribes have developed codes for domestic violence, but they have not developed them for sexual assault. One advocate, B., who conducted a training for southwestern tribes on sexual assault, says participants said they did not need to develop codes because the "feds will take care of rape cases." B. then asked how many cases of rape had been federally prosecuted, and the participants discovered that not one case of rape had ever reached the federal courts. Additionally, there is inadequate jail space in many tribal communities. When the tribal jail is full, the tribe has to pay the surrounding county to house its prisoners. Given the financial constraints, tribes are reluctant to house prisoners for any length of time. Most important, as sociologist Luana Ross notes, incarceration has been largely ineffective in reducing crime rates in the dominant society, much less in Native communities. "The white criminal justice system does not work for white people; what makes us think it's going go work for us?" she asks.

> The criminal justice system in the United States needs a new approach. Of all the countries in the world, we are the leader in incarceration rates—higher than South Africa and the former Soviet Union, countries that are perceived as oppressive to their own citizens. Euro-America builds bigger and better prisons and fills them up with criminals. Society would profit if the criminal justice system employed restorative justice….Most prisons in the United States are, by design, what a former prisoner termed the devil's house. Social environments of this sort can only produce dehumanizing conditions.[14]

Similarly, policing under tribal control or the BIA (Bureau of Indian Affairs) is not necessarily an improvement, as can be attested to by the countless charges of police brutality by the BIA or tribal police. For example, in the mid-1990s, Indian children in Montana were calling the reservation police "terminators." Tribal leaders say that is how bad a reputation the tribal police had. "The common sentiment, is the cops are the enemy of the people," said Clara Spotted Elk, who was a member of a special law enforcement committee for the Northern Cheyenne tribe in Montana. At a congressional hearing in 1994, she and other tribal leaders told the Native American Affairs Subcommittee of the House Natural Resources Committee that the BIA fails to adequately train and supervise reservation police, and disregards complaints about brutality and other misconduct. The House panel called the hearing in 1993 after brutality charges, ranging from beatings to spraying suspects with mace, were made against BIA police in five Western states. The committee watched a brief videotape of a BIA officer slamming a woman's head into a wall on the Wind River Reservation in Wyoming. The woman had been arrested for disorderly conduct. Under questioning from the panel, a BIA official insisted the incident did not constitute police brutality.[15] Nearly 10 years later, in 2002, the entire police force on the Rocky Boys Indian Reservation in Montana was placed on probation by the Chippewa Cree Business Committee because of allegations of police brutality.[16]

As a number of studies have demonstrated, more prisons and more police do not lead to lower crime rates.[17] The Rand Corporation found that California's "three strikes" legislation, which requires life sentences for three-time convicted felons, did not reduce the rate of "murders, rapes, and robberies that many people believe to be the law's principal targets."[18] In fact, changes in crime rates often have more to do with fluctuations in employment rates than with increased police surveillance or increased incarceration.[19] Concludes Steven Walker, "Because no clear link exists between incarceration and crime rates, and because gross incapacitation locks up many low-rate offenders at a great dollar cost to society, we conclude as follows: gross incapacitation is not an effective policy for reducing serious crime."[20] Criminologist Elliott Currie similarly finds that "the *best* face put on the impact of massive prison increases, in a study routinely used by prison supporters to prove that 'prison works,' shows that prison growth seems not to have 'worked' at all for homicide or assault, barely if at all for rape."[21]

Relying on the criminal justice system as the primary approach toward ending violence does not address the reality of police and other forms of state violence in Native communities. Some recent reported examples in the U.S. and Canada follow:

February 26, 2003 — Minneapolis, Minnesota. A group of American Indians, including a pregnant woman, who said they were beaten, falsely imprisoned, and terrorized during a raid of their home, filed a lawsuit against several Minneapolis police officers. According to the lawsuit filed in U.S. district court, six relatives and two friends who were in the home at the time claim that their race and location in one of Minnesota's roughest neighborhoods led police officers to mistreat them. Officers had obtained a warrant based on information that residents were selling drugs. No guns were found by officers at the home and none of the eight plaintiffs has been prosecuted for a crime in connection to the raid, the lawsuit said. The plaintiffs say the raid at the Little Earth Housing Project lasted over three hours and as many as 15 Minneapolis police officers were involved. Wayne Long Crow said he was sitting in a bed with his hands in the air when one officer struck him in the head with the butt end of a rifle, tearing open his scalp. Another plaintiff, Harold Groskruetz, said two officers slammed him into broken glass on the floor, cutting open his head. After he was handcuffed and bleeding, one of the officers kicked him in the head when he complained about the treatment of his wife. Two people were arrested after police found crack cocaine in a toy box. The lawsuit states that officers conducted a full search of the home and turned up nothing until another officer arrived and searched the toy box. The lawsuit accuses the officer of planting the drug. Each plaintiff is seeking damages in excess of $50,000.[22]

January 30, 2003 — Pine Ridge, South Dakota. A judge in South Dakota sentenced a former police officer for the Oglala Lakota Tribe to life in prison for raping a woman and her daughter. Tancrede Hamel, 28, pleaded guilty to the rapes. He has a prior conviction of raping a girl on the Pine Ridge Reservation.[23]

January 2003 — Minneapolis, Minnesota. Two unidentified Minneapolis police officers were seen manhandling an American Indian man before leaving him and a woman outside in freezing temperatures. Two residents of the Little Earth Housing Project in south Minneapolis told community leaders and police investigators that they saw two officers drag the man and woman from the back seat of a marked squad car late on a Friday night. The witnesses said they saw officers assault the man in a parking lot before leaving him unconscious after midnight. The temperature was two degrees above zero. "They left them out to freeze," said Ellie Webster, executive director of Little Earth Community Partnership. She also said that off-duty officers who took the man to a hospital later told a Little Earth security supervisor that someone had urinated on the man's upper torso and head. The man and woman are homeless.

The charges are similar to those of a decade ago, when two Indian men who were drunk were stuffed into the trunk of a Minneapolis squad car to be taken to a detoxification center. In 1995, Charles Lone Eagle and John Boney were awarded $100,000 each by a Hennepin County jury after jurors found that officers Michael Lardy and Marvin Schumer had violated their human and civil rights. The officers said they put the men in the trunk as the quickest way to get them medical attention.[24]

November, 2002—Winnipeg, Manitoba. Nahanni Fontaine, an employee of the Southern Chiefs' Organization, reported that three boys were asleep in a house when police officers burst in, started beating them, and then called for more help. "There were 16 officers in that little house for three youth," she said. "The youth were taken outside, were handcuffed, were stomped in the face, were kicked in the stomach, were choked."[25]

June 2001—Cleveland, Ohio. An off-duty Cleveland police officer shot and killed 20-year-old Joseph Finley, who was Cherokee and Seminole. The Cleveland police were accused of covering up the shooting that happened on June 29, 2001. Officer James Toomey found Finley in his garage and, assuming he was a burglar, warned him repeatedly not to move, according to police. When Finley jumped up, Toomey shot him in the chest, abdomen, back, arms, and legs. The coroner said Finley died of about 14 gunshot wounds; three were in the back.[26]

October 2000—Sioux Falls, South Dakota. Yankton Sioux tribal members complained that Wagner police chief Ed Zylstra used excessive force while arresting an American Indian homeless woman. They say Zylstra threw Sharon K. Gullikson to the ground in the middle of Main Street, handcuffed her, then yanked her up by the cuffs, cutting her wrist. Gullikson was charged with disorderly conduct and resisting arrest. This incident was not the first time the police chief and the city have been at odds with the tribe. In April 2000, tribal members accused Zylstra and his officers of racial profiling. Zylstra and the city denied the charges. They say they were stopping tribal members to serve outstanding warrants. Several of those who witnessed Gullikson's arrest last week say the woman did nothing to provoke Zylstra. "He grabbed her by the wrist and slammed her wickedly, right to the concrete," said Larry Weddell, who watched the arrest from across the street. "She landed on her face and chest. Dust flew up when she hit. He kneed her in the back, put the handcuffs on her, then jerked her off the ground by the handcuffs. She never attacked him. She wasn't trying to get away or assault him. There was no need for this attack."

Gullikson said she went to the Wagner Food Center, a local grocery store, then shopped for earrings in a pawn shop, buying a pair for 25 cents. As she was walking in front of James Drug, she saw Zylstra drive up but kept walking until he honked the horn. She said Zylstra told her she was under arrest for trespassing and panhandling at the grocery store. "The next thing I knew, I was face down. My glasses broke, and my head hit the pavement," she said. "He kneeled on my kidney. At night, it ached for a while. I'm scared of him. A lot of homeless people are scared of him. They're scared of getting hurt," she said."[27]

September 2000 — Saskatoon, Saskatchewan. Police officers in Saskatoon took a Native man, Darrell Night, put him in a police car, drove him far from the city's downtown, and dropped him off to walk home in freezing weather after taking away his coat. He survived, and on telling his story, it came out that police officers had regularly taken Native people out into the cold with no warm clothing, leaving them to freeze. The police would then blame their deaths on alcohol. Two other young aboriginal men did not survive such incidents — their bodies were found separately in the same area where Darrell Night was dropped off.

Constable Dan Hatchen and Constable Ken Munson of Saskatoon city police were charged with police brutality but were put back on the payroll during the trial. The Saskatchewan police commission ruled they deserved to be paid, because the two officers had been cooperative and honest throughout the investigation. In Saskatchewan, aboriginal people make up 11 percent of the population but close to 74 percent of the inmate population in provincial jails and 61 percent of inmates in federal institutions. Starting in November, 2001, Saskatchewan spent more than $2 million on its own aboriginal justice inquiry. The Commission on First Nations and Metis Peoples and Justice Reform made many recommendations, among them considering sentencing alternatives with input from First Nations and Metis elders; and establishing a "therapeutic court" to deal with certain issues, including domestic violence.

Futhermore, the president of the provincial association of police chiefs acknowledged publicly that police from across Saskatchewan are alleged to have taken aboriginals and abandoned them in remote areas. The Federation of Saskatchewan Indian Nations says more than 300 complaints have been received.[28]

July 2000 — Lake Andes, South Dakota. A simple assault charge was filed against a Lake Andes police officer, Michael Atwood, accused of choking a 12-year-old American Indian boy in a city park on the Fourth of July. He was allowed to keep working. The boy, Ben Cournoyer, and two 11-year-old friends admit they were spray-painting profanity on picnic tables, which brought Atwood to the park. The three were charged with vandalism. The three boys and three adult witnesses say a lecture from Atwood turned physical when he grabbed Cournoyer by the neck and lifted him up off the ground. "He grabbed me around the neck, choked me, and lifted me up by my neck. I was barely on my tippie-toes," said Cournoyer, a seventh-grader from Lake Andes.[29]

June 1999 — St. Paul. The St. Paul City Council unanimously agreed to pay $92,500 to settle a police brutality lawsuit filed by a Minneapolis man who alleged that two officers handcuffed him, sprayed him with a chemical irritant, and dumped him in the snow near the Minneapolis border. The council, without debate, also agreed to pay up to $30,000 for attorneys' fees and costs, ending the suit before trial. City officials acknowledged that the officers violated police policy when they didn't take Michael Greenleaf (Red Lake Chippewa), who was intoxicated, to a hospital after spraying him with a chemical irritant in the incident on November 15, 1997. Greenleaf, then 38, also was put in jeopardy when the officers left him outside wearing only a light jacket with the temperature at 20 degrees. The police officers also used racist epithets during the incident.[30]

March 1998 — Calgary, Alberta. A First Nations woman, Connie Jacobs, and her son Ty were shot to death by police who called to respond to a domestic violence incident. No charges were filed against Dan Voller, the police officer who murdered them.[31]

November 1997 — Plymouth, Massachusetts. The United Indians of New England have an annual protest in Plymouth, Massachusetts on Thanksgiving. In 1997, violence erupted when police attacked the demonstrators with pepper spray in an attempt to halt the march. Twenty-three protesters were arrested. They filed suit against the police for brutality. Lloyd Gray (Onondaga) stated that he was pepper-sprayed and his head was bashed into the ground. Eventually, the protesters dropped the suit in return for a $135,000 donation made to the United Indians of New England as well as an agreement to let the protesters continue to have their annual marches.[32]

In addition to innumerable incidents of police brutality, Native peoples, including Native women, are overrepresented in prisons and jails. According to a 2000 study, Native women make up only 8 percent of the women's population in South Dakota, but 35 percent of the state's women's prison population.[33] For Native peoples generally, incarceration rates are high. In Montana, for instance, 16 percent of prisoners were Native in 2000, compared with just 6 percent of the state population. In 2000, 19 percent of prisoners were American Indian and Alaska Native in North Dakota, a state where just 5 percent of the population is Native.

Wyoming Indians made up 2 percent of the state population and 7 percent of the prison population in 2000. In 2000, the rate was comparable in Minnesota, where Indians were 1 percent of the general population and 7 percent of the prison population, and to Nebraska, where Indians make up 1 percent of the population and 5 percent of the prison population.

In 2000, South Dakota had the highest percentage of imprisoned women in the Plains. Some 21 percent of the state's prisoners were Native, compared with just 8 percent of the state population. And in 2000, 37 percent of the state prison population in Alaska was Native, compared with 16 percent of the general population.[34] (It should be noted that these statistics often undercount American Indians who often get miscategorized into other racial/ethnic groups.)

As a result of the death of Cindy Sohappy (discussed at greater length in Chapter 2), Earl Devaney, inspector general of the Department of Interior, conducted an investigation into detention facilities in Indian country in 2004. In testimony to the Senate Select Committee of Indian Affairs on June 23, 2004, Devaney reported that, in the previous three years, there were deaths at 27 out of a total of 74 detention facilities he visited. In all, there were 10 deaths and 41 suicide attempts. For instance, he testified that "at the BIA-operated Hopi Adult and Juvenile Facility in Arizona, an intoxicated inmate died of asphyxiation in 2003. According to the Acting Lead Correctional Officer, this occurred because the two officers on duty were 'more interested in cleaning up the office than observing inmates.'" Devaney also found that there were over 500 serious incidents (including attempted murders and suicide attempts) that were never reported to the Bureau of Indian Affairs.[35]

Gender Violence and the State

All women of color, including Native women, live in the dangerous intersections of gender and race. Within the mainstream antiviolence movement in the U.S., women of color who survive sexual or domestic abuse are often told that they must pit themselves against their communities, often stereotypically portrayed as violent, to begin the healing process. Communities of color, meanwhile, often pressure women to remain silent about sexual and domestic violence in order to maintain a "united front" against racism. The analysis in this chapter argues for the need to adopt antiviolence strategies that are mindful of the larger structures of violence that shape the world in which we live. Our strategies to combat violence within communities (sexual/domestic violence) must be informed by approaches that also combat violence directed against communities, including state violence—police brutality, prisons, militarism, racism, colonialism, and economic exploitation.

Mainstream remedies for addressing sexual and domestic violence in the U.S. have proven inadequate for combating sexual and domestic violence, especially for women of color. The answer is not simply to provide "multicultural services" to survivors. Rather, the analysis of and strategies around addressing gender violence must also address how gender violence is a tool of racism, economic oppression, and colonialism, as well as patriarchy. We must recognize how colonial relationships, as well as race and class relations, are themselves gendered and sexualized.

As discussed in Chapter 1, when a woman of color suffers abuse, this abuse is not just an attack on her identity as a woman, but on her identity as a person of color. The issues of colonial, race, class, and gender oppression cannot be separated. Hence, the strategies employed to address violence against women of color must take into account their particular histories and the complex dynamics of violence.

Beyond the Politics of Inclusion and Cultural Competency

As the antiviolence movement has attempted to become more "inclusive," attempts at multicultural interventions against domestic violence have unwittingly strengthened white supremacy within the antiviolence movement. All too often, inclusivity has come to mean that the "domestic violence model," which developed largely with the interests of white, middle-class women in mind, should simply add a multicultural component to it. Antiviolence multicultural curricula are often the same as those produced by mainstream groups, with some "cultural" designs or references added to this preexisting model. Most domestic violence programs servicing communities of color do not have dramatically different models from the mainstream's, except for "community outreach workers" or bilingual staff. And women of color are constantly called upon to provide domestic violence service providers with "cultural sensitivity programs" in which we are supposed to explain our cultures, sometimes in 30 minutes or less. Even with trainings as long as 40 hours, only one or two of those hours are devoted to "cultural diversity." It is naively assumed that "the culture" of people of color is simple, easy to understand, homogenous, and that such understanding requires little or no substantive engagements with communities. Furthermore, those people who are marginalized *within* communities of color, such as lesbian, gay, bisexual, and transgendered (LGBT) or queer people, people with disabilities, sex workers, or addicts, are often marginalized within these "cultural" representations.

Of course, many women of color in domestic violence programs have been active in expanding notions of "cultural competency" to be more politicized, less simplistic, and less dependent on the notion of culture as a static concept. However, cultural competency, no matter how reenvisioned, is limited in its ability to create a movement that truly addresses the needs of women of color because the lives and histories of women of color call on us to radically rethink all models currently developed for addressing domestic violence.

An alternative approach to "inclusion" is to place women of color at the center of the organizing and analysis of domestic violence. What if we do not make any assumptions about what a domestic violence *program* should look like, but instead ask: What would it take *to end violence against women of color?* What would this movement look like? What if we do not presume that this movement would necessarily have anything we take for granted in the current domestic violence movement? Beth Richie suggests we need to go beyond just centering our analysis on women of color. Rather, she asks, what if we centered our attention on those abused women most marginalized within the category of "women of color?" This approach is of utmost importance because it is within this context, she argues, that we must ultimately "be accountable not to those in power, but to the powerless."[36] She is not suggesting that we have a permanent category in the center of analysis (i.e., women of color), but that we constantly shift the center of analysis to multiple perspectives to ensure that we are developing a holistic strategy for ending violence.

In her essay "Disloyal to Feminism: Abuse of Survivors Within the Domestic Violence Shelter System," Emi Koyama examines some of the possible ramifications of locating women of color, particularly women of color who have been criminalized by the state, such as sex workers, at the center of our analysis and work. Koyama suggests that some of the components now seen as integral to domestic violence programs are ones we would not necessarily continue to use. In particular, she critiques the "shelter system" for mirroring the abusive patterns of control that women in battering relationships seek to leave, and for isolating women from their communities.[37] As Isabel Gonzalez of Sista II Sista (a young women's community-based organization in Brooklyn) argues, the domestic violence shelter system is often modeled on a pattern similar to the prison system—where women's activities are monitored and policed, and where they are cut off from their friends and families.[38] In fact, some shelters have gone so far as to conduct background searches on clients and have them arrested if they have outstanding warrants. As Jael Silliman notes, many antiviolence activists in other countries do not rely on shelters as their primary strategy to address violence. Rather than assume that the absence of a shelter system is a sign of "underdevelopment," perhaps we can learn from these alternative approaches.[39]

Possible Remedies

Anchoring violence against women within the larger context of racism, colonialism, and inequality. The antiviolence movement has always contested the notion of home as a safe place because the majority of the violence that women suffer happens at home. Furthermore, the notion that violence happens "out there," inflicted by the stranger in the dark alley, prevents us from recognizing that the home is, in fact, the place of greatest danger for women. However, the strategies the domestic violence movement employs to address violence are actually premised on the danger coming from "out there" rather than from at home. Reliance on the criminal justice system to address gender violence would make sense if the threat was a few crazed men whom we can lock up. But the prison system is not equipped to address a violent culture in which an overwhelming number of people batter their partners, unless we are prepared to imprison hundreds of millions of people.

State violence — in the form of the criminal justice system — cannot provide true safety for women, particularly women of color, when it is directly implicated in the violence women face. Unfortunately, the remedies that have been pursued by the mainstream antiviolence movement have often strengthened rather than undercut state violence. The antiviolence movements have been vital in breaking the silence around violence against women and in providing critically needed services to survivors of sexual and domestic violence. These movements have also become increasingly professionalized in providing services. As a result, they are often reluctant to address sexual and domestic violence within the larger context of institutionalized violence.[40]

For instance, many state coalitions on domestic/sexual violence have refused to take stands against the anti-immigration backlash and its violent impact on immigrant women, arguing that this issue is not a sexual/domestic violence issue. Yet as the immigration backlash intensifies, many immigrant women do not report abuse for fear of deportation. Mainstream antiviolence advocates have increasingly demanded longer prison sentences for batterers and sex offenders as a frontline approach to stopping violence against women.[41] However, the criminal justice system has always been brutally oppressive toward communities of color. In 2003, almost three out of four prison admissions and ninety percent of those imprisoned for drug offenses are Black or Latino.[42] Two thirds of men of color in California between the ages of 18 and 30 have been arrested.[43] Six of every 10 juveniles in federal custody are American Indian. Two thirds of women in prison are women of color.[44]

Prisons serve to disguise the economic hardships of these communities because prisoners are not included in unemployment statistics. They then serve to exacerbate these problems within the same communities. In addition, when the state allocates resources by population, they count prisoners as part of the community in which the prison is located, primarily white rural areas. Thus, the imprisonment of mass numbers of people of color leads to the draining of resources from communities of color.[45]

The Thirteenth Amendment expressly permits the slavery of prisoners. Uncompensated prison labor is a multimillion-dollar industry and undercuts unionized labor, forcing more people out of jobs and into poverty and thus making them more vulnerable to committing crimes of poverty. Companies that profit from exploitation of prison labor include TWA, McDonald's, Compaq, Texas Instruments, Sprint, Microsoft, MCI, Victoria's Secret, IBM, Toys R Us, AT&T, Eddie Bauer, Nordstrom, Honeywell, Lexus, and Revlon.[46]

Furthermore, public funds are diverted directly from public education and social services to prison construction. Since education is one of the more effective ways to prevent future incarceration, essentially some youth are being tracked toward higher education and others are being tracked into prison.

According to a 2001 study *Cellblocks or Classrooms?: The Funding of Higher Education and Corrections and Its Impact on African American Men* sponsored by the Justice Policy Institute, there were more Black men in prison than in college.[47] Prisoners become seen as nonpersons, deserving of any type of abuse or enslavement. They may lose their right to vote. Eighty percent of experimental drugs are tried on prisoners. Women in prison are routinely sexually abused with no recourse for justice. Prisoners lack adequate nutrition and medical care, much less anything rehabilitative. The denial of media access to prisons ensures that this abuse continues unnoticed by the public.[48] Three out of four women in prison are mothers who routinely lose custody of their children while in prison.[49] When men of color are imprisoned they too are prevented from fulfilling familial responsibilities. Prisons effectively prevent communities of color from raising physically and psychologically healthy children.[50] In addition to suffering the brutalizing effects of prison, Native prisoners are also finding that the state uses incarceration to seize the tribal trust funds guaranteed to them by treaty rights. The Native American Project of Columbia Legal Services (CLS) and the Colville Confederated Tribes have filed suit against the state of Washington for seizing trust fund disbursements from tribal members since 1997.[51]

Under such conditions, it is problematic for women of color to go to the state for the solution to the problems that the state has had a large part in creating. Consider these examples:[52]

> An undocumented woman calls the police because of domestic violence. Under current mandatory arrest laws, the police must arrest someone on domestic violence calls. Because the police cannot find the batterer, they arrest her and have her deported. (Tucson)

> An African-American homeless woman calls the police because she has been the victim of group rape. The police arrest her for prostitution. (Chicago)

> An African-American woman calls the police when her husband, who is battering her, accidentally sets fire to their apartment. She is arrested for setting the fire. (New York)

> A Native woman calls the police because she is the victim of do-
> mestic violence, and she is shot to death by the police. (Alert Bay,
> Canada)[53]

The *New York Times* recently reported that the effect of strengthened anti-domestic violence legislation is that battered women kill their abusive partners less frequently; however, batterers do *not* kill their partners less often.[54] In addition, as Beth Richie notes in her study of Black women in prison, and as Luana Ross describes in her study of incarcerated American Indian women, women of color are generally in prison as a direct or indirect result of gender violence. For example, Richie and Ross document how women of color involved in abusive relationships are often forced to participate in men's criminal activities.[55] Abused women often end up in jail as a result of trying to protect themselves. For instance, over 40 percent of the women in prison in Arizona were there because they murdered an abusive partner.[56] The criminal justice system, rather than solving the problems of violence against women, often revictimizes women of color who are survivors of violence.[57]

In addition, those who go to prison for domestic violence are disproportionately people of color. Julie Ostrowski reports that of the men who go to domestic violence courts in New York, only 12 percent are white. Half of them are unemployed, and the average income of those who are employed is $12,655.[58] But the issue is not primarily that antiviolence advocates are supporting the prison-industrial complex by sending batterers and rapists to jail, since many antiviolence advocates simply say, "If someone is guilty of violence, should they not be in jail regardless of their racial background?" The co-optation of the antiviolence movement by the criminal justice system has far-reaching effects beyond the immediate victims of domestic violence. The Right has been very successful at using antiviolence rhetoric to mobilize support for a repressive anti-crime agenda that includes "three strikes" legislation and antidrug bills. These anti-crime measures then make abused women more likely to find themselves in prison if they are coerced by partners to engage in illegal activity. When men of color are disproportionately incarcerated because of these laws that have been passed in part through the co-optation of antiviolence rhetoric, the entire community—particularly women, who are often the community caretakers—is negatively impacted. For instance, the Violence Against Women Act was attached to a repressive anticrime bill that was then heralded by antiviolence advocates as "feminist" legislation.

Increasingly, domestic violence advocates are coming to recognize the limitations of the criminal justice system. This recognition gave rise to the joint statement by INCITE! Women of Color Against Violence and Critical Resistance, "Gender Violence and the Prison Industrial Complex: Interpersonal and State Violence Against Women of Color."[59] This document critiques the antiviolence movement's reliance on state violence as the primary strategy for eradicating violence against women in general, and women of color in particular. Since this statement was developed, many prominent activists and organizations have signed it, including the National Coalition Against Domestic Violence. (The statement follows this chapter.)

Restorative justice and peacemaking. In critiquing mainstream strategies against domestic violence, we must answer the question, what are the strategies that can end violence against women? Unfortunately, many of the alternatives to incarceration promoted under the previously described restorative justice model have not developed sufficient safety mechanisms for survivors of domestic/sexual violence. On the one hand, these models seem to have much greater potential for dealing with crime effectively; if we want perpetrators of violence to live in society peaceably, justice models which allow the community to hold him/her accountable make sense. On the other hand, in addressing domestic/sexual violence, these models work only when the community unites in holding perpetrators accountable. And in cases of sexual and domestic violence, the community often sides with the perpetrator, not the victim, because of the patriarchal values they have internalized. So in many Native American communities, as well as other areas where these models are in operation, they are often used to pressure adult sexual violence survivors to "reconcile" with their families, and "restore" the community.

Models of restorative justice proposed by anti–domestic violence advocates tend to be located within the criminal justice system, as illustrated by the important but flawed anthology *Restorative Justice and Family Violence*.[60] What unites these essays for the most part, is an inability to think outside the traditional criminal justice/social service model for addressing violence. What seems to be at stake for the contributors of this book is whether or not restorative justice programs should be added as an appendage to the current criminal justice/social service model as the primary strategy for addressing violence. No contributor considers how some of the principles involved in restorative justice programs might be helpful in considering completely different strategies for eradicating violence. There are reasons why this tendency happens—some domestic violence advocates argue that restorative justice only works if it's backed by the threat of incarceration. This approach can actually strengthen the criminal justice system, with all its inherent racism, rather than challenge it. Prison abolitionist Stanley Cohen argues that alternative models are typically co-opted to serve state interests, increase the net of social control, and often lose their community focus as they become professionalized.[61] When programs are administered by the state, the state usually requires that someone with a professional degree oversee these programs. This professionalization hinders communities from doing the work on the grassroots level. Indeed, the history of prison reform shows how often reform programs actually strengthen the prison system, increasing the number of people who fall under its purview.[62]

For instance, women religious reformers in the nineteenth century advocated reforms for women prisoners, who were being kept in the same brutal institutions with men. These reformers imagined women prisoners not as "criminal, fallen women" deserving harsh treatment, but as "sick" or "wayward" women in need of a cure or proper retraining. They fought for the establishment of sex-segregated "reformatories" to provide women the guidance they needed to fulfill their domestic roles. As a result, great numbers of women suddenly found themselves in the criminal justice system receiving domesticity training.[63] As Luana Ross points out, the outgrowth of this ideology is that women often find themselves in prison longer than men—until they can prove they have been "cured."[64] Simply adding restorative justice to the present criminal justice system is likely to further strengthen the criminal justice apparatus, particularly in communities of color that are deemed in need of "restoration." In addition, as discussed in Chapter 8, continued emphasis on criminal justice reforms diverts our attention from grassroots political-organizing strategies which do have the potential to address root causes of violence.

We face a dilemma: On the one hand, the incarceration approach promotes the repression of communities of color without really providing safety for survivors. On the other hand, restorative justice models often promote community silence and denial around issues of sexual/violence without concern for the safety of survivors.

Thus our challenge is, how do we develop community-based models of accountability in which the community will actually hold the perpetrator accountable? There are no simple solutions to violence against women of color, but we will not develop effective strategies unless we stop marginalizing women of color. When we center women of color in the analysis, it becomes clear that we must develop approaches that address interpersonal, state (e.g., colonization, police brutality, prisons), and structural (e.g., racism, poverty) violence simultaneously. In addition, we find that by centering women of color in the analysis, we may actually build a movement that more effectively ends violence not just for women of color but for all people.

Structural Change, Social Change

Today, more community-based organizations are developing strategies that do not primarily rely on the state to end domestic violence. These interventions are not based in what are typically known as "domestic violence" programs, and they often do not receive sufficient attention for their innovation and creation. Because these models attempt to get at the root causes of violence, they do not offer simple panaceas for addressing this problem. This work does suggest some possible directions that the antiviolence movement could take in eradicating violence, including sexual and domestic violence. Providing services to survivors is important, but services alone will not stop domestic violence. It becomes critical that we create more space to ponder how to end domestic violence in communities of color. If we do, some directions we might take could include the following strategies.

Develop interventions that address state violence and interpersonal violence simultaneously. In one model intervention, Communities Against Rape and Abuse (CARA) in Seattle, began monitoring incidents of police brutality shortly after they were established in 1999. They found that the majority of police officers involved with brutality were responding to domestic violence charges in poor neighborhoods of color. As a result, CARA began organizing around the issue of prison abolition from an antiviolence perspective. In the program book for a 2002 prison-abolition film festival cosponsored with Critical Resistance, CARA outlined its philosophy:

> Any movement seeking to end violence will fail if its strategy supports and helps sustain the prison industrial complex. Prisons, policing, the death penalty, the war on terror, and the war on drugs all increase rape, beatings, isolation, oppression, and death. As an anti-rape organization, we cannot support the funneling of resources into the criminal justice system to punish rapists and batterers, as this does not help end violence. It only supports the same system that views incarcerations as a solution to complex social problems like rape and abuse. As survivors of rape and domestic violence, we will not let the antiviolence movement be further co-opted to support the mass criminalization of young people, the disappearance of immigrants and refugees, and the dehumanization of poor people, people of color, and people with disabilities. We support the anti-rape movement that builds sustainable communities on a foundation of safety, support, self-determination, and accountability.

Also significant about CARA is the manner in which they have followed Beth Richie's mandate to organize around the women of color who are least acceptable to the mainstream public. In particular, the group began a campaign against Children Requiring a Caring Kommunity (CRACK), which pays women (and some men) who are substance abusers to be sterilized and focuses primarily on recruiting women from poor communities of color. (See Chapter 4.) CARA's organizing framework emphasizes how an organization that targets substance abusers necessarily targets survivors of violence. Furthermore, CARA is unique in organizing specifically around women with disabilities. In the CRACK campaign, for instance, they address the manner in which the success of CRACK is dependent on the notion of "crack babies" as being "damaged goods" because they may have disabilities.

Emphasize base-building approaches that view domestic violence survivors as potential organizers rather than clients. Long-time activist Suzanne Pharr argues that one of the ways in which the domestic violence movement fails as a violence-reduction movement is its focus on providing services to "clients" instead of seeing survivors as potential antiviolence activists or organizers. Because they are focused on providing services, rather than building a sustainable antiviolence movement, those involved in antiviolence work tend to be professionals who may or may not be interested in challenging the societal norms and structures that give rise to violence.

One organization that focuses on base-building—recruiting people who are not currently activists to become activists—is Sista II Sista in Brooklyn. This organization of young women of color addresses violence against girls in the neighborhood committed both by the police and by other members of the community. Sista II Sista created a video project documenting police harassment after two girls were killed by the police. (One girl was sexually assaulted as well.) In addition, it recently created a community accountability program called Sisters Liberated Ground, which organizes members to monitor violence in the community without relying upon the police. Sista II Sista recruits young women to attend freedom schools which provide political education from an integrated mind-body-spirit framework, then trains girls to become activists on their own behalf.

Develop accountability strategies that do not depend on a romanticized notion of "community" and that ensure safety for survivors. As Pharr's analysis suggests, the success of community accountability models will always be limited as long as survivors are seen as "clients" rather than as organizers. Furthermore, community accountability models will be limited in their success if they are not implemented in the community itself. One group that has developed a model for accountability within communities is Friends Are Reaching Out (FAR Out) in Seattle, an organization which works with queer and LGBT communities of color. The premise of this model is that when people are abused, they become isolated. The domestic violence movement further isolates them through the shelter system because they cannot tell their friends or family members where they are. In addition, the domestic violence movement does not work with the people who could most likely hold perpetrators accountable—their friends and family.

The FAR Out model encourages people to have conversations with friends and developing friendship groups so they are less likely to become isolated. These groups develop processes to talk openly about relationships, since most people tend to keep their sexual relationships private. If we are talking more openly, it is easier for friends to hold us accountable. If a person knows s/he is going to share her/his relationship dynamics openly, it is more likely that s/he will be accountable in the relationship.

Perpetrators will listen to the people they love before they will listen to court-mandated orders, contends FAR Out. And given the homophobia in the criminal justice system, involving law enforcement is more difficult in queer communities. What has made this model work is that it is based on preexisting friendship networks. As a result, it develops the capacity of a community to handle domestic violence.

At the same time, it is important to critically assess community resources for their accountability to survivors of violence.

Sometimes it is easy to underestimate the amount of intervention that is required before a perpetrator can really change his behavior. Often a perpetrator will subject her/himself to community accountability measures but eventually will tire of them. If community members are not vigilant about holding the perpetrator accountable *for years* and instead assume that he or she is "cured," the perpetrator can turn a community of accountability into a community that enables abuse.

Expand our definition of community. Given the high level of mobility in the U.S., the challenge is to develop accountability structures when people can so easily leave communities, or when these communities may not really exist. Part of establishing community accountability processes may involve developing communities themselves. In addition, it is important to expand our notion of community to include communities based on religious affiliations, employment, hobbies, and athletics, and develop strategies based in those communities. For instance, one man was banished from a community for committing incest. As a result, he simply moved out of that area. But because he was a well-known academic, the family made sure he was held accountable in the academic community by making sure that when he gave talks in different communities, his history of incest was exposed.

Traci West's *Wounds of the Spirit* looks to church communities as possible sites for building strategies of accountability. What is particularly noteworthy about *Wounds of the Spirit* is West's attempt to locate at least some crisis intervention services within community structures (in this case, the church), rather than in separately constituted agencies that often force women to leave their communities (or in the criminal justice system). Her approach also involves communities holding social service agencies accountable to those communities.[65]

Build transnational relationships in the fight to end violence against women. Currently, the mainstream domestic violence model in the U.S. is exported to other countries as the model for addressing violence. However, in many countries where reliance on the state is not an issue or a possibility, other organizations have developed creative strategies for addressing violence that can inform the work done in the U.S. Masum, a women's organization in Pune, India, addresses violence through accountability strategies that do not rely on the state. The members of Masum actively intervene in domestic violence cases by using such nonviolent tactics as singing outside a perpetrator's house until he stops his abuse. Masum reports that it has been able to work on this issue without community backlash because it simultaneously provides needed community services such as microcredit, health care, and education. After many years, this group has come to be seen as a needed community institution, and thus, has the power to intervene in cases of gender violence where its interventions might be resisted.

Another model is from Brazil, the Movement of Landless People (known as Movimento dos Trabalhadores Rurail Sem Terra, or MST). This movement is based in networks of families which claim privately owned territory that is not being used. The families set up tents and fences and defend the land, an action which is called an "occupation." If they manage to gain control of the land, they form a settlement in which they build houses and more permanent structures. Over the past 20 years, 300,000 families have been involved in these occupations. Families rather than individuals take part in this resistance. About 20 families form a nucleus, which is coordinated by one man and one woman. The nuclei are then organized into the following sectors: production/cooperation/employment; trading; education; gender; communication; human rights; health; and culture. Since the MST cannot utilize the state to address domestic violence, it must develop accountability structures from within. Both men and women participate in the gender sector. This sector is responsible for ensuring that women are involved in all decision-making positions and are equally represented in public life. Security teams are made up of women and men. The gender team trains security to deal with domestic violence.

All issues are discussed communally. As time progresses, participants report that domestic violence decreases because interpersonal relationships are communal and transparent. Because women engage in "physical" roles, such as being involved in security, women become less likely to be seen as "easy targets" for violence; and the women also think of themselves differently. Sectors and leadership roles rotate so that there is less of a fixed, hierarchical leadership. Hierarchical leadership tends to promote power differentials and hence abuse. This leadership model helps prevent the conditions of abuse from happening in the first place. This model suggests community accountability strategies need to be more holistic. We need to focus not only on intervening when violence happens, but on creating communities where violence becomes unthinkable.

Organize outside the nonprofit industrial complex. Anti-violence and social justice organizations within the U.S. largely operate within the 501(c)3 nonprofit model. Activists and organizers often have difficulty conceiving of developing structures outside this model. At the same time, however, social justice organizations across the country are critically rethinking their investment in the 501(c)3 system. Particularly because of the negative impact of the current recession on foundation support, as well as increased surveillance on social justice groups through "homeland security," social justice organizations are assessing other possibilities for funding social change that do not rely so heavily upon state structures.

In spring of 2004, INCITE! Women of Color Against Violence co-organized a conference with Grace Chang, a professor of women's studies at the University of California–Santa Barbara, called "The Revolution Will Not Be Funded: Beyond the Non-Profit Industrial Complex." At the conference, which attracted 600 attendees, activist and scholar Dylan Rodriguez defined the nonprofit–industrial complex as the set of symbiotic relationships which link political and financial technologies of state to create owning-class control and surveillance over public political ideology, including and especially emergent progressive and leftist social movements. He argued that the nonprofit–industrial complex (NPIC) is the natural corollary to the prison industrial complex (PIC); the PIC overtly represses dissent, while the NPIC manages and controls dissent through incorporating it into the state apparatus. In her presentation, panelist Suzanne

Pharr observed that the early development of antiviolence organizations within the nonprofit system coincided with the era of Reaganomics. As a response to the slashing of government services, the women's movement organized itself into nonprofits to provide the services that the government was no longer providing. As a result, the antiviolence movement essentially became a "cover" for state defunding.

The NPIC contributes to a mode of organizing that is ultimately unsustainable. To radically change society, we must build mass movements that can topple current capitalist hierarchy. The NPIC encourages us to think of social justice organizing as a career—you do the work if you can get paid for it. A mass movement, however, requires the involvement of millions of people, most of whom cannot get paid to do the work. Or, as Arundhati Roy says, "Resistance does not carry with it a paycheck."[66] By trying to do grassroots organizing using a careerist model, we are essentially asking a few people to work more than full-time hours to make up for the work that needs to be done by millions of people.

Also, because our funding comes from foundations rather than from the people we claim to represent, the NIPC does not have an incentive to increase "membership," or the base. Instead, we become preoccupied with developing what Paula Rojas calls "smoke and mirrors" forms of organizing that look good to fenders, but that do not actually increase the number of people doing organizing work, or that do not really build power.

As Paula Rojas, Anannya Bhattacharjee, and Adjoa Jones de Almeida pointed out at the Revolution Will Not Be Funded Conference, we must look outside the U. S. for alternative models for social change. In India and throughout Latin America, social movements are not dominated by nonprofits; movement building is funded by the constituents. These movements have made alliances with nonprofits and developed their own nonprofit organizations to fund specific aspects of their work. But these nonprofits are truly *accountable* to social movements from which they sprang and are not necessarily seen as parts of the movement. Furthermore, when such nonprofits are "defunded," it does not significantly impact the movement because its resources come primarily from constituents.

It might be helpful to think about developing antiviolence organizing projects in the U.S. that are not nonprofits, but are funded by their constituents. People of good conscience who work in mainstream antiviolence organizations could then play a critical role and support these basebuilding efforts and develop accountability to movements. Such an approach would require a shift in our thinking. Instead of seeing domestic and sexual violence agencies as the antiviolence movement, we would work to develop an independent antiviolence movement *supported* by nonprofit domestic and sexual violence agencies.

Conclusion

Activist and scholar Beth Richie asks, "What if funding to combat domestic violence had been located instead in agencies other than criminal justice?"[67] Perhaps we would be organizing around providing affordable housing for women, so they could leave their abusers. Or perhaps we would be working to end poverty, so women would not be trapped in abusive relationships by economics.

By decentering the criminal justice approach to sexual and domestic violence, we can expand the strategies we employ. Increasingly, human rights organizations such as Amnesty International advocate that states act with "due diligence" to prevent domestic or sexual violence. However, this due diligence is often equated with increased criminalization. What if demands for due diligence focused less on criminalization and more on the U.S. ensuring economic, social, and cultural rights that decrease women's vulnerability to violence?

Such an approach might be particularly relevant for Native communities, because the response by many in the federal government and the mainstream media to social ills faced by Native peoples is more funding for tribal law enforcement. Two recent *USA Today* articles, for instance, paint a picture of lawlessness in

Indian Country and suggest that it would be solved through more police and prisons. In 1999, Janet Reno provided $89 million for tribal law enforcement as a solution to "crime."[68] At the same time, however, there was no call for increased funding for housing, social services, economic development, or health care.

One element that models from other countries share is a reliance upon strategies other than "crisis intervention" to develop community accountability. We must recognize that the criminal justice approach cannot stop domestic violence — it only works at the point of crisis, and it does not prevent abuse from occurring. Of course, it is important not to simply appropriate such models without assessing current conditions in the U.S. Strategies to prevent and respond to domestic violence are much more effective when they address the underlying structural and cultural conditions in the community which make abuse possible. In short, radical social change is necessary to end violence against women.

Furthermore, Native and non-Native communities must meet the challenge to develop programs which address sexual violence from an anticolonial, antiracist framework, so that we don't attempt to eradicate acts of personal violence while strengthening the apparatus of state violence. Nothing less than a holistic approach toward eradicating sexual violence can be successful. As Ines Hernandez-Avila states,

> We must imagine a world without rape. But I cannot imagine a world without rape, a world without misogyny, without imagining a world without racism, classism, sexism, homophobia, ageism, historical amnesia and other forms and manifestations of violence directed against those communities that are seen to be "asking for it "Even the Earth is presumably "asking for it…"
>
> What do I imagine then? From my own Native American perspective, I see a world where sovereign indigenous peoples continue to plunge our memories to come back to our originality, to live in dignity and carry on our resuscitated and ever-transforming cultures and traditions with liberty….I see a world where native women find strength and continuance in the remembrance of who we really were and are…a world where more and more native men find the courage to recognize and honor — that they and the women of their families and communities have the capacity to be profoundly vital and creative human beings.[69]

INCITE! Women of Color and Critical Resistance Statement: Gender Violence and the Prison Industrial Complex

We call social justice movements to develop strategies and analysis that address both state *and* interpersonal violence, particularly violence against women. Currently, activists/movements that address state violence (such as anti-prison, anti-police brutality groups) often work in isolation from activists/movements that address domestic and sexual violence. The result is that women of color, who suffer disproportionately from both state and interpersonal violence, have become marginalized within these movements. It is critical that we develop responses to gender violence that do not depend on a sexist, racist, classist, and homophobic criminal justice system. It is also important that we develop strategies that challenge the criminal justice system and that also provide safety for survivors of sexual and domestic violence. To live violence free-lives, we must develop holistic strategies for addressing violence that speak to the intersection of all forms of oppression.

The anti-violence movement has been critically important in breaking the silence around violence against women and providing much-needed services to survivors. However, the mainstream anti-violence movement has increasingly relied on the criminal justice system as the front-line approach toward ending violence against women of color. It is important to assess the impact of this strategy.

- Law enforcement approaches to violence against women *may* deter some acts of violence in the short term. However, as an overall strategy for ending violence, criminalization has not worked. In fact, the overall impact of mandatory arrest laws for domestic violence have led to decreases in the number of battered women who kill their partners in self-defense, but they have not led to a decrease in the number of batterers who kill their partners. Thus, the law protects batterers more than it protects survivors.

- The criminalization approach has also brought many women into conflict with the law, particularly women of color, poor women, lesbians, sex workers, immigrant women, women with disabilities, and other marginalized women. For instance, under mandatory arrest laws, there have been numerous incidents where police officers called to domestic incidents have arrested the woman who is being battered. Many undocumented women have reported cases of sexual and domestic violence, only to find themselves deported. A tough law and order agenda also leads to long punitive sentences for women convicted of killing their batterers. Finally, when public funding is channeled into policing and prisons, budget cuts for social programs, including women's shelters, welfare and public housing are the inevitable side effect. These cutbacks leave women less able to escape violent relationships.

- Prisons don't work. Despite an exponential increase in the number of men in prisons, women are not any safer, and the rates of sexual assault and domestic violence have not decreased. In calling for greater police responses to and harsher sentences for perpetrators of gender violence, the anti-violence movement has fueled the proliferation of prisons which now lock up more people per capita in the U.S. than any other country. During the past fifteen years, the numbers of women, especially women of color in prison has skyrocketed. Prisons also inflict violence on the growing numbers of women behind bars. Slashing, suicide, the proliferation of HIV, strip searches, medical neglect and rape of prisoners has largely been ignored by anti-violence activists. The criminal justice system, an institution of violence, domination, and control, has increased the level of violence in society.

- The reliance on state funding to support anti-violence programs has increased the professionalization of the anti-violence movement and alienated it from its community-organizing, social justice roots. Such reliance has isolated the anti-violence movement from other social justice movements that seek to eradicate state violence, such that it acts in conflict rather than in collaboration with these movements.

- The reliance on the criminal justice system has taken power away from women's ability to organize collectively to stop violence and has invested this power within the state. The result is that women who seek redress in the criminal justice system feel disempowered and alienated. It has also promoted an individualistic approach toward ending violence such that the only way people think they can intervene in stopping violence is to call the police. This reliance has shifted our focus from developing ways communities can collectively respond to violence.

In recent years, the mainstream anti-prison movement has called important attention to the negative impact of criminalization and the build-up of the prison industrial complex. Because activists who seek to reverse the tide of mass incarceration and criminalization of poor communities and communities of color have not always centered gender and sexuality in their analysis or organizing, we have not always responded adequately to the needs of survivors of domestic and sexual violence.

- Prison and police accountability activists have generally organized around and conceptualized men of color as the primary victims of state violence. Women prisoners and victims of police brutality have been made invisible by a focus on the war on our brothers and sons. It has failed to consider how women are affected as severely by state violence as men. The plight of women who are raped by INS officers or prison guards, for instance, has not received sufficient attention. In addition, women carry the burden of caring for extended family when family and community members are criminalized and warehoused. Several organizations have been established to advocate for women prisoners; however, these groups have been frequently marginalized within the mainstream anti-prison movement.
- The anti-prison movement has not addressed strategies for addressing the rampant forms of violence women face in their everyday lives, including street harassment, sexual harassment at work, rape, and intimate partner abuse. Until these strategies are developed, many women

will feel shortchanged by the movement. In addition, by not seeking alliances with the anti-violence movement, the anti-prison movement has sent the message that it is possible to liberate communities without seeking the well-being and safety of women.

- The anti-prison movement has failed to sufficiently organize around the forms of state violence faced by LGBTI communities. LGBTI street youth and trans people in general are particularly vulnerable to police brutality and criminalization. LGBTI prisoners are denied basic human rights such as family visits from same sex partners, and same sex consensual relationships in prison are policed and punished.

- While prison abolitionists have correctly pointed out that rapists and serial murderers comprise a small number of the prison population, we have not answered the question of how these cases should be addressed. The inability to answer the question is interpreted by many anti-violence activists as a lack of concern for the safety of women.

- The various alternatives to incarceration that have been developed by anti-prison activists have generally failed to provide sufficient mechanism for safety and accountability for survivors of sexual and domestic violence. These alternatives often rely on a romanticized notion of communities, which have yet to demonstrate their commitment and ability to keep women and children safe or seriously address the sexism and homophobia that is deeply embedded within them.

We call on social justice movements concerned with ending violence in all its forms to:

- Develop community-based responses to violence that do not rely on the criminal justice system *and* which have mechanisms that ensure safety and accountability for survivors of sexual and domestic violence. Transformative practices emerging from local communities should be documented and disseminated to promote collective responses to violence.

- Critically assess the impact of state funding on social justice organizations and develop alternative fundraising strategies to support these organizations. Develop collective fundraising and organizing strategies for anti-prison and anti-violence organizations. Develop strategies and analysis that specifically target state forms of sexual violence.

- Make connections between interpersonal violence, the violence inflicted by domestic state institutions (such as prisons, detention centers, mental hospitals, and child protective services), and international violence (such as war, military base prostitution, and nuclear testing).

- Develop an analysis and strategies to end violence that do not isolate individual acts of violence (either committed by the state or individuals) from their larger contexts. These strategies must address how entire communities of all genders are affected in multiple ways by both state violence and interpersonal gender violence. Battered women prisoners represent an intersection of state and interpersonal violence and as such provide an opportunity for both movements to build coalitions and joint struggles.

- Put poor/working class women of color in the center of their analysis, organizing practices, and leadership development. Recognize the role of economic oppression, welfare "reform," and attacks on women workers' rights in increasing women's vulnerability to all forms of violence and locate anti-violence and anti-prison activism alongside efforts to transform the capitalist economic system.

- Center stories of state violence committed against women of color in our organizing efforts.

- Oppose legislative change that promotes prison expansion, criminalization of poor communities and communities of color and thus state violence against women of color, even if these changes also incorporate measure to support victims of interpersonal gender violence.

- Promote holistic political education at the everyday level within our communities, specifically how sexual violence helps reproduce the colonial, racist, capitalist, heterosexist, and patriarchal society we live in as well as how state violence produces interpersonal violence within communities.

- Develop strategies for mobilizing against sexism and homophobia *within* our communities in order to keep women safe.
- Challenge men of color and all men in social justice movements to take particular responsibility to address and organize around gender violence in their communities as a primary strategy for addressing violence and colonialism. We challenge men to address how their own histories of victimization have hindered their ability to establish gender justice in their communities.
- Link struggles for personal transformation and healing with struggles. We seek to build movements that not only end violence, but that create a society based on radical freedom, mutual accountability, and passionate reciprocity. In this society, safety and security will not be premised on violence or the threat of violence; it will be based on a collective commitment to guaranteeing the survival and care of all peoples.

Chapter 8

U.S. Empire and the War Against Native Sovereignty

What disturbed so many U.S. citizens about the attacks on the World Trade Center was that their sense of "safety at home" was disrupted. Until 9/11, many people believed that terrorism was something that happened in other countries, while our "home" was a place of safety. But the notion that terrorism only happens in other countries makes it difficult to grasp that the U.S. is built on a foundation of genocide, slavery, and racism. Likewise, the belief that violence happens "out there," inflicted by the stereotypical stranger in a dark alley, makes it difficult to recognize that the home is, in fact, the place of greatest danger for women. The antiviolence movement has always pointed to evidence that home is the most dangerous place for women, and shown how our "home" in the U.S. has never been a safe place for people of color.

While the antiviolence movement has contributed this important piece of analysis (discussed at greater length in Chapter 7), some of its strategies to defeat violence are, indeed, based on the premise that violence happens "out there," rather than at home. For instance, the antiviolence movement relies on the criminal system as its primary tool to address domestic and sexual violence. That reliance is based on the false notion that the perpetrators of violence are a few crazed strangers that we need to lock up. As I have argued, this strategy will not transform a rape culture which implicates the majority of men.

Furthermore, after 9/11 many organizations reported sharp increases in attacks in LGBT communities, demonstrating the extent to which gays and lesbians are often seen as "aliens" whose sexuality threatens white, nuclear families held up as the building blocks of U.S. society. U.S. empire has always been reified by enforced heterosexuality and binary gender systems. By contrast, Native societies were not necessarily structured through binary gender systems. Rather, some of these societies had multiple genders and people did not fit rigidly into particular gender categories.[1] Thus, it is not surprising that the first peoples targeted for destruction in Native communities were those who did not neatly fit into Western gender categories.

Because the U.S. empire is built on a foundation of heteropatriarchy, it cannot "liberate" other countries from the effects of homophobia and sexism. So mainstream feminist support for the war on terror — in the interest of helping women in Afghanistan fight sexism and homophobia — ultimately helped the Bush administration push its sexist and homophobic policies and its support of the Christian Right at home. As Trishala Deb and Rafael Mutis of the Audre Lorde Project in New York argue,

> One of the central messages of colonization is the assertion that we are not entitled to autonomy over our own bodies — they are simply machines to be used in sweatshops, prisons, and farms. Devoid of our own self-determination regarding sexuality and gender, we are as disposable as any other piece of equipment that has lost its use.
>
> As Lesbian, Gay, Bisexual, Transgender and Two Spirit People of Color in the United States, we need to insist that we will not accept more lies about the War on Terrorism's potential to liberate any person or nation. We need to make the connections between the misogyny, homophobia and racism of this war effort with the overall agenda that the U.S. government is rolling out on all these fronts.[2]

U.S. Empire Within the U.S.

Many Indian tribes came out in support of the U.S. "war against terror." However, it is important to understand that this war against "terror" is really an attack against Native sovereignty, and that consolidating U.S. empire abroad is predicated on consolidating U.S. empire *within* U.S. borders. For example, the Bush administration continues to use the war on terror as an excuse to support anti-immigration policies and the militarization of the U.S./Mexico border. After the Clinton and Bush II administrations spent $20 billion on border enforcement, in June 2003 the U.S. launched Operation Desert Safeguard, Operation Desert Grip, and Operation Triple Strike. These policies will, among other things, add 200 more Border Patrol agents, increase Border Patrol encampments, raid smugglers' homes, and provide 225 million rounds of hollow-point bullets as ammunition. As a result of this increased militarization, more than 300 migrants die each year, according to the Bureau of Customs and Border Protection. (This figure does not include people whose bodies end up on the Mexico side of the border.) This number is a tenfold increase from 10 years ago.[3]

The Justice Department has also announced that it is entering the names and descriptions of nearly 300,000 people who are overstaying visas or otherwise staying in the country illegally into its criminal databank. Half of those on the list are from Mexico. This information will be available to local police making routine traffic stops. In 2003, a congressional amendment to the Patriot Act explicitly empowered local cops to enforce immigration laws and to exempt them from liability under federal civil rights law for acts carried out in apprehending the undocumented.[4]

Still, many Native peoples may not see anti-immigration policies as attacks against Native sovereignty. But what is at stake for the U.S. government is its ability to determine *who can be on these lands*. By instituting repressive immigration policies, the U.S. government is once again asserting that it—and not indigenous nations—should determine who can be on these lands. That is why popular media often feature stories of American Indians serving on border control, to present the picture that Native peoples support the interests of the U.S. over the interests of their own nations. In one example, *People* magazine ran an article about 21 Native people who form Shadow Wolves, an elite U.S. Customs Service unit formed about 30 years ago. According to *People*, "It is fitting and perhaps ironic that descendants of America's original — and violently dispossessed — inhabitants are helping to protect their own homeland from new invaders."[5]

Furthermore, Bush has used the argument that the U.S. needs to harness domestic energy reserves to support the "war on terror" as a pretext to increase energy resource extraction in the U.S. And as the vast majority of energy resources are on indigenous lands, and almost all uranium mining takes place on or near Native lands, the rhetoric of developing U.S. domestic energy resources is a veiled attack against Native sovereignty. Former White House speechwriter David Frum offers a laudatory analysis of Bush in *The Right Man*,

> For Bush, the point of energy conservation was not for Americans to USE less, but for Americans to IMPORT less. For him, energy was first and foremost a national security issue. He had warned in 2000, "As a result of our foreign oil imports skyrocketing, America is at the mercy more than ever of foreign governments and cartels."[6]

The U.S. government is not encouraging conservation or the consumption of less energy, but rather that people in the U.S. use domestic rather than foreign resources. These resources will come from indigenous lands. Consequently, Native peoples are increasingly vulnerable to U.S. policy. Bush continues to support drilling in the Arctic National Wildlife Refuge (home to the Gwich'in people) while he opposes making sport utility vehicles more fuel efficient. Since the proposed drilling would affect the calving grounds of the caribou the Gwich'in depend on, this project could be genocidal to the Gwich'in peoples. Another huge blow to Native sovereignty was the recent congressional act to locate a permanent high-level nuclear waste repository on Yucca Mountain, which is on Western Shoshone lands. (See Chapter 3 for more details.)

Before the U.S. attacks other countries, it tests its weapons on indigenous peoples in the Americas; military and nuclear testing also takes place almost exclusively on Native lands. Native women have been disproportionately impacted by nuclear testing in the Pacific Islands and on the Nevada test site on Shoshone land. In Canada, the Inuit have been subjected to NATO war exercises that have been wreaking environmental havoc where they live. The 18,000 low-level flights that take place each year over Inuit land create so much noise they disrupt the wildlife and destroy the hearing of the Inuit. In addition, oil falls from the jets and poisons their water supply. Since the Inuit depend on wildlife for their subsistence, flights threaten their existence. Two jets that crashed contained an extremely toxic substance, hydrazine, but NATO was not required to publish any results of the study regarding the potential effects of this crash. NATO considers the Inuit to be expendable casualties, as illustrated by one of its promotional brochures:

> One can spend a one-hour mission at low-level and never see another human being. The only humans are occasional Inuit families who hunt and fish out of small camps on a seasonal basis.[7]

Canada's Department of Defense has disregarded any complaints of the Inuit, arguing that any negative health effects can be attributed to poor nutrition.[8]

Apparently, again, Native peoples do not qualify as human beings. Similarly, at the First People of Color Environmental Justice Summit in Washington, D.C., in 1991, representatives from the Western Shoshone nation reported that low-level flying also takes place on their land. According to the Shoshone, the flying was supposed to take place over the cattle pasturage until the Humane Society interceded and said this would be inhumane to the cattle. Consequently, the war exercises were redirected to take place over Indian people instead. It is clear that when we look at the casualties of the "war on terror" we must look at the unacknowledged casualties in Indian country.

U.S. Exceptionalism

Bush's war against terrorism is a clear attempt of the U. S. government to assert military and economic power throughout the
world. Unilateralism has become the watch word of this administration. And Bush has undermined several multilateral processes:
the administration has withheld support for the Kyoto Accords;
refused to support a permanent tribunal to investigate war crimes;
and boycotted the U.N. Conference Against Racism. The U.S. also
undermines U.N. processes through economic and political coercion, forcing other member countries to support U.S. policies. The
lead up to the U.N. Security Council vote on the resolution which
paved the way for the war against Iraq offers a very clear example
of this kind of blackmail.[9] In contrast, Native peoples have been
very interested in engaging international law, arguing that as descendants of indigenous nations, they deserve protection under
international human rights laws. Some activists have been lobby-
ing the U.N. to pass the Draft Declaration on the Rights of
Indigenous Peoples which would recognize the *collective* human
rights of indigenous peoples. This protection would allow their
sovereignty rights to take precedence over U.S. or other nation-states' domestic laws. As Sharon Venne states,

> The aim of Indigenous Peoples is not to be assimilated into the
> state that has colonized and dispossessed them, but to persist as In-
> digenous Peoples within their territories….Indigenous Peoples are
> not minorities under international law. The evolving Draft Decla-
> ration is striving to incorporate the right of self-determination for
> Indigenous Peoples into an international instrument. It is the right
> under which historical wrongs committed through the coloniza-
> tion process may be redressed.[10]

The constant undermining of the U.N. by the U.S. hinders the
ability of indigenous nations to gain recognition as sovereign
nations under international law.

And as Bush increases spending to support the military, he
takes money away from social services. We can expect to see more
cuts in federal spending for tribally based programs. Already, for
instance, former attorney general John Ashcroft shifted monies

from tribally based domestic violence programs to support "homeland security." Because Native peoples are at the bottom of the socioeconomic ladder in this country, they are disproportionately impacted by cuts in social spending. Native women, in particular, are burdened with taking care of their communities as the economy worsens and their access to social services declines.

Nevertheless, Native women activists have been heroic in their struggles to end violence in Native communities. A multitude of tribally-based domestic violence programs have developed in Indian country to address violence against women and children. The "war on terror," however, makes it much more difficult to address violence within this country. In addition, war escalates rates of sexual/domestic violence in both the U.S. and in the countries it is at war with. The connection is illustrated by the 2002 murders of Teresa Nieves, Andrea Floyd, Jennifer Wright, and Marilyn Griffin, who were killed by their military partners within days of each other at Fort Bragg, North Carolina.[11] The Miles Foundation[12] reports rates of domestic violence as much as two to five times higher in military homes. In addition, there have been over 80 allegations of sexual misconduct against female soldiers by their fellow soldiers.[13] Yet, at the 2002 National Coalition Against Domestic Violence conference held in Orlando, Florida, an artist named MeloD mounted an exhibit celebrating U.S. troops and George Bush. According to her handout,

> These visually stimulating images serve as a wake up call for all of man-kind, while at the same time they celebrate the shared patriotic spirit of the *American people*. They convey indisputable certainties while showing that the hope of tomorrow is based upon the values of our forefathers. Freedom has a very dear price and our patriotism is as strong today as when our ancestors and our sons and daughters paid that price![14]

Notwithstanding the obvious point that it has been indigenous peoples and people of color, not white people, who have paid the price to build the U.S., it is simply inconsistent to say it is not okay to beat your partner, but it is okay to bomb civilians in Iraq. We cannot end violence in Native communities, or in any community for that matter, while supporting violence in other countries.

And just as we have to think beyond the state as the "answer" to violence, we need to think beyond the nation-state as the appropriate form of governance for the world. In particular, we must call into question the notion that the U.S. can ever be the guarantor of peace and freedom and recognize the U.S. for the colonial, settler nation that it is. With slogans like "peace is patriotic," many in the antiwar movement are not calling the legitimacy of the U.S. into question. And organizing work to combat the "decline in civil liberties" has been especially popular since 9/11. The implications of this work is that Bush administration policies signal a decline in the democratic ideals found in the U.S. Constitution.

In looking to the U.S. Constitution as the basis for our democratic "ideals," one is immediately struck with many contradictions. Generally speaking, liberal discourse (and even many sectors of "radical" discourse) dismiss these contradictions as aberrations from otherwise admirable democratic ideals—white supremacy, genocide, and imperialism are unfortunate mistakes made by the U.S., but do not fundamentally constitute the U.S. itself.[15] But white supremacy, colonialism, and economic exploitation are inextricably linked to U.S. democratic ideals rather than aberrations from it. The "freedom" guaranteed to some individuals in society has always been premised upon the radical unfreedom of others. Very specifically, the U.S. could not exist without the genocide of indigenous peoples. Otherwise visitors to this continent would be living under indigenous forms of governance rather than under U.S. empire.

Indeed, an examination of U.S. democratic ideals reveals the extent to which they are inextricably linked to capitalism and racial exclusion. Liberals and progressives maintain that these democratic ideals are based on notions of citizenship, where individuals engage each other in "reasoned" debate within the public sphere to help shape public policy. However, citizenship and the public sphere are concepts that are based in exclusivity. The public sphere has been articulated as the arena in which "citizens," or property owners, could publicly debate exercises of state power. Because citizenship has been the basis for engagement in the public sphere, the bourgeoisie argued that excluding non–property owners from the public sphere was consistent. This move has allowed the bourgeoisie to consolidate power, while masking their will to power. As theorist Jurgen Habermas articulates,

> Nevertheless, the liberal model sufficiently approximated reality so that the interest of the bourgeois class could be identified with the general interest....If everyone, as it might appear, had the chance to become a "citizen," then only citizens should be allowed into the political public sphere, without this restriction amounting to an abandonment of the principle of publicity. On the contrary, only property owners were in a position to form a public that could legislatively protect the foundations of the existing property owner....Only from them, therefore, was an effective representation of the general interest to be expected.[16]

Unfortunately, while Habermas argues that the public sphere is fundamentally based on exclusion, he contradicts himself by continuing to hold it up as a model for addressing conflict within society. In fact, it is a consistent practice among progressives to bemoan the genocide of Native peoples, but in the interest of political expediency, implicitly sanction it by refusing to question the legitimacy of the settler nation responsible for this genocide. It is incumbent upon all people who benefit from living on Native lands to consider how they can engage in social justice struggles without constantly selling out Native peoples in the interest of political expediency *in the short term*. I say "short term" because it is fundamentally nonsensical to expect that we can fundamentally challenge white supremacy, imperialism, and economic exploitation within the structures of U.S. colonialism and empire *in the long term*.

In questioning the legitimacy of the U.S., it necessarily follows that we question the nation-state as an appropriate form of governance. Doing so allows us to free our political imagination to begin thinking of how we can begin to build a world we would actually want to live in. Such a political project is particularly important for colonized peoples seeking national liberation because it allows us to differentiate "nation" from "nation-state." Helpful in this project of imagination is the work of Native women activists who have begun articulating notions of "nation" and "sovereignty" which are separate from nation-states. Whereas nation-states are governed through domination and coercion, indigenous sovereignty and nationhood is predicated on interrelatedness and responsibility. As Crystal Ecohawk (Pawnee) writes,

> Sovereignty is an active, living process within this knot of human, material and spiritual relationships bound together by mutual responsibilities and obligations. From that knot of relationships is born our histories, our identity, the traditional ways in which we govern ourselves, our beliefs, our relationship to the land, and how we feed, clothe, house and take care of our families, communities and Nations.[17]

Similarly, Ingrid Washinawatok (Menominee) writes,

> While sovereignty is alive and invested in the reality of every living thing for Native folks, Europeans relegated sovereignty to only one realm of life and existence: authority, supremacy and dominion. In the Indigenous realm, sovereignty encompasses responsibility, reciprocity, the land, life and much more.[18]

This interconnectedness exists not only among the nation's members but among all creation, human and nonhuman. As Venne writes,

> Our spirituality and our responsibilities define our duties. We understand the concept of sovereignty as woven through a fabric that encompasses our spirituality and responsibility. This is a cyclical view of sovereignty, incorporating it into our traditional philosophy and view of our responsibilities. There it differs greatly from the concept of western sovereignty which is based upon absolute power. For us absolute power is in the Creator and the natural order of all living things; not only in human beings...Our sovereignty is related to our connections to the earth and is inherent. The idea of a nation did not simply apply to human beings. We call the buffalo, the wolves, the fish, the trees, and all are nations. Each is sovereign, and equal part of the creation, interdependent, interwoven, and all related.[19]

These models of sovereignty are not based on narrow definitions of nationhood. It is interesting to me, for instance, how non-Indians often presume that if Native people regained their landbases, that non-Indians would be exiled from those landbases. Yet, a much more inclusive vision of sovereignty is articulated by Native women activists. For instance, Native activist

Lakota Harden of Women of All Red Nations (WARN) and the Indigenous Women's Network describes how indigenous sovereignty is based on freedom for all peoples:

> If it doesn't work for one of us, it doesn't work for any of us. The definition of sovereignty [means that]…none of us are free unless all of us are free. We can't, we won't turn anyone away. We've been there. I would hear stories about the Japanese internment camps…and I could relate to it because it happened to us. Or with Africans with the violence and rape, we've been there too. So how could we ever leave anyone behind?[20]

Activist Sammy Toineeta (Lakota) distinguishes between a chauvinistic notion of "nationalism" and a flexible notion of "sovereignty:"

> Nationalism is saying, our way is the only right way….I think a real true sovereignty is a real, true acceptance of who and what's around you. And the nationalist doesn't accept all that….Sovereignty is what you do and what you are to your own people within your own confines, but there is a realization and acceptance that there are others who are around you. And that happened even before the Europeans came, we knew about the Indians. We had alliances with some, and fights with some. Part of that sovereignty was that acceptance that they were there.[21]

There are local organizing models that rely on the dual strategy of what Sista II Sista describes as "taking power" and "making power." On one hand, it is necessary to engage in oppositional politics to corporate and state power by taking power. Yet if we only engage in the politics of taking power, we will have a tendency to replicate the hierarchical structures in our movements. So it is also important to "make power" by creating those structures within our organizations, movements, and communities that model the world we are trying to create. Many groups in the U.S. often try to create separatist communities based on egalitarian ideals. If we "make power" without also trying to "take power," we ultimately support the political status quo by failing to dismantle structures of oppression that will undermine us.

Roberto Mendoza (Muscogee) makes an important critique of some indigenous approaches toward "making power." He notes that Native thinkers valorize "Native solutions" to our problems without spelling out what they are. Native activists are fond of saying, "We won't follow socialism or capitalism, we'll do things the Indian way." Often then the political strategy espoused is one that advocates that Native nations simply separate from the larger colonial system rather than contest the U.S. itself. For instance, Vine Deloria, whose analysis and activism was and is central to the development of the Red Power movement, argued that there was nothing particularly problematic with the U.S. political or economic system. "It is neither good nor bad, but neutral."[22] Similarly, a Cherokee explained why he is not a revolutionary: "We, the Native people have NEVER been a part of your (non-Native) society, therefore our acts are not of the revolutionist; rather a separate People seeking to regain what is rightfully and morally ours."[23] This separatist sentiment is reflected in the following joke: "A survey was taken and only fifteen percent of the Indians thought that the United States should get out of Vietnam. Eighty-five percent thought they should get out of America!"[24]

Indian people, while espousing separatism, have not necessarily articulated a critique of global or U.S. structures of oppression. Native activist Lee Maracle argues that many sectors of Native sovereignty movements "did not challenge the basic character, the existence or the legitimacy of the institutions or even the political and economic organization of America, but rather, they addressed the long-standing injustice of expropriation."[25] And, she notes, it was the power of this U.S. political/economic system that has devastated organizations like the American Indian Movement.[26]

This approach is not sufficient to dismantle multinational capitalism, argues Mendoza, because it does not "really address the question of power. How can small communities tied in a thousand ways to the capitalist market system break out without a thorough social, economic and political revolution within the whole country?"[27] A separatist approach can contribute to a reluctance to engage with other social justice movements. Mendoza concludes, "I feel that dialogue and struggle with Left forces are necessary rather than rejection and isolation."[28]

We are faced with the challenge of developing organizing models that make power and take power. The community models described in Chapter 7, such as those used by Sista II Sista, exemplify this approach. Another important model is Sisters in Action for Power based in Portland, Oregon. Most members are under 18. Its mission is to develop the power of communities of color and low-income communities through grassroots coalition-building and campaigns. The organization draws from an analysis of colonialism as the root cause of gender, race, and class oppression and which continues to shape our realities, our bodies, and our connections to each other. Sisters in Action for Power holds that this colonial system is based on four pillars: taking the land; use of force; killing of culture; and control of mind, body, and spirit. Their work has three components:

- **Issue campaigns.** Issue campaigns are a series of strategic activities, actions, and projects organized to make changes within institutions and influence dominant culture around a specific issue. Members identify issues most affecting them. Then the group examines the issue to get to its root cause and to determine how it affects other issues. They conduct research to learn who benefits, who loses, and how, under the current conditions. Based on this information, the group determines its demands and then builds support by mobilizing allies. Through the campaign, it builds membership.

- **Leadership Development.** Sisters in Action for Power has a formalized program designed to build collective power and to develop members' organizing and critical-thinking skills. The purpose of the campaign is to develop the leadership skills of the members. Potential members can become involved in Healthy Girl Space. From there, girls have the option of joining the Girls in Action for Power training program, which can take several years. Those who graduate can become paid interns and then staff-apprentices.

- **Modeling the Vision.** This sector of Sisters in Action for Power, often missing in traditional organizing projects, is based on the philosophy that we should model the vision for change in the here and now, and that we must make changes within ourselves and our organizations. This

modeling takes place through a variety of structures and
activities that connect mind, body, and spirit, such as
teamwork activities, self-reflection, journaling,
self-defense classes, cooking, and revolutionary therapy.
Just as members support each other in the political work,
they support each other in each other's personal work to
decolonize their minds, bodies, and spirits.[29]

Another example of a group that makes and takes power is
the Native Americans for a Clean Environment based in
Tahlequah, Oklahoma, the group that forced Kerr-McGee to close
its nuclear conversion facility in Oklahoma, and eventually cease
its operations in the U.S. altogether. (See Chapter 3 for more.)
Kerr-McGee has been linked to Karen Silkwood's suspicious
death in 1974, after her efforts to make the company's disregard
for the safety of its workers from nuclear contamination public.
Pamela Kingfisher, another leader in this struggle, says one thing
missing in the group's activist work was "modeling the vision." In
addition to fighting Kerr-McGee, Kingfisher maintains that it was
important to fight for an alternative vision.

And at that point, about a year earlier, I'd already started saying,
you know all we're doing is fighting. I'm so wore out. I got to work
on something I believe in. We realized that we weren't building
economic development—clean economic development for that
community, and we should have been working with the city
council. We should have been working with the businesses
because as soon as that plant shut down, all of these nasty new-
comers started coming in and going, we'll come in and build this
and we'll do that, and we'll save your little town since you lost all
this money…

We figured out we had media, law, all this stuff, and we had
six strategies. So we said, okay, this is a six-stream strategy. But as
Cherokee people, that's not a good number for us. Our magic
numbers are four and seven, and those are very magical, very
spiritual numbers for us. We've got six; we need one more. And
we sat there. I thought about it, and I went home. We had it up on
the wall on big papers. We looked at it. And I had a dream, and I
came back, and I said you know what we left out? We left out
spirituality. And we weren't doing the spiritual work. So we very
quickly got my cousin, Eagle Kingfisher, to come on our board of

directors. He had been on it early on and fell out. He's old and elder. So I went to Eagle and I asked him to come back on our board and give us spiritual [guidance].

And we always had a prayer. We always opened everything with the prayers. And we realized we've got to move spirituality to the front. So we started taking medicine men down to the plant and praying for the land under that plant. And praying for land where they had their sludge ponds…

You can study about organizing, but unless you do it with a full heart and your ceremonies intact and your spiritual people behind you, and your medicine people with you, it won't work. I just believe you have to have spirituality in everything you do. Within our schools, our languages, our education, everything has to be centered. It has to be in the middle. It has to be the center of the work we do. And that is the difference with Native communities. We open with prayers. We don't open with, oh here's who I am and the chest stuck out at the microphone. We offer our humble prayers. And ask the creator to guide us.[30]

The project of creating a new world governed by an alternative system not based on domination, coercion, and control, does not depend on an unrealistic goal of being able to fully describe a utopian society for all at this point in time. From our position of growing up in a patriarchal, colonial, and white supremacist world, we cannot even fully imagine how a world that is not based on structures of oppression might operate. Nevertheless, we can be part of a collective, creative process that can bring us closer to a society not based on domination. To quote Jean Ziegler from the 2003 World Social Forum held in Pôrto Alegre, Brazil: "We know what we don't want, but the new world belongs to the liberated freedom of human beings. There is no way; you make the way as you walk. History doesn't fall from heaven; we make history."

Endnotes

Chapter 1: Sexual Violence as a Tool of Genocide

1   Susan Brownmiller, *Against Our Will* (Toronto: Bantam Books, 1986).
2   Kimberle Crenshaw, "The Intersection of Race and Gender," in Critical Race Theory, ed. Kimberle Crenshaw, et al. (New York: New Press, 1996).
3   Neferti Tadiar, "Sexual Economies of the Asia-Pacific," in *What's in a Rim? Critical Perspectives on the Pacific Region Idea*, ed. Arif Dirlik (Boulder: Westview Press, 1993).
4   Ibid.
5   Ann Stoler, *Race and the Education of Desire* (Chapel Hill: Duke University Press, 1997).
6   Ibid.
7   Ella Shohat and Robert Stam, *Unthinking Eurocentrism* (London: Routledge, 1994).
8   James Rawls, *Indians of California: The Changing Image* (Norman: University of Oklahoma, 1997).
9   Ibid.
10   Andre Lopez, *Pagans in Our Midst* (Mohawk Nation: Awkesasne Notes, n.d.).

11   Albert Cave, "Canaanites in a Promised Land," *American Indian Quarterly*, (Fall 1988); H.C. Porter, *The Inconstant Savage* (London: Gerald Duckworth & Co., 1979); Robert Warrior, "Canaanites, Cowboys, and Indians," in *Voices from the Margin*, ed. R.S. Sugirtharajah (Maryknoll: Orbis, 1991).

12   Robert Berkhofer, *The White Man's Indian* (New York: Vintage, 1978).

13   David Stannard, *American Holocaust* (Oxford: Oxford University Press, 1992).

14   David Wrone and Russell Nelson, eds., *Who's the Savage?* (Malabar: Robert Krieger Publishing, 1982).

15   Ibid.

16   Ibid.

17   Ibid.

18   Ibid.

19   Stannard, *American Holocaust.*

20   Wrone and Nelson, *Who's the Savage?*

21   Press conference, Chicago, Illinois, August 17, 1990.

22   Andrea Hermann and Maureen O'Donnell, "Indians Rap Thompson over Burial Site Display," *Chicago Sun Times*, August 17, 1990. As a result of the organizing efforts of Native people in Illinois, the site was eventually closed, but the remains were not reburied when the next governor took office.

23   Terry Pedwell, "Flaherty Slammed by Opposition over Native Health-Care Comments" (Canadian Press, January 21, 2002 ; available from http://www.bluecorncomics.com/stype215.htm.)

24   Aime Cesaire, *Discourse on Colonialism* (New York: Monthly Review Press, 1972).

25   Stoler, *Race and the Education of Desire.*

26   Ellen Bass and Laura Davis, *Courage to Heal* (Harper & Row: New York, 1988).

27   Celia Haig-Brown, *Resistance and Renewal* (Vancouver: Tilacrum, 1988).

28   Chrystos, *Fugitive Colors* (Vancouver: Press Gang, 1995).

29   Frantz Fanon, *Wretched of the Earth* (New York: Grove Press, 1963).

30   Michael Taussig, *Shamanism, Colonialism and the Wild Man* (Chicago: University of Chicago Press, 1991).

31   Native American Women's Health Education Resource Center, "Discrimination and the Double Whammy." (Lake Andes, South Dakota: 1990).

32   Sonia Shah, "Judge Rules Rape of Aboriginal Girl 'Traditional'" (Women's E-News, November 29, 2002; available from http://www.feminist.com/news/news126.html.)

33 Ibid.
34 Taussig, *Shamanism, Colonialism and the Wild Man*.
35 Fanon, *Wretched of the Earth*.
36 Tadiar, "Sexual Economies of the Asia-Pacific."
37 Stoler, *Race and the Education of Desire*.
38 Kirpatrick Sale, *The Conquest of Paradise* (New York: Plume, 1990).
39 Wrone and Nelson, *Who's the Savage?*
40 Ibid.
41 Bartolome de Las Casas, *Devastation of the Indies*, trans. Herma Briffault (Baltimore: John Hopkins University Press, 1992).
42 *Sand Creek Massacre: A Documentary History* (New York: Sol Lewis, 1973).
43 Angela Davis, *Women, Race and Class* (New York: Vintage, 1981).
44 Eugene Genovese, *Roll, Jordan, Roll* (New York: Vintage, 1976).
45 Clifton Johnson, ed., *God Struck Me Dead* (Cleveland: Pilgrim Press, 1969).
46 Herbert Gutman, *Black Family in Slavery and Freedom* (Vintage: New York, 1976).
47 Thomas Almaguer, *Racial Faultlines* (Berkeley: University of California, 1994).
48 Karen Warren, "A Feminist Philosophical Perspective on Ecofeminist Spiritualities," in *Ecofeminism and the Sacred*, ed. Carol Adams (New York: Continuum, 1993).
49 Stannard, *American Holocaust*.
50 Mary Daly, *Gyn/Ecology* (Boston: Beacon Press, 1978); Andrea Dworkin, *Woman Hating* (New York: E.P. Dutton, 1974); Anne Barstow, *Witchcraze* (New York: Dover, 1994); Barbara Ehrenreich and Deirdre English, *For Her Own Good* (Garden City: Anchor, 1979); Rosemary Radford Ruether, ed., *Religion and Sexism* (New York: Simon & Schuster, 1974); Rosemary Radford Ruether, *New Woman, New Earth* (Minneapolis: Seabury Press, 1975); Stannard, *American Holocaust*.
51 Matilda Joslyn Gage, *Women, Church and State* (Watertown, MA: Persephone Press, 1980).
52 Stannard, *American Holocaust*.
53 Ehrenreich and English, *For Her Own Good*.
54 Stannard, *American Holocaust*.
55 Wrone and Nelson, *Who's the Savage?*
56 Barry O'Connell, ed., *On Our Own Ground: The Complete Writings of William Apess, a Pequot* (Amherst: University of Massachusetts, 1992).
57 Shohat and Stam, *Unthinking Eurocentrism*.

58   M. Annette Jaimes and Theresa Halsey, "American Indian Women: At the Center of Indigenous Resistance in North America," in *State of Native America*, ed. M. Annette Jaimes (Boston: South End Press, 1992).

59   Paula Gunn Allen, *The Sacred Hoop* (Boston: Beacon, 1986).

60   Jaimes and Halsey, "American Indian Women"

61   Tom Holm, "Patriots and Pawns," in *State of Native American*, ed. M. Annette Jaimes (Boston: South End Press, 1992).

62   Jane Richardson, *Law and Status among the Kiowa Indians* (New York: JJ Augustin, 1940).

63   "Anishinabe Values/Social Law Regarding Wife Battering," *Indigenous Woman* 1, no. 3 (n.d.). See similar viewpoints in Charon Asetoyer, "Health and Reproductive Rights," in *Indigenous Women Address the World*, ed. Indigenous Women's Network (Austin: Indigenous Women's Network, 1995); Division of Indian Work Sexual Assault Project, "Sexual Assault Is Not an Indian Tradition," (Minneapolis: n.d.).

64   Mary Rowlandson, *A Narrative of the Captivity and Removes of Mrs. Mary Rowlandson* (Fairfield: Ye Talleon Press, 1974).

65   June Namias, *White Captives* (Chapel Hill: University of North Carolina Press, 1993). I am not arguing that the nonpatriarchal nature of Native societies is the only reason white women may have chosen to live with their captors, but that it is a possible explanation for why many chose to stay.

66   Lopez, *Pagans in Our Midst*.

67   Ibid.

68   It is difficult to ascertain the true nature of Indian captivity of white people based on these narratives because of their anti-Indian bias. For instance, *A Narrative of the Horrid Massacre by the Indians of the Wife and Children of the Christian Hermit* sets out to prove that Indians are so biologically cruel that there is nothing else for whites to do than exterminate them. However, even the narrator admits that Indians killed his family because he "destroyed their village." He further states that Natives "are kind and hospitable, but toward those who *intentionally* [italics mine] offend them, the western savage [sic] is implacable. *A Narrative of the Horrid Massacre by the Indians of the Wife and Children of the Christian Hermit* (St. Louis: Leander W. Whiteney and Co., 1833). June Namias suggests that captivity of white people became more brutal as the conquest drove Native people to the point of desperation. She also says that since captivity narratives by Jesuits seem to be the most graphic in nature, it is possible that they embellished their stories to enhance their status as martyrs and encourage greater funding for their missions. Namias, *White Captives*. Francis

Jennings argues also that there were some practices of torture among the Iroquois, though not other northeastern tribes, and that it became more pronounced as the conquest against them became more brutal. He states, however, that Native people never molested women or girls. Francis Jennings, *Invasion of the Americas* (New York: Norton, 1975). Richard Drinnon believes that most male captives were killed, except that some might have been adopted into the tribe to replace those that had been killed in battle. Women and children were not killed. Richard Drinnon, *Facing West* (New York: Schocken Books, 1980). All of these discussions are based on Native practices after colonization and the infusion of violence into their societies.

69   James Seaver, *Narrative of the Life of Mrs. Mary Jemison* (New York: Corinth Books, 1975).

70   Ibid.

71   Carol Adams, *Neither Man nor Beast* (New York: Continuum, 1994).

72   Andrea Dworkin, *Pornography* (New York: Periree, 1981).

73   Namias, *White Captives*.

74   Jane Caputi, *Age of Sex Crime* (Bowling Green, OH: Popular Press, 1987).

75   Allen, *The Sacred Hoop*.

76   Paula Gunn Allen, "Violence and the American Indian Woman," in *The Speaking Profits Us*, ed. Maryviolet Burns (Seattle: Center for the Prevention of Sexual and Domestic Violence, 1986).

77   Roy Harvey Pearce, *Savagism and Civilization* (Baltimore: John Hopkins Press, 1965).

78   Rawls, *Indians of California*.

79   Laura Flanders, "What Has George W. Ever Done for Women?" *The Guardian*, March 26, 2004.

80   Ellie Smeal, Fund For a Feminist Majority, 2001.

81   RAWA, "The U.S. Bares Its Fangs to Its Flunkeys," http://rawa.fancymarketing.net/attacke.htm, August 21, 1998.

82   E. Raymond Evans, "Fort Marr Blackhouse," *Journal of Cherokee Studies* 2, no. 2 (1977).

83   Homi Bhabha, "Of Mimicry and Men," in *Tensions of Empire*, ed. Frederick Cooper and Ann Laura Stoler (Berkeley: University of California Press, 1997); Edward Said, *Orientalism* (New York: Vintage, 1994).

84   Wrone and Nelson, *Who's the Savage?*

85   Mark Brunswick and Paul Klauda, "Possible Suspect in Serial Killings Jailed in New Mexico," *Minneapolis Star and Tribune*, May 28, 1987.

86   "Indian Being Tried for Rape with No Evidence," *Fargo Forum*, January 9, 1995.

87   Lawrence Greenfield and Steven Smith, "American Indians and Crime," (Washington, D.C.: Bureau of Justice Statistics: U.S. Department of Justice, 1999).

88   Davis, *Women, Race and Class.*

89   Paula Giddings, *Where and When I Enter* (New York: Bantam Books, 1984).

90   Dona Antonia, lecture, University of California-Davis, 1996.

91   Amnesty International, "Mexico: Under the Shadow of Impunity," March 9, 1999, http://web.amnesty.org/library/ index/eng AMR410021999?open&of=eng-2am

92   Catherine MacKinnon, "Postmodern Genocide," *Ms.*, July/August 1993.

93   Greenfield and Smith, *American Indians and Crime.* Native youth are also 49% more likely to be victimized by violent crime than the next highest ethnic group—African Americans. National Center for Victims of Crime, http://www.ncvc.org.

94   Promotional material from Public Relations: Mahoney/Wasserman & Associates, Los Angeles, CA, n.d.

95   Joe Brinkley, "CIA Reports Widespread Immigrant Sexual Slavery," *San Francisco Examiner*, April 2, 2000.

96   Neferti Tadiar, "Colonization and Violence Against Women of Color," lecture, The Color of Violence: Violence Against Women of Color Conference, University of California-Santa Cruz, April, 2000.

97   Ibid.

98   Anannya Bhattacharjee, In *Whose Safety? Women of Color and the Violence of Law Enforcement* (Philadelphia: American Friends Service Committee, 2001).

99   Bill Hewitt, "A Wave of Murders Terrorizes the Women of Ciudad Juarez," People, August 25, 2003; Evelyn Nieves, "To Work and Die in Juarez," *Mother Jones*, May/June, 2002.

100   Amnesty International, Mexico, "Intolerable Killings: Ten years of abductions and murders in Ciudad Juarez and Chihuahua," August 11, 2003.

101   Linda Diebel, "500 Missing: Aboriginal Canadians Take Fight for Justice for Invisible Victims to U.N.," *Toronto Star*, November 30, 2002.

102   This information was conveyed by Department of Justice representatives at the Strategic Planning Meeting on Crime and Justice Research in Indian Country (Portland, Oregon), October 14-15, 1998 and the Mending the Sacred Hoop Faculty Development Session (Memphis, Tennessee) May 21-23, 1998.

103   The Indian Civil Rights Act was passed ostensibly to protect the civil rights of Indian peoples, but the effect of this act was to limit tribal sov-

ereignty over tribal members if tribal acts infringed on the "civil rights" of its members, as understood by the U.S. government. Consequently, tribes are limited in the types of strategies and punishments they can use to address sexual violence to the types of strategies and punishments that are seen as acceptable by the U.S. government.

104 For history of Indian policy, see Sharon O'Brien, *American Indian Tribal Governments* (Norman: University of Oklahoma, 1989); Luana Ross, *Inventing the Savage: The Social Construction of Native American Criminality* (Austin: University of Texas Press, 1998); Carole Goldberg, *Planting Tail Feathers* (Los Angeles: American Indian Studies Center, UCLA, 1997). For more resources on current criminal justice policy, see the website of the Tribal Law and Policy Institute, Los Angeles, CA <www.tribal-institute.org.>

105 Sarah Deer, "Expanding the Network of Safety: Tribal Protection Orders and Victims of Sexual Assault," unpublished paper.

106 Ibid.

107 Ibid.

108 Stoler, *Race and the Education of Desire.*

Chapter 2: Boarding Schools and the Case for Reparations

1 David Wallace Adams, *Education for Extinction* (Topeka: University of Kansas Press, 1995).

2 The off-reservation schools are Wahpeton, Pierre, and Flandreau, South Dakota; Talequah and Anadarko, Oklahoma; Salem, Oregon; Riverside, California; and Santa Fe, New Mexico. See Gayle Raymer, "Indian Boarding Schools: Tools of Forced Assimilation, 1870–1934"; http://www.humboldt.edu/~go1/kellogg/boardingschools.html

3 Adams, *Education for Extinction.*

4 Ibid.

5 Richard Pratt, "The Advantages of Mingling Indians with Whites," in *Americanizing the American Indians: Writings by the "Friends of the Indian" 1880-1990*, ed. Francis Prucha (Cambridge: Harvard University Press, 1973).

6 Richard Trennart, "Educating Indian Girls at Nonreservation Boarding Schools, 1878-1920," in *The Way We Lived*, ed. Frederick Binder and David Reimers (Lexington, KY: DC Heath and Company, 1982).

7 K. Tsianina Lomawaima, *They Called it Prairie Light* (Lincoln: University of Nebraska Press, 1994).

8   Adams, *Education for Extinction.*

9   Wendy Holliday, "Hopi History: The Story of Alcatraz Prisoners," Hopi Cultural Preservation Office, 1998. http://www.nps.gov/ alcatraz/tours/hopi/hopi-h1.htm

10   Binder and Reimers, *The Way We Lived.*

11   "Hello New Federalism Goodbye BIA," *American Eagle,* no. 2 (1994). Incidentally, after the allegations of abuse became public, the BIA merely provided a counselor for the abused children, who then used his sessions with them to write a book.

12   Jeff Hinkle, "A Law's Hidden Failure," *American Indian Report* XIX, no. 1 (2003).

13   "Child Sexual Abuse in Federal Schools," *Ojibwe News,* January 17, 1990.

14   Hinkle, "A Law's Hidden Failure."

15   Ibid.

16   Adams, *Education for Extinction*; Suzan Harjo, "A Native Child Left Behind," *Indian Country Today,* July 2, 2004.

17   Kim Christensen and Kara Briggs, "Chemawa Warnings Date To '89," *The Oregonian,* February 20, 2004.

18   Matt Kelley, "The Hurt That Never Goes Away," *News from Indian Country,* May 1999.

19   Carol Adams, *Neither Man nor Beast* (New York: Continuum, 1994); Lomawaima, *They Called it Prairie Light;* Brenda Child, *Boarding School Seasons* (Lincoln: University of Nebraska Press, 1998); Devon Mihesuah, *Cultivating the Rosebuds* (Urbana: University of Illinois Press, 1993).

20   Royal Commission on Aboriginal Peoples, 1991 #1786; http://www.ainc-inac.gc.ca/ch/rcap/sg/sg31_e.html#104

21   Royal Commission on Aboriginal Peoples, 1991 #1786; http://www.ainc-inac.gc.ca/ch/rcap/sg/sg31_e.html#104

22   Truth Commission into Genocide in Canada, "Hidden from History: The Canadian Holocaust," (2001).

23   Suzanne Fournier, "Gatherers Mark School's Grim Litany of Death," *The Province,* June 4, 1996.

24   James Brooke, "Indian Lawsuits on School Abuse May Bankrupt Canada Churches," *New York Times,* November 2, 2000.

25   Tim Giago, "Catholic Church Can't Erase Sins of the Past," *Indian County Today,* December 15, 1994.

26   U.S. Senate Subcommittee on Indian Affairs of the Committee on Interior and Insular Affairs, "Indian Child Welfare Program," (Washington, D.C.: U.S. Senate, 1974).

27   Ibid.

28 Ibid.

29 Ibid.

30 Luana Ross, *Inventing the Savage: The Social Construction of Native American Criminality* (Austin: University of Texas Press, 1998).

31 Sephen Pevar, *The Rights of Indians and Tribes* (Carbonodale, IL: Southern Illinois University Press, 1992).

32 Lisa Demer, "Tribes Accuse Dfys Care," *Anchorage Daily News*, December 23 2002.

33 Celia Haig-Brown, *Resistance and Renewal* (Vancouver: Tilacrum, 1988).

34 Royal Commission on Aboriginal Peoples, 1991 #1786; http://www.ainc-inac.gc.ca/ch/rcap/sg/sg32_e.html#105

35 The "Bad Man" clause holds that if a "man" acting on behalf of the U.S. government harms Native peoples, and the injured parties complain to the U.S. with no redress, then they are entitled to redress.

36 Valerie Tallman, "Tribes Speak out on Toxic Assault," *Lakota Times*, December 18, 1991.

37 Sherry Wilson (Native activist), in discussion with the author, July 11, 2001.

38 Ward Churchill, *Struggle for the Land* (Monroe: Common Courage, 1993).

39 Doug McAdam, *Political Process and the Development of Black Insurgency, 1930-1970* (Chicago: University of Chicago Press, 1982).

40 Traci West, *Wounds of the Spirit* (New York: New York University Press, 1999).

41 Andrea Smith, *Sacred Sites, Sacred Rites* (New York: National Council of Churches, 1998); Jace Weaver, "Losing My Religion," in *Unforgotten Gods: Native American Religious Identity*, ed. Jace Weaver (Maryknoll, NY: Orbis, 1998).

42 Jonathan Edwards, *The Works of Jonathan Edwards*, vol. 1 (Peabody, MA: Hendrickson Publishers, 1998).

43 Ibid., vol. 2.

Chapter 3: Rape of the Land

1   Jane Caputi, *Gossips, Gorgons and Crones* (Santa Fe: Bear Publishing, 1993).
2   Francis Jennings, *Invasion of the Americas* (New York: Norton, 1975).
3   Ibid.
4   Ibid.
5   Francis Paul Prucha, ed., *Documents of United States Indian Policy*, 2nd ed. (Lincoln: University of Nebraska Press, 1990).
6   Ibid.
7   Ibid.
8   John Eidsmoe, *Columbus and Cortez: Conquerors for Christ* (Green Forest, AR: New Leaf Press, 1992).
9   Ibid.
10   Pat Robertson, *The Turning Tide* (Dallas: Word Books, 1993).
11   Commission for Racial Justice, United Church of Christ, *Toxic Wastes and Race* (New York: Public Data Access, 1987).
12   Cesar Chavez, "Farm Workers at Risk," in *Toxic Struggles*, ed. Richard Hofrichter, 163-170 (Philadelphia: New Society Publishers, 1993); Robert Wasserstrom and Richard Wiles, *Field Duty: U.S. Farmworkers and Pesticide Safety* (Washington, D.C.: World Resources Institute, 1988).
13   Winona LaDuke, "A Society Based on Conquest Cannot Be Sustained," in Hofrichter, *Toxic Struggles,* 98-106.
14   Ibid.
15   Valerie Tallman, "Tribes Speak Out on Toxic Assault," Lakota Times, December 18, 1991, and Shundahai Network, Nevada, "The Nevada Test Site History," http://www.shundahai.org/nevada_test_site_history.htm
16   Native Americans for a Clean Environment, "Radwaste Fertilizer," *Wise News*, February 8, 1991; available from http://www.antenna.nl/wise/346/3465.html.
17   Jessie DeerInWater, "The War against Nuclear Waste Disposal," *Sojourner,* June 1992, 15.
18   Tallman, "Tribes Speak Out."
19   Shundahai Network, "What Is Depleted Uranium," Nevada, http://www.shundahai.org/d_u.htm
20   Larry Johnson, "Iraqi Cancers, Birth Defects Blamed on U.S. Depleted Uranium," *Seattle Post-Intelligencer,* November 12, 2002.
21   Correspondence between Michael Matz, Alaska Coalition and Women of All Red Nations, December 3, 1991.

22   For fuller accounts of this struggle, see also Al Gedicks, *The New Resource Wars* (Boston: South End Press, 1993); Zoltan Grossman, "Unlikely Alliances: Treaty Conflicts and Environmental Cooperation between Native American and Rural White Communities," Ph.D. dissertation, (Madison: University of Wisconsin, 2002); Justine Smith, "Custer Rides Again—This Time on the Exxon Valdez," in *Defending Mother Earth*, ed. Jace Weaver, (Maryknoll, NY: Orbis, 1996); Rick Whaley and Walt Bressette, *Walleye Warriors* (Philadelphia: New Society Publishers, 1994).

23   Justine Smith, "Native Sovereignty and Social Justice: Moving toward an Inclusive Social Justice Framework," in *Dangerous Intersections: Feminist Perspectives on Population, Environment and Development*, ed. Jael Silliman and Ynestra King, 202-213 (Boston: South End Press, 1999).

24   Gedicks, *The New Resource Wars*; Grossman, "Unlikely Alliances: Treaty Conflicts and Environmental Cooperation Between Native American and Rural White Communities,"; Smith, "Custer Rides Again," in *Defending Mother Earth,* Weaver; Whaley and Bressette, *Walleye Warriors.*

25   Robert Crawford, "The Politics of Whales," *Dignity Report* 5, Fall (1998): 4-7.

26   The Deep Ecology Platform, according to the Foundation for Deep Ecology www.deepecology.org, is as follows:
      1) The well-being and flourishing of human and nonhuman life on Earth have value in themselves (synonyms: inherent worth; intrinsic value; inherent value). These values are independent of the usefulness of the nonhuman world for human purposes.
      2) Richness and diversity of life forms contribute to the realization of these values and are also values in themselves.
      3) Humans have no right to reduce this richness and diversity except to satisfy vital needs.
      4) Present human interference with the nonhuman world is excessive, and the situation is rapidly worsening.
      5) The flourishing of human life and cultures is compatible with a substantial decrease of the human population. The flourishing of nonhuman life requires such a decrease.
      6) Policies must therefore be changed. The changes in policies affect basic economic, technological structures. The resulting state of affairs will be deeply different from the present.
      7) The ideological change is mainly that of appreciating life quality (dwelling in situations of inherent worth) rather than adhering to an

increasingly higher standard of living. There will be a profound awareness of the difference between big and great.

27   Michael Zimmerman, "Deep Ecology and Ecofeminism," in *Reweaving the World*, ed. Irene Diamond and Gloria Feman Orenstein, 138-154 (San Francisco: Sierra Club, 1990).

28   Starhawk, "Feminist Earth-Based Spirituality and Ecofeminism," in *Healing the Wounds*, ed. Judith Plant, 174-185 (Philadelphia: New Society, 1989).

29   Foundation for Deep Ecology, "Deep Ecology Platform."

30   Marie Wilson, "Wings of the Eagle," in *Healing the Wounds*, ed. Judith Plant, 212-218 (Philadelphia: New Society, 1989).

31   Katsi Cook, lecture, Indigenous Women's Network conference, White Earth reservation, September 17, 1994.

32   National Wildlife Federation, *Dioxin and the Pulp and Paper Industry*, http://www.nwf.org/water/facts/cwapulp/html

33   National Wildlife Federation, *Toxic Chemicals Threaten Our Children and Our Future* , http:/www.nwf.org/water/facts/txefet.html

34   Ibid.

35   Ibid.

36   DES, or diethylstilbestrol, is a synthetic version of estrogen, a common female hormone. Beginning in the mid-to-late 1940s, DES was prescribed to pregnant women at high risk for miscarriage and other serious pregnancy complications. DES was later found to not only be ineffective at preventing miscarriages, but harmful to fetuses under five months old. In 1971, after an FDA recall, doctors stopped prescribing DES to pregnant women. In the U.S. an estimated 5 to 10 million persons were exposed to DES from 1938 to 1971, including pregnant women prescribed DES, and their children.

37   Patricia Whitten and Frederick Naftolin, "Xenoestrogens and Neurendocrine Development," in *Prenatal Exposure to Environmental Toxicants: Developmental Consequences*, ed. H.L. Nedleman and D. Bellinger (Baltimore: Johns Hopkins University Press, 1994).

38   Tanabe Kannan, "Critical Evaluation of Polichlorinated Biphenyl Toxicity in Terrestrial and Marine Mammals," *Archives of Environmental Contamination and Toxicology* 18 (1989): 850-857.

39   DeNeen Brown, "Toxic-Tainted Arctic Animals Passing Poisons on to Inuit," *Washington Post*, May 28, 2001.

40   Knight, "Pollution in Arctic."

41   Wilkiverse Universe, "Hanford Site," http://hanford-site.wikiverse.org/

42   Jennifer Hemmingsen, "Glowing Fish Put Tribes at Risk Along Columbia," *Indian Country Today*, March 23, 2002.

43   Caputi, *Gossips, Gorgons and Crones.*

44   Ibid.

45   Valerie Tallman, "Toxic Waste of Indian Lives," *Covert Action* 17, Spring (1992): 16-22.

46   Lakota Harden, "Black Hills Paha Sapa Report," (Rapid City, SD: 1980).

47   "Contaminated Milk in Mohawk Women," *Sojourner*, April 1994, 11.

48   Jane Dibblin, *Day of Two Suns* (London: Virago Press, 1988).

49   Ibid.

50   Environmental Health Perspectives 105 (1997), available from ehpnet1.niehs.nih.gov/docs/1997/105-9/focus-full.html

51   Lijon Eknilang, "Horror in the Marshall Islands," *Earth Island Journal*, Spring 1996, http://www.earthisland.org/eijournal/new_articles.cfm?articleID=391&journalID=59

52   Haunani Kay Trask, "Keynote Address," lecture, Color of Violence Conference, University of California-Santa Cruz, April 2000.

53   Mililani Trask, lecture, University of Michigan, March 2003.

54   Environmental Health Perspectives, September 1997, Volume 105, ehpnet1.niehs.nih.gov/docs/1997/105-9/focus-full.html.

55   Hofrichter, *Toxic Struggles.*

56   Population Institute, "Annual Report," 1991. See also Zero Population Growth, fundraising appeal, n.d.; Population Committee of Sierra Club, Los Angeles Chapter, and Population Institute fundraising appeal, which states that population growth is the root cause of poverty, hunger, and environmental destruction.

57   Sierra Club, "Frequently Asked Questions about Population," http://www.sierraclub.org/population/faq.asp

58   Maria Mies and Vandana Shiva, *Ecofeminism* (London: Zed, 1993.)

59   Ibid.

60   "Mythconceptions," *New Internationalist*, October (1987): 9.

61   Betsy Hartmann, *Reproductive Rights and Wrongs: The Global Politics of Population Control.* (Boston: South End Press, 1995).

62   Carol Adams, *Neither Man Nor Beast.* (New York: Continuum, 1994).

63   Ibid.

64   "Controversy Over Sterilization Pellet," *Political Environments* 1, Spring (1994): 9; Judy Norsigian, "Quinacrine Update," *Political Environments* 3, Spring (1996): 26-27.

65   Garrett Hardin, *New Ethics for Survival.* (New York: Viking Press, 1972).

66   Llecture, EcoVisions and Ecofeminist Conference, Alexandria, VA, March 19-20, 2004.

67   Patience Idemudia and Kole Shettima, "World Bank Takes Control of UNCED's Environmental Fund," in *Fifty Years is Enough*, ed. Kevin Danaher, 107-111 (Boston: South End Press, 1994.)

68   Russell Chandler, "Belief Behind Bars," Moody 89, July/August (1989): 28-30; Pratap Chatterjee, "World Bank Failures Soar to 37.5% of Completed Projects in 1991," in Danaher, *Fifty Years is Enough*, 137-138; Idemudia and Shettima, "World Bank Takes Control," in Danaher, *Fifty Years is Enough*, 107-111; Vandana Shiva, "International Institutions Practicing Environmental Double Standards," in Danaher, *Fifty Years is Enough*, 102-106.

69   Fatima Mello, speech, Ninth Annual Conference, "The Fight for Abortion Rights and Reproductive Freedom," Hampshire College, Amherst, MA, April 1, 1995.

70   Population-Environment Balance, "Why Excess Immigration Damages the Environment," *Carrying Capacity Network* 2 (1992): 31-32.

71   Population-Environment Balance, "U.S. Borders Open to Mass Immigration and Terrorism," Action Alert, August 2003, http://www.balance.org/alerts/index.html

72   Political Ecology Group, "A Defeat for the Greening of Hate," *Call to Action*, Summer (1988): 1-2.

73   "Anti-Immigration Group Loses Sierra Club Vote," *Associated Press*, April 21, 2004.

74   Political Ecology Group, educational materials, Political Ecology Group, San Francisco, California, n.d.

75   Virginia Abernathy, "Consumption, Population, and the Environment Conference," Boston Theological Institute, Weston, MA, Nov 9-11, 1995.

76   Carrying Capacity Network, *Carrying Capacity Network* Focus 2, no. 3 (1992).

77   Ibid.

78   Cathi Tactaquin, National Network for Immigrant and Refugee Rights, Oakland, California. Conversation with author.

79   Bill DeValle, speech, Environmental Law Conference, Eugene Oregon, February 1998.

80   Michael Novick, *White Lies, White Power* (Monroe: Common Courage Press, 1995).

81   Ibid.

Chapter 4: "Better Dead than Pregnant"

1   Ines Hernandez-Avila, "In Praise of Insubordination, or What Makes a Good Woman Go Bad?" in *Transforming a Rape Culture*, ed. Emilie Buchwald, Pamela R. Fletcher, and Martha Roth (Minneapolis: Milkweed, 1993), 375-92.

2   David Stannard, *American Holocaust* (Oxford: Oxford University Press, 1992).

3   Ibid., 131.

4   Paul Wagman, "U.S. Goal: Sterilizations of Millions of World's Women," *St. Louis Post-Dispatch*, April 22, 1977.

5   Henry Kissinger, "National Security Study Memorandum 2000," (Washington, D.C.: National Security Council, 1974).

6   Bruce Johansen, "Reprise/Forced Sterilizations: Native Americans" and the "Last Gasp of Eugenics," *Native Americas* 15, Winter (1998): 44-47.

7   "Survey Finds 7 in 10 Hospitals Violate DHEW Guidelines on Informed Consent for Sterilization," *Family Planning Perspectives* 11, no. 6 (November/December, 1979): 366.

8   Johansen, "Reprise/Forced Sterilizations," 44-47.

9   Gayle Mark Jarvis, "The Theft of Life," *WARN Report*, n.d., 13-16.

10 General Accounting Office, "Investigation of Allegations Concerning Indian Health Services B-164031(5); HRD-77-3," (Washington, D.C.: General Accounting Office, 1976)..

11 Ibid.

12 "Oklahoma: Sterilization of Women Charged to I.H.S.," 11-12.

13 Jarvis, "Theft of Life," 13-16.

14 Dorothy Roberts, *Killing the Black Body* (New York: Pantheon Books, 1997).

15 Johansen, "Reprise/Forced Sterilizations," 44-47.

16 Pat Bellanger, "Native American Women, Forced Sterilization, and the Family," in *Every Woman Has a Story*, ed. Gayla Wadnizak Ellis, 30-35 (Minneapolis: Midwest Villages and Voices, 1982).

17 Charles Warren et al., "Assessing the Reproductive Behavior of On- and Off-Reservation American Indian Females: Characteristics of Two Groups in Montana," *Social Biology* 37, Spring/Summer (1990): 69-83.

18 Helena Temkin-Greener et al., "Surgical Fertility Regulation among Women on the Navajo Indian Reservation, 1972-1978," *American Journal of Public Health* 71, no. 4 (1981): 403-407.

19 Warren et al., "Assessing Reproductive Behavior," 69-83.

20   Jarvis, "Theft of Life," 13-16.

21   Ibid.

22   Johansen, "Reprise/Forced Sterilizations," 44-47.

23   Ibid.

24   General Accounting Office, "Investigation of Allegations."

25   Ibid.

26   Ibid.

27   Ibid.

28   Ibid.

29   Ibid.

30   "Sterilization and Abortions," *Federal Register*, 42 CFR, Parts 50 and 441, November 8, 1978.

31   Lin Krust and Charon Assetoyer, *A Study of the Use of Depo-Provera and Norplant by the Indian Health Services* (Lake Andes, South Dakota: Native American Women's Health Education Resource Center, 1993)

32   Ibid.

33   Owain Johnson, "Peru Apologizes for Sterilizing Indians," *United Press International*, July 24, 2002.

34   Ibid.

35   Luis Sinco, "Sterilization Plan Fuels Controversy," *Detroit News*, April 17, 1998; available from http://www.detroitnews.com/1998/nation/9804/17/04170085.htm>.

36   Theryn Kigvamasud'Vashi, "Fact Sheet on Positive Prevention/Crack (Children Requiring a Caring Kommunity)," (Seattle: Communities Against Rape and Abuse, 2001).

37   Ibid.

38   Karen Garloch, "Addicts Get Cash for Birth Control," *Charlotte Observer*, July 22, 2003.

39   Roberts, *Killing the Black Body*.

40   KigvamasudVashi, "Fact Sheet on Positive Prevention."

41   Joelle Brouner, "From One Damaged Baby to Another: Why People with Disabilities Should Oppose Crack and the Effort to Positively Prevent You and Me" (Seattle: Communities Against Rape and Abuse, 2001).

42   Roberts, *Killing the Black Body*.

43   Ibid.

44   Elizabeth Cook-Lynn, *Why I Can't Read Wallace Stegner and Other Essays* (Madison: University of Wisconsin Press, 1998).

45   Michael Dorris, *The Broken Cord* (New York: Harper & Row, 1989).

46   Cook-Lynn, *Why I Can't Read Wallace Stegner*.

47   Roberts, *Killing the Black Body*.

48   Gretchen Long, "Norplant: A Victory, Not a Panacea for Poverty," *The National Lawyers Guild Practitioner* 50, no. 1 (n.d.).

49   Debra Hanania-Freeman, "Norplant: Freedom of Choice or a Plan for Genocide?" *EIR*, May 14, 1993, 18-23.

50   Ibid.

51   For example, the Dalkon Shield was approved for use by the FDA, and was later implicated in the deaths and sterility of several women. Dowie and Johnston describe the manufacturer's suppression of data that indicated its health hazards in order to assure its FDA approval. Mark Dowie and Tracy Johnston, "A Case of Corporate Malpractice and the Dalkon Shield," in *Seizing Our Bodies*, ed. Claudia Dreifus, 105-120 (Toronto: Vintage Press, 1977).

52   Doris Haire, "How the F.D.A. Determines the 'Safety' of Drugs–Just How Safe Is 'Safe'?" (Washington, D.C.: National Women's Health Network, 1982).

53   Mike Masterson and Patricia Gutherie, "Taking the Shot," *Arizona Republic* ,1986.

54   Krust and Assetoyer, "Study of Use of Depo-Provera."

55   Gena Corea, "Testimony: Board of Public Inquiry on Depo-Provera," 1993.

56   Mike Masterson and Patricia Gutherie, "Taking the Shot," *Arizona Republic* ,1986.

57   Ibid.

58   Krust and Assetoyer, "Study of Use of Depo-Provera.".

59   Stephen Minkin, "Depo-Provera: A Critical Analysis," (San Francisco: Institute for Food and Development, n.d.).

60   Solomon Sobel, "Testimony Before Public Board of Inquiry Re: Depo-Provera," Department of Health and Human Services; Food and Drug Administration, Docket No. 78n (1982).

61   Karen Branan and Bill Turnley, *Ultimate Test Animal* (1984), documentary film.

62   Ibid.

63   Krust and Assetoyer, "Study of Use of Depo-Provera."

64   Corea, "Testimony."

65   Sobel, "Testimony."

66   Masterson and Guthrie, "Taking the Shot."

67   Feminist Women's Health Centers, "Depo-Provera (the Shot)," (1997), <http://www.fwhc.org/bcdepo.htm>

68   Mildred Hanson, "Injectable Contraceptive Arouses Controversy. Yes, Depo-Provera at Last!" *WomanWise*, Fall (1993): 6-10.

69   Sharon Todd, "New Reproductive Technologies: Norplant, Depo-Provera and RU-486," *Womanist Health Newsletter*, n.d.

70   Masterson and Gutherie, "Taking the Shot."

71   Ibid.

72   Ibid.

73   Ibid.

74   Ibid.

75   Ibid.

76   Hanania-Freeman, "Norplant," 18-23.

77   Deborah Cadbury, *Human Laboratory* (London: BBC, 1995), documentary film; Sharon Cohen, "Norplant Lawsuits Flourish Along with Women's Reports of Problems," *Associated Press*, http://www.africa 2000.com/SNDX/norplant.htm; Hanania-Freeman, "Norplant," 18-23.

78   Masterson and Gutherie, "Taking the Shot."

79   Ibid.

80   Ibid.

81   Hanania-Freeman, "Norplant," 18-23.

82   Roberts, *Killing the Black Body*.

83   Hanania-Freeman, "Norplant," 18-23; Sharon Todd, *Womanist Health Newsletter* (Chicago Women's Health Education Project, 1993).

84   Krust and Assetoyer, "Study of Use of Depo-Provera."

85   Joseph, "India's Population 'Bomb',"12-15; Mehta, "Science and Ethics," 26-28.

86   Krust and Assetoyer, "Study of Use of Depo-Provera."

87   Branan and Turnley, *Ultimate Test Animal*.

88   Ibid.

89   Petition can be found on the web at http://www.wanaral.org/s01 takeaction/200307101.shtml

90   Kari Schinder, Anna Jackson, and Charon Asetoyer, "Indigenous Women's Reproductive Rights," (Lake Andes, South Dakota: Native American Women's Reproductive Rights, 2002).

91   State Congress of North Carolina, "House Bill 1430, Norplant Requirement/Funds." General Assembly of North Carolina (1993).

92   Mary Williams Walsh, "Abortion Horror Stories Spur Inquiry: Questions Raised after Women Allege Hospital Denied Them Anesthesia," *Los Angeles Times*, April 3, 1992, A5.

93   Ibid.

94   Ibid.

95   Ibid.

96   Justine Smith, "Native Sovereignty and Social Justice: Moving Toward an Inclusive Social Justice Framework," in *Dangerous Intersections: Feminist Perspectives on Population, Environment, and Development,*

ed. Jael Silliman and Ynestra King, 202-213 (Boston: South End Press, 1999).

97   Rosalind Patchesky, *Abortion and Woman's Choice*, rev. ed. (Boston: Northeastern University Press, 1990); Smith, "Native Sovereignty"; Rickie Solinger, *Beggars and Choosers* (New York: Hill and Wang, 2001).

98   Solinger, *Beggars and Choosers*.

99   Ibid.

100   Martha Saxton, "Disability Rights," in *The Abortion Wars*, ed. Rickie Solinger, 374-393 (Berkeley: University of California Press, 1998). Ibid.

101   Rashmi Luthra, "Toward a Reconceptualization of 'Choice': Challenges at the Margins," *Feminist Issues* 13, Spring (1993): 41-54.

102   In 1994, the National Abortion and Reproductive Rights Action League (NARAL) held a strategy session for its state chapters, which I attended. Michelman and her associates claimed that this name change was reflective of NARAL's interest in expanding its agenda to new communities, and informed consent around contraceptives would be included in this expanded agenda. I asked how much of NARAL's budget was going to be allocated to this new agenda. Their reply: none. They were going to issue a report on these new issues, but they were going to work only on the issues NARAL had traditionally worked on.

103   Betsy Hartmann, *Reproductive Rights and Wrongs: The Global Politics of Population Control* (Boston: South End Press, 1995).

104   Gloria Feldt, *The War on Choice* (New York: Bantam Books, 2004).

105   Jennifer Nelson, *Women of Color and the Reproductive Rights Movement* (New York: New York University Press, 2003); Patchesky, *Abortion and Woman's Choice*.

106   Committee on Women, Population and the Environment, internal correspondence, 1999.

107   Lee Rainwater, *And the Poor Get Children* (Chicago: Quadrangle Books, 1960).

108   Ibid.

109   Hartmann, *Reproductive Rights and Wrongs:*.

110   Cadbury, *Human Laboratory*.

111   Hartmann, *Reproductive Rights and Wrongs*.

112   Feldt, *The War on Choice*.

113   Andrea Smith, "Bible, Gender and Nationalism in American Indian and Christian Right Activism," PhD dissertation (Santa Cruz: University of California-Santa Cruz, 2002).

114 Beth Richie, "Plenary Presentation," paper presented at the The Color of Violence: Violence Against Women of Color, University of California-Santa Cruz, 2000.

115 Hartmann, *Reproductive Rights and Wrongs.*

116 Sheryl Blunt, "Saving Black Babies," *Christianity Today* 47, (February 2003).

117 Ibid.

118 Jael Silliman et al., *Undivided Rights* (Boston: South End Press, 2005).

119 Papers surveyed which focused solely on abortion rights include the following: Robin Toner, "Abortion Rights Marches Vow to Fight Another Bush Term," *New York Times*, April 26, 2004, A1; "Abortion-rights Marchers Crowd D.C.," *Connecticut Post*, April 26, 2004; Timothy Phelps, "Demonstration in D.C.," *New York Newsday*, April 26, 2004, A05; Renee Gadoua, "A Woman Should Decide," *Syracuse Post-Standard*, April 26, 2004, B1; Eman Varoqua, "N.J. Supporters Form Large Column for Rights," *The Record*, April 26, 2004, A01; Gail Gibson, "Thousands Rally for Abortion Rights," *Baltimore Sun*, April 26, 2004, 1A; Elizabeth Wolfe, "Rights March Packs Mall," *The [Memphis] Commercial Appeal*, April 26, 2004, A4; Tammie Smith, "Marchers Call for 'A Choice' About Reproductive Rights," *Richmond Times Dispatch*, April 26, 2004, A1; "Marchers Say Bush Policies Harm Women," *Marin Independent Journal*, April 26, 2004, Nation/World Section; Melissa Segars, "Rally for Women's Rights," *[Madison] Capital Times*, April 26, 2004, 1A; Kathy Stephenson, "Utahns Take Part in D.C. and at Home," *Salt Lake Tribune*, April 26, 2004, A6; Bob Dart, "Abortion-Rights Backers March," *Dayton Daily News*, April 26, 2004, A1; Erin Madigan, "Hundreds of Thousands March for Abortion Rights," *Milwaukee Journal Sentinel*, April 26, 2004, 3A; Tom Diemer, "Thousands Rally for Choice: 500,000 to 800,000 March in D.C. in Support of Abortion Rights," *Cleveland Plain Dealer*, April 26, 2004, A1; Lawrence O'Rourke, "Thousands Rally for Abortion Rights," *[Minneapolis] Star Tribune*, April 26, 2004, 1A; Joseph Ryan, "Abortion Rights Supporters Jump in to Rejuvenate Cause," *Chicago Daily Herald*, April 26, 2004, 15; Annie Sweeney, "Chicagoans Head to D.C. for Pro-Choice March," *Chicago Sun-Times*, April 25, 2004, 18; Jonathan Riskind, "Supporters of Abortion Rights Seek Forefront," *Columbus Dispatch*, April 25, 2004, 1A; Carla Marinucci, "Hundreds of Thousands in D.C. Pledge to Take Fight to Polls," *San Francisco Chronicle*, April 26, 2004, A1; and Kelli Wynn, "Hundreds Go to D.C. for March Today," *Dayton Daily News*, April 25, 2004, B1.

120 Barbara Major, "Keynote Address," National Women's Studies Association National Conference, New Orleans, June 2003.

121   These representatives were unaware that most Native women do not have ready access to abortion service anyway because the Hyde Amendment prohibits federal funding for abortion services, and Indian Health Services (where most Native women receive health care) is a federal agency.

122   Native American Women's Health Education Resource Center, *Indigenous Women's Reproductive Rights and Pro-Choice Page*, http://www.nativeshop.org/pro-choice.html.

123   Herbert Aptheker, *Racism, Imperialism, and Peace* (Minneapolis: MEP Press, n.d.).

124   Patricia Hill Collins, *Black Feminist Thought* (London: Routledge, 1991).

125   Testimony of Scott Matheson to the U.S. Senate, hearings on Indian sacred sites, 1989.

Chapter 5: *"Natural Laboratories"*

1   The source of information for this vaccination controversy and any other citations about this program can be found in Traditional Dena'ina, "Summary Packet on Hepatitis B Vaccinations," (Sterling, AK: 1992). They can be reached at: Traditional Dena'ina Health Committee, P.O. Box 143, Sterling, AK 99672.

2   Brian McMahon et al., "A Comprehensive Programme to Reduce the Incidence of Hepatitis B Virus Infection and Its Sequelae in Alaskan Natives," *The Lancet* (November 14, 1987): 1134-1135.

3   Alan Phillips, "Vaccination Myths," http://www.relfe.com/vaccine.html

4   Charles Norman, "Hepatitis B Vaccine—Dangerous or Safe?" *The Voice* 6 (December 3, 1998): 1, 4..

5   Brian James McMahon, M.D. Department of Health and Human Services, Alaska Native Medical Center. Letter to the author, November 18, 1988.

6   Robert Redfield et al., "Disseminated Vaccinia in a Military Recruit with Human Immunodeficiency Virus (HIV) Disease," *Medical Intelligence* 316, no. 11 (1987): 673.

7   See http://www.naturalparenting.com/vaccines.html. Their information is compiled from *Mothering* magazine, #84..

8   Law Firm of Allen Rothenberg, http://www.injurylawyer.com/envMercury.htm

9   Erich Bloch, "United States Arctic Research Plan" (Washington D.C.: Interagency Arctic Research Policy Committee, July 1987): 220.

10 Interagency Arctic Research Policy Committee, 1997, #1428 as reported by Mills and Atcheson. Also, the National Research Council says that "the Arctic is an excellent natural laboratory for some types of social science research because the relevant variables can be isolated more easily than in more complex societies." National Research Council, *Arctic Contributions to Social Science and Policy Research* (Washington, DC: National Academy Press, 1993).

11 Kenaitze Indian Tribe Newsletter, March 1991, which promoted the immunization program.

12 CDC Protocol #1016, "Evaluation of the Safety, Immunogenicity, and Protective Efficacy of an Inactivated Hepatitis A Vaccine in Healthy Children," December 4, 1990.

13 Reported at the People of Color Environmental Justice Summit. See also Shelly Davis, "Parents Balk at Secret Immunization Programs for Hepatitis," *News from Indian Country*, Mid-September (1993).

14 J.H. Jones, *Bad Blood: The Tuskegee Syphilis Experiment* (New York: Free Press, 1993).

15 J.C. Murdoch, Professor of General Practice, Rural Clinical School, Letter, September 30, 1988.

16 Traditional Dena'ina, "Summary Packet on Hepatitis B Vaccinations, n.d.

17 General Accounting Office, "Investigation of Allegations Concerning Indian Health Services B-164031(5); HRD-77-3," (Washington, D.C.: General Accounting Office, 1976).

18 Ibid.

19 Ibid.

20 Ibid.

21 Ibid.

22 Ibid.

23 Luana Ross, *Inventing the Savage: The Social Construction of Native American Criminality* (Austin: University of Texas Press, 1998).

24 Stormy Ogden, speech, Color of Violence conference, University of California-Santa Cruz, April 2000.

25 Matt Kelley, "Lost Tribes: The U.S. Government Promised to Provide Indians with HealthCare, but Underfunding Is Jeopardizing the System," *Associated Press*, January 27, 2003.

26 Walking Shield American Indian Society, http://www.walking shield.org/The_Need.htm. Also, California Rural Indian Health Board, "Fact Sheet: The Appalling Health Status of American Indians," September 2004. http://www.crihb.org/campaign/FactSheet.pdf

27 Mary Ann Mills, speech, WARN Forum, Chicago, IL, September 1993.

28   *Physicians' Desk Reference* (PDR), (Oradell, NJ: Medical Economics, 1991) 1292-1293.

29   James Rawls, *Indians of California: The Changing Image* (Norman: University of Oklahoma, 1997).

Chapter 6: Spiritual Appropriation as Sexual Violence

1   Mary Douglas, *Purity and Danger* (London: Routledge, 1995), 41.

2   Philip Deloria, *Playing Indian* (New Haven: Yale University Press, 1998).

3   Dennis Tedlock and Barbara Tedlock, *Teachings from the American Earth — Indian Religion and Philosophy*. (New York: Liveright, 1975): xi, xiii.

4   Winona LaDuke, "A Society Based on Conquest Cannot Be Sustained," in *Toxic Struggles*, ed. Richard Hofrichter (Philadelphia: New Society Publishers, 1993).

5   For fuller discussion on this issue, see Vine Deloria, *God Is Red* (Golden, CO: North American Press, 1992); Jace Weaver, *That the People Might Live* (Oxford: Oxford University Press, 1997).

6   Vine Deloria, "A Native American Perspective on Liberation," *Occasional Bulletin of Missionary Research* (July 1977), 16..

7   Sharon O'Brien, "A Legal Analysis of the American Indian Religious Freedom Act," in *Handbook of American Indian Religious Freedom*, ed. Christopher Vecsey, (New York: Crossroad, 1991), 27-43.

8   Laurie Anne Whitt, "Cultural Imperialism and the Marketing of Native America," in *Natives and Academics: Researching and Writing About American Indians*, ed. Devon Mihesuah (Lincoln: University of Nebraska Press, 1998). See also Tom Greaves, ed., *Intellectual Property Rights for Indigenous Peoples: A Sourcebook* (Oklahoma City: Society for Applied Anthropology, 1994).

9   Rayna Green, "The Tribe Called Wannabee," *Folklore* 99 (1988): 30–35.

10   Haunani-Kay Trask, *From a Native Daughter: Colonialism and Sovereignty in Hawai'i* (Monroe: Common Courage Press, 1993), 185–94.

11   Ibid., 191.

12   Justine Smith, conversation with author, February 17, 1994.

13   Will Roscoe, *The Zuni Man-Woman* (Albuquerque: University of New Mexico Press, 1991), 187

14   Ibid., 188.

15   Andy Rooney, "Indians Have Worse Problems," *Chicago Tribune*, March 4, 1992.

16   Jim Lockhart, "AIM Protests Film's Spiritual Misrepresentation," *News from Indian Country,* late September (1994): 10.

17   Green, "The Tribe Called Wannabee," 30-55.

18   Annie Sprinkle, "How to Have Energy Orgasms," http://www.heck.com/annie, n.d.; The Lineage of the Twisted Hairs and the Sweet Medicine SunDance Path, http://www.dtmms.org, n.d.

19   Golden Wind Dreamers Lodge, "Spiritual Sexuality," (Phoenix: n.d.).

20   L.A. Justice, *Indian Love Signs* (Boca Raton: Globe Communications, 1999).

21   Ibid, 62.

22   Ibid, 33.

23   "Shaman Sentenced for Sex Abuse," *News from Indian Country,* Mid-June 1996.

24   David Melmer, "Sexual Assault," *Indian Country Today,* April 30-May 7, 1996.

25   Todd Cooper, "Man Tells of Herek's Betryal of Trust," *Omaha World Herald,* June 8, 2003.

26   Brian Crescente, "Suspect May Have Approached More Kids," *Rocky Mountain News,* May 14, 2002.

27   Walt Wiley, "Two Die in Solstice Sweat Lodge Ceremony," *Sacramento Bee,* June 22, 2002.

28   Winona (Stevenson) Wheeler, "every word is a bundle: Cree Intellec-

29   tual Traditions and History," unpublished paper, 1998.

Chapter 7: Anticolonial Responses to Gender Violence

1   Ward Churchill, *Struggle for the Land* (Monroe: Common Courage, 1993).

2   Callie Rennison, "Violent Victimization and Race, 1993-1998," (Washington, D.C.: Bureau of Justice Statistics, 2001).

3   Lucy Eldersveld Murphy, "Autonomy and the Economic Roles of Indian Women of the Fox-Wisconsin Riverway Region, 1763-1832," in *Negotiators of Change: Historical Perspectives on Native American Women,* ed. Nancy Shoemaker, 72-89 (New York: Routledge Press, 1995); Theda Purdue, "Women, Men and American Indian Policy: The Cherokee Response to 'Civilization'," in Shoemaker, *Negotiators of Change.*

4   Paula Gunn Allen, *The Sacred Hoop* (Boston: Beacon, 1986).

5   Lee Maracle, *I Am Woman* (North Vancouver: Write-On Press Publishers, 1988).

6   Troy Armstrong, Michael Guilfoyle, and Ada Pecos Melton, "Native American Delinquency: An Overview of Prevalence, Causes and Correlates," in *Native Americans, Crime, and Justice*, ed. Marianne Nielsen and Robert Silverman, 46-53 (Boulder: WestView Press, 1996).

7   Rupert Ross, *Return to the Teachings* (London: Penguin, 1997); James Zion and Elsie B. Zion, "'Hazho's Sokee'—Stay Together Nicely: Domestic Violence under Navajo Common Law," in Nielsen and Silverman, *Native Americans*, 96-113.

8   Ross, *Return to Teachings*.

9   Elizabeth Barker, "The Paradox of Punishment," in *Abolitionism: Towards a Non-Repressive Approach to Crime*, ed. Herman Bianchi and Rene van Swaaningen, 90-95 (Amsterdam: Free University Press, 1985).

10 Ross, *Return to Teachings*.

11 Zion and Zion, "Hazho's Sokee."

12 Rupert Ross, "Leaving Our White Eyes Behind: The Sentencing of Native Accused," in Nielson and Silverman, *Native Americans*, 152-169.

13 This information was conveyed by U.S. Department of Justice representatives at the Strategic Planning Meeting on Crime and Justice Research in Indian Country (Portland, OR), October 14-15, 1998, and the Mending the Sacred Hoop Faculty Development Session (Memphis, TN) May 21-23, 1998.

14 Luana Ross, "Native Women in Prison," lecture given at the University of California, Berkeley, 1998.

15 Meredith Cohn, "Indian Reservation Officials Testify at House Hearing," *States News Service*, March 18, 1994.

16 "Reservation Cops All Placed On Probation," *Associated Press*, December 6, 2002.

17 Elliott Currie, *Crime and Punishment in America* (New York: Metropolitan Books, 1998); Steven Donziger, *The Real War on Crime* (New York: HarperCollins, 1996); Samuel Walker, *Sense and Nonsense About Crime* (Belmont, WA: Wadsworth Publishing Company, 1998)

18 Walker, *Sense and Nonsense*.

19 Steve Box and Chris Hale, "Economic Crisis and the Rising Prisoner Population in England and Wales," *Crime and Social Justice* 17 (1982): 20-35; Mark Colvin, "Controlling the Surplus Population: The Latent Functions of Imprisonment and Welfare in Late U.S. Capitalism," in *The Political Economy of Crime*, ed. B.D. MacLean (Scarborough:

Prentice-Hall, 1986); Ivan Jankovic, "Labour Market and Imprisonment," *Crime and Social Justice* 8 (1977): 17-31.

20 Walker, *Sense and Nonsense.*

21 Currie, *Crime and Punishment.*

22 "Indians Meet with Minneapolis Police and Mayor after Filing Lawsuit," *Star Tribune*, February 26, 2003.

23 "Man Sentenced for Rape of Woman and Her Daughter," *Associated Press*, January 29, 2003.

24 Chris Graves and Howie Padilla, "Olson to Investigate Indians' Claim of Brutality," *Star Tribune*, January 30, 2003, 1A.

25 Kevin Rollanson, "Natives Accuse Force of Racism," Assembly of Manitoba Chiefs, November 2002; available from http://www.manitobachiefs.com/news/2002/nbnov02/11120203.html

26 Martin Kuz, "Officer James Toomey Didn't Waste Any Bullets When He Killed Bug Finley: The Question, Was It Just?" *Plains Dealer*, December 25, 2002.

27 "Complaint Filed Against Police Chief," *Associated Press*, October 26, 2000.

28 "Aboriginal Group Says Calls Flooding Into Police Abuse Hotline," *Canadian Press Newswire*, September 20, 2000; "Aboriginal-Police Tension Festers, Families Say," *Star Phoenix*, December 26, 2002, A12.

29 Lee Williams, "He Grabbed Me around Neck," *Argus Leader*, December 15, 2000.

30 "St. Paul Will Pay $92,500 to Settle Police Brutality Lawsuit," *Associated Press*, June 17, 1999.

31 CBC News, "Connie Jacobs Inquiry," *CBC News Online*, July 2, 2004, available at http://www.cbc.ca/news/background/aboriginals/jacobs.html.

32 Tatsha Robertson, "Parade Takes Step toward Healing," *Boston Globe*, November 21, 1999, B7.

33 Terry Woster, "State-Tribal Panel to Study Jails," *Argus Leader*, August 1, 2002.

34 indanz.com, "Behind Bars: Native Incarceration Rates Increase," *indianz.com*, July 13, 2001, available at http://www.indianz.com/News/show.asp?ID=law/7132001-1.

35 Earl Devaney, "Statement of Earl E. Devaney, Inspector General, Department of Interior," in *Indian Tribal Detention Facilities* (Capital Hill Hearing Testimony: Senate Indian Affairs, 2004).

36 Beth Richie, Plenary Address, Color of Violence: Violence Against Women of Color conference, Santa Cruz, CA, April 2000.

37 Emi Koyama, *"Disloyal to Feminism,"* paper, 2002.

38 Isabel Gonzalez, Sista II Sista Activist, statements made at Ford Foundation meeting on Domestic Violence, Clinton, TN, March 2003.

39 Jael Silliman, Ford Foundation officer, statements made at Ford Foundation meeting on domestic violence, Clinton, TN, March 2003.

40 "Now You See it, Now You Don't: The State of the Battered Women's Movement," *off our backs* 31 (2001): 10; Susan Schecter, *Women and Male Violence: The Visions and Struggles of the Battered Women's Movement* (Boston: South End Press, 1982).

41 For a history and critique of this position, see Schneider, 2000.

42 Marc Mauer, *Race to Incarcerate* (New York: New Press/WW Norton, 1999).

43 Donziger, *The Real War.*

44 Prison Activist Resource Center, available from http://www.prisonactivist.org.

45 Ibid.

46 Ibid.

47 Ibid.

48 Ibid.

49 Endnote Text

50 Ibid.

51 Silja J.A. Talvi, "Indian Prisoners in Washington State Fight Seizure of Tribal Trust Fund Distribution," *Indian Country Today*, July 24, 2002.

52 The sources for the information in examples 1, 2, and 3 come from my experiences as a rape crisis counselor or from stories I have heard from other antiviolence activists.

53 Turtle Island Native Network, 2003 available from http://www.turtleisland.org/news/news-women.htm.

54 Fox Butterfield, "Study Shows a Racial Divide in Domestic Violence Cases," *New York Times*, May 18, 2000, A16.

55 Beth Richie, *Compelled to Crime: The Gender Entrapment of Black Battered Women* (New York: Routledge, 1996); Luana Ross, *Inventing the Savage: The Social Construction of Native American Criminality* (Austin: University of Texas Press, 1998).

56 Nancy Jurik and Russ Winn, "Gender and Homicide: A Comparison of Men and Women Who Kill," *Violence and Victims* 5, no. 4 (1990): 236.

57 Ross, *Inventing the Savage.*

58 Julie Ostrowski, "Race Versus Gender in the Court Room," *Africana.com*, May 4, 2004, available at http://www.africana.com/articles/daily/bw20040504domestic.asp.

59 INCITE! Women of Color Against Violence, http://www.incite-national.org.

60   Heather Strang and John Braithwaite, eds., *Restorative Justice and Family Violence* (Cambridge: Cambridge University Press, 2002).

61   Stanley Cohen, "Community Control: To Demystify or to Reaffirm?" in Bianchi and van Swaaningen, *Abolitionism*, 127-132.

62   Michel Foucault, *Discipline and Punish* (New York: Vintage Books, 1977); Edgardo Rotman, "The Failure of Reform," in *The Oxford*

Chapter 8: The War Against Native Sovereignty

1   Sue-Ellen Jacobs, Wesley Thomas, and Sabine Lang, eds., *Two-Spirit People* (Urbana: University of Illinois Press, 1999); Paula Gunn Allen, *The Sacred Hoop* (Boston: Beacon, 1986). I do not mean that Native concepts of gender and sexuality correspond with contemporary Western concepts of "gay," "lesbian," or "queer;" Allen's book sometimes gives the misleading impression that they do. I also do not mean to suggest that Native communities today have not internalized homophobia, or should be seen as utopic havens for those who identify as LGBT in mainstream society. Note the recent Cherokee Nation ban on same-sex marriages: Chad Previch, "Cherokee Council Bans Gay Unions," *The Oklahoman*, June 15, 2004.

2   Author correspndence.

3   Guadalupe Castillo, "Border Enforcement Sends Migrants to Their Death," *NNIRR News*, Spring/Summer (2003): 8-9.

4   Bill Van Auken, "Stop the Persecution of Immigrant Workers," *World Socialist Website*, September 11, 2004.

5   Richard Jerome and Ron Arias, "The Shadows Know," *People*, October 21, 2002, 99-103.

6   David Frum, *The Right Man* (New York: Random House, 2003).

7   Marie Wadden, *Nitassinan* (Vancouver: Douglas & McIntyre, 1996).

8   Ibid.

9   "Rash of Wife Killings at Fort Bragg Leaves the Base Wondering Why," *New York Times*, July 27, 2002..

10   Sharon Venne, *Our Elders Understand Our Rights* (Penticton, British Columbia: Theytus Books, 1998). See also Vine Deloria, *Behind the Trail of Broken Treaties* (Austin: University of Texas Press, 1985); Haunani-Kay Trask, *From a Native Daughter: Colonialism and Sovereignty in Hawai'i* (Monroe: Common Courage Press, 1993).

11   "Rash of Wife Killings at Fort Bragg Leaves the Base Wondering Why," *New York Times*, July 27, 2002..

12   Available at The Miles Foundation, members.aol.com_ht_a/ milesfdn/myhomepage/

13   Thomas Fields-Mayer, "The Pentagon Investigates Sexual Misconduct among Troops in Iraq," *People*, February 23, 2004, 67-68.

14   MeloD, available at www.domesticviolenceseries.com.

15   Carl Boggs, *The End of Politics* (New York: Guilford Press, 2000).

16   Jurgen Habermas, *The Structural Transformation of the Public Sphere*, trans. Thomas Burger (Cambridge: MIT Press, 1999).

17   Crystal Echohawk, "Reflections on Sovereignty," *Indigenous Woman* 3,

18   Ingrid Washinawatok, "Sovereignty Is More Than Just Power," *Indigenous Woman* 2, no. 6 (1999): 23-24.

19   Sharon Venne, "The Meaning of Sovereignty," *Indigenous Woman* 2, no. 6 (1999): 27-30.

20   Lakota Harden (Native activist), in discussion with the author, July 13, 2001.

21   Sammy Toineeta (Lakota activist), in discussion with the author, March 15, 2001.

22   Vine Deloria, *Custer Died for Your Sins* (Norman: University of Oklahoma, 1988).

23   Council on Interracial Books for Children, *Chronicles of American Indian Protest* (Greenwich, CT: Fawcett, 1971).

24   Deloria, *Custer Died for Your Sins.*

25   Lee Maracle, *I Am Woman* (North Vancouver: Write-On Press Publishers, 1988).

26   It should be noted that AIM is not a monolithic entity, and many sectors have organized against U.S. empire here and abroad.

27   Roberto Mendoza, *Look! A Nation is Coming!* (Philadelphia: National Organization for an American Revolution, 1984).

28   Ibid. At the same time, because of the relatively small numbers of Native peoples in the U.S, we have often had to create some of the most creative and effective alliances with other communities in their struggles for sovereignty. See Smith, 2002.

29   Andrea Smith, "Bible, Gender and Nationalism in American Indian and Christian Right Activism," paper (Santa Cruz: University of California-Santa Cruz, 2002).

30   Pamela Kingfisher (a leader of the fight to close the Kerr-McGee facility), in discussion with author, June 16, 2001.

Resource Guide

ORGANIZATIONS

Boarding School Healing Project
The Boarding School Healing Project (BSHP) seeks to document abuses so Native communities can begin healing from boarding school abuses, and demand justice from churches and the U.S. government.
c/o Andrea Smith
3700 Haven Hall
Program in American Culture
University of Michigan
Ann Arbor, MI
PHONE: (734) 231-1845

Communities Against Rape and Abuse
Communities Against Rape and Abuse (CARA) is an organization spearheaded by survivors who are marginalized from

mainstream sexual assault services and who are working to undermine the root causes of sexual violence.
801-23rd A South Avenue
Suite G-1
Seattle, WA 98144
PHONE: (206) 322-4856
WEBSITE: http://www.cara-seattle.org

Honor the Earth

Honor the Earth works to create awareness and support for Native environmental issues and to develop needed financial and political resources for the survival of sustainable Native communities. Honor the Earth develops these resources by using music, the arts, the media, and Indigenous wisdom to ask people to recognize our joint dependency on the Earth.
2104 Stevens Avenue South
Minneapolis, MN 55404
PHONE: (612) 879-7529
WEBSITE: http://www.honorearth.org

INCITE! Women of Color Against Violence

INCITE! Women of Color Against Violence is a national activist organization of radical feminists of color advancing a movement to end violence against women of color and their communities through direct action, critical dialogue, and grassroots organizing. INCITE!
WEBSITE: http://www.incite-national.org

Indigenous Environmental Network

The IEN is a network of Indigenous Peoples empowering Indigenous Nations and communities towards sustainable livelihoods, demanding environmental justice, and maintaining the Sacred Fire of our traditions.
P.O. Box 485
Bemidji, MN 56619
PHONE: (218) 751-4967
WEBSITE: http://www.ienearth.org

The Indigenous Women's Network
The Indigenous Women's Network supports the self-determination of Indigenous women, families, communities, and Nations in the Americas and the Pacific Basin. The IWN supports public education and advocacy for the revitalization of our languages and culture, elimination of oppression, the attainment of self-sufficiency, and the protection of Mother Earth for future generations.
Alma de Mujer
13621 FM 2769
Austin, TX 78726
PHONE: (512) 258-3880
WEBSITE: http://indigenouswomen.org

Mending the Sacred Hoop Technical Assistance Project
MSH-TA is a Native American program that provides training and technical assistance to our American Indian and Alaskan Native relations in order to eliminate violence in the lives of women and their children.
202 East Superior Street
Duluth, MN 55802
PHONE: (218) 722-2781 or (888) 305-1650
WEBSITE: http://www.msh-ta.org

National Aboriginal Health Organization
The National Aboriginal Health Organization, an Aboriginal de-signed and controlled body, influences and advances the health and well-being of Aboriginal Peoples using knowledge-based strategies.
56 Sparks Street, Suite 400
Ottawa, Ontario
K1P 5A9
PHONE: (613) 237-9462
TOLL FREE: (877) 602-4445
WEBSITE: http://www.naho.ca

National Council of Urban Indian Health

The National Council of Urban Indian Health was founded in 1998 to meet the unique health care needs of the urban Indian population through education, training, and advocacy.
501 Capitol Court, NE Suite 100
Washington, DC 20002
PHONE: (202) 544-0344
WEBSITE: http://www.ncuih.org

National Indian Health Board

The National Indian Health Board advocates on behalf of all tribal governments and American Indians/Alaskan Natives in their efforts to provide quality health care.
101 Constitution Ave. N.W., Suite 8-B02
Washington, DC 20001
PHONE: (202) 742-4262
WEBSITE: http://www.nihb.org

Native American Circle, Ltd.

Native American Circle, Ltd. (NAC) is a non-profit victim advocacy organization. NAC's programs are available to tribes operating batterer intervention and victim services programs. NAC also aids survivors of domestic violence, sexual assault and stalking crimes, and non-Indian programs desiring to offer culturally competent victim services.
P.O. Box 149
Avery, TX. 75554
PHONE: (866) 622-3872
WEBSITE: http://www.nativeamericancircle.org

Native American Rights Fund

The Native American Rights Fund (NARF) is a non-profit organization that provides legal representation and technical assistance to Indian tribes, organizations and individuals nationwide.
1506 Broadway
Boulder, CO 80302
PHONE: (303) 447-8760
WEBSITE: http://www.narf.org

Native American Women's Health Education Resource Center
The Resource Center, founded by the Native American Community Board, provides educational programs locally, nationally, and internationally including the Domestic Violence Program, AIDS Prevention Program, Child Development Program, and the Youth Wellness Program among many others.
PO Box 572
Lake Andes, SD 57356
PHONE: (605) 487-7072
WEBSITE: http://www.nativeshop.org

Seventh Generation Fund
The Seventh Generation Fund is the only Native American intermediary foundation and advocacy organization dedicated to promoting and maintaining the uniqueness of Native Peoples and our nations. SGF's work has grown in vision and direction over the decades to reach Indigenous community-based projects with a dynamic integrated program of issue advocacy, small grants, technical assistance, management training and leadership development.
P.O. Box 4569
Arcata, CA 95518
PHONE: (707) 825-7640
WEBSITE: http://www.7genfund.org

Sista II Sista
Sista II Sista was created as a response to the lack of community spaces that focused on the experience of young women of color. It was also seen as a proactive space where young women of color could tap into their collective power to fight against injustice.
89 St. Nicholas Avenue
Brooklyn, NY 11237
PHONE: (718) 366-2450
WEBSITE: http://www.sistas.org

Sister Song
The Sister Song Women of Color Reproductive Health Collective is made up of local, regional and national grassroots organizations

in the U.S. The organization is committed to educating women of color on reproductive and sexual health and rights, and improving access to health services, information and resources that are culturally and linguistically appropriate through community organizing, self-help and human rights education.
P.O. Box 311020
Atlanta, GA 31131
WEBSITE: http://www.sistersong.net

Sisters in Action for Power
Sisters in Action for Power is an intergenerational, multiracial, community-based organization. We build and strengthen the leadership development and organizing skills of low income women and women and girls of color.
1732 NE Alberta
Portland, OR 97211
PHONE: (503) 331-1244
WEBSITE: http://volunteermatch.org/orgs/org35280.html

Women of Color Alliance
The Women of Color Alliance strives to unite women of color in a strong common bond to challenge destructive racial disharmony by actively leading our families and society, honoring our powerful cultural diversity, and responding to humanity's call for love, respect, compassion, and service.
P. O. Box 603
Meridian, ID 83680 US
PHONE: (208) 344-4914
WEBSITE: http://www.wocaonline.org

JOURNALS

Akwesasne Notes
Akwesasne Notes is a journal for Native and Natural peoples and has been known for the last 26 years as "the Voice of Indigenous Peoples." *Akwesasne Notes* is a news journal dedicated to reporting

on the issues and concerns of Native Peoples, and to the presentation, preservation, perpetuation, and portrayal of Native cultures throughout the world.
Kahniakehaka Nation
Akwesasne Mohawk Territory
P.O. Box 366
via Rooseveltown, NY 13683
PHONE: (518) 358-3326

Indian Country Today
"The Nation's Leading American Indian News Source"
3059 Seneca Turnpike
Canastota, NY 13032
PHONE: (888) 327-1013
WEBSITE: http://www.indiancountrynews.com

Native American Times
"America's Largest Independent Native American News Source"
12833 East 41st Street
Tulsa, OK 74169
PHONE: (918) 438-6548
WEBSITE: http://nativetimes.com

News From Indian Country
Indian Country Communications, Inc. is an independent, Indian-owned, reservation based business that has been publishing *News From Indian Country* for two decades.
8558N County Road K
Hayward, Wisconsin 54843-5800
WEBSITE: http://www.indiancountrynews.com

Index

About South End Press

South End Press is a nonprofit, collectively run book publisher with more than 250 titles in print. Since our founding in 1977, we have tried to meet the needs of readers who are exploring, or are already committed to, the politics of radical social change. Our goal is to publish books that encourage critical thinking and constructive action on the key political, cultural, social, economic, and ecological issues shaping life in the United States and in the world. In this way, we hope to give expression to a wide diversity of democratic social movements and to provide an alternative to the products of corporate publishing.

Through the Institute for Social and Cultural Change, South End Press works with other political media projects — Alternative Radio; Speakout, a speakers' bureau; and Z *Magazine* — to expand access to information and critical analysis, movements and to provide an alternative to the products of corporate publishing.

Write or e-mail southend@southendpress.org for a free catalog, or visit our Web site at www.southendpress.org.

Related Titles from South End Press

Disposable Domestics:
Immigrant Women Workers in the Global Economy
Grace Chang
0-89608-617-8 paper $18.00

All Our Relations
Winona LaDuke
0-89608-599-6 paper $16.00

Sweatshop Warriors:
Immigrant Women Workers Take On the Global Factory
Miriam Ching Yoon Louie
0-89608-638-0 paper $18.00

De Colores Means Everyone:
Latina Views for a Multicolored Century
Elizabeth Martinez
0-89608-533-X paper $18.00